Indispensable immigrants

The wine porters of northern Italy
and their saint, 1200–1800

Lester K. Little

Manchester University Press

Published by Manchester University Press
Altrincham Street, Manchester M1 7JA, UK
www.manchesteruniversitypress.co.uk

British Library Cataloguing-in-Publication Data is available

Library of Congress Cataloging-in-Publication Data is available

ISBN 978 1 5261 1669 7 *paperback*

First published by Manchester University Press in hardback 2015

This edition first published 2017

The publisher has no responsibility for the persistence or accuracy of URLs for any external or third-party internet websites referred to in this book, and does not guarantee that any content on such websites is, or will remain, accurate or appropriate.

Printed by Lightning Source

For Emilia, Miri, Fiona, and Lucien, and
in memory of Bob Brentano:
may all four know the joy of discovering
teachers and friends like him.

Another regular feature: the urban proletariat could not maintain itself, let alone increase, without the help of continuous immigration. The city, in addition to the eternal mountain immigrant willing to do any kind of work, had the obligation and the opportunity to attract from all over a throng of proletarians in order to meet its needs . . . These indispensable immigrants . . .

Fernand Braudel, *The Mediterranean and the Mediterranean World in the Age of Philip II*

Contents

Figures

Prologue: The setting, the main characters, and two questions

Our story is set in northern Italy within a rectangle of the earth's surface that would fit comfortably within the bounds of Kansas but with a range in elevation going from sea level to well over 4,000 m. Five million years ago a quarter or so of it lay under the sea, the lowest parts several hundred metres under. Our story, though, will deal with only a bit over a 10,000th of that period, or about six centuries, and the action will take place mainly between sea level and elevations of up to 1,200 m.

Seen at a glance from outer space, the outstanding features of this setting are clearly the arc of mountains ringing the north, west, and south sides; the flat land in the centre; and the opening out to the sea in the east (see Figure 1). The Alpine summits on the north and west sides generally reach heights in the range of 2,000 to 3,500 m, but with Monte Rosa and Mont Blanc, the tallest, reaching 4,634 and 4,810 m respectively. Meanwhile, on the south side, the tallest peaks among the Apennines barely exceed 1,800 m. The valleys that cut into the faces of both these mountain ranges send rivers of varying dimensions down towards the centre of the plain, where they eventually join the River Po (see Figure 2). Only the Adige on the north side and the Reno on the south, along with the few rivers to their east, empty directly into the Adriatic Sea. After its own descent from the Maritime Alps, the Po passes Turin at a height above sea level of some 239 m; the point where the Ticino coming down from Switzerland joins it near Pavia is at a height of about 77 m. The Po falls to 61 m near Piacenza, 45 m at Cremona, and so on to 9 m as it passes just north of Ferrara and branches out into the broad delta that finally brings it down to sea level. This topography assumes a key role in the story.

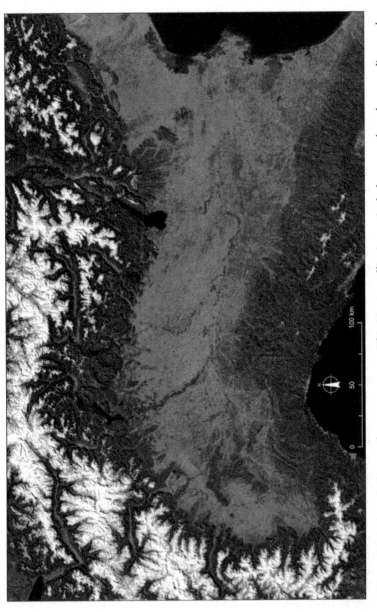

Figure 1 Northern Italy seen from outer space. This Nasa satellite image includes more than the area discussed in the text, namely some of the French Alps and nearly half of Switzerland.

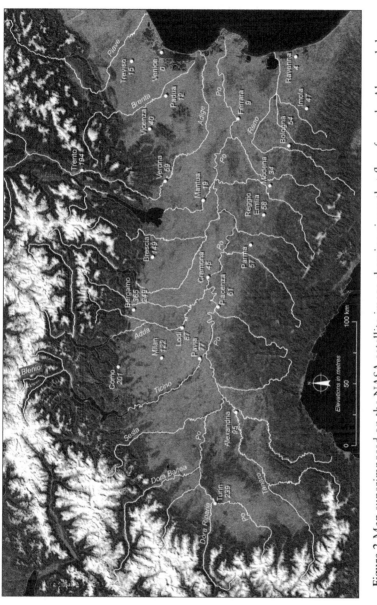

Figure 2 Map superimposed on the NASA satellite image showing rivers that flow from the Alps and the Apennines into the Po Valley plain and eventually the Adriatic Sea, plus the cities that figure in this study.

Alberto, the leading protagonist, was a wine porter in the city of Cremona, where he lived until his death in 1279. Some said he was from Villa d'Ogna, others said Bergamo. Although the first claim was correct, the second was not really wrong, given that Villa d'Ogna is a village up in Bergamo's mountainous hinterland.

How and when he went from his birthplace to Cremona we can only guess. The year had to be fairly close to the middle of the 1200s. We are reasonably safe in imagining him, a poor peasant, leaving home and the fields where he has worked since boyhood. He walks past the parish church of Saint-Matteo to the edge of the village, and starts down the road to the valley floor and the river that runs through it. The village is Villa d'Ogna, a pastoral and agricultural community situated in the orbit of the town of Clusone at an elevation of about 550 m. The river is the Serio, which originates 25 km or so further north, up at nearly 3,000 m in the pre-Alps. He has no reason to go up in that direction. In the winter the whole upper valley is closed off by snow, while in the summer it is mainly shepherds who take their flocks up there to pasture. Instead, Alberto follows the river in its hasty descent of some 300 m and 33 km to where it skirts the eastern edge of the city of Bergamo.

The year is somewhere close to AD 1250, give or take. The Holy Roman Emperor Frederick II, Wonder of the World, is at the end of his intensely fascinating life, hounded to the last by the fourth of the popes he has known – all of them either trained in the law or surrounded by men who were – who have striven to build up the papal monarchy at the expense of his empire with their claims to control Rome and much of central and northern Italy. Kublai Khan, at the other end of Eurasia, is about to take supreme command of the Mongols' great empire, which stretches from the Pacific Ocean to the Black Sea. Ferdinand III, king of Castile, is completing his conquest – *reconquista*, the Spanish Christians call it – of Seville, thereby raising high the bars of both crusading and sainthood for his French counterpart, Louis IX. The new kind of religious orders founded a generation ago by Saints Francis and Dominic have become the vanguard of Latin Christianity at home in Italy, elsewhere in Europe, and in the vast stretches of Mongol territory where Franciscan friars have gone to preach. The Polo brothers, merchants of Venice, will soon be following the route of those friars accompanied by their son and nephew, Marco, to arrive eventually at the court of the Great Khan himself.

Architecture, meanwhile, has been going through one of those rare moments of daring innovation of structural technique, Gothic vaulting in this case, beginning a century ago in a small area centring on Paris and now spreading out from there. Nothing like it has been seen since the introduction of the spherical pendentive in sixth-century Constantinople, an invention that permitted the circular base of a dome to rest upon a square support, or will again before the introduction of the steel-frame skyscraper in late-nineteenth-century Chicago. Similar in audacity to Gothic vaulting are the complex yet coherently organised summaries of knowledge being constructed by scholars: in medicine at Salerno, in law at Bologna, or in theology at Paris.[1] One of these, another Alberto, a Dominican theologian who is the teacher of Thomas Aquinas, will soon be delivering a series of sermons in Augsburg that announce a radical change in Christian social thought, discarding the Old Testament-style fulminations against cities as cesspools of sin, greed, and corruption in favour of an appreciation of them for their light, beauty, erudite culture, and dense populations.[2]

Villa d'Ogna knew nothing of these matters. No one there knew or much cared who the Holy Roman emperor was, or the pope either for that matter. No friars preached there, and no long-distance traders passed through. There was no stunning architecture to be seen or holders of academic degrees from Bologna to be found. Stories about Jews and Saracens there may well have been, but the notion that in the wide world beyond their mountains entire peoples existed who were neither adherents to nor opponents of Christianity had not penetrated. Everybody, though, had heard about cities and their peculiar mix of wondrous sights, strange people, lively distractions, and terrifying dangers for both body and soul; besides, word also had it that cities harboured opportunities to earn and even stash away some money.

Once he notes the land flattening out and the river slowing down, Alberto sees a promontory thrust up more than 100 m from the plain and topped with a ring of walls surrounding a forest of towers. To him it is a timeless mirage. He would not have been impressed to hear that Bergamo was at first a Celtic settlement and was thus part of Cisalpine Gaul – or Gaul-on-this-side-of-the-Alps from the Roman point of view – or that the Romans had conquered it in the third century BC and then connected it by road to *Mediolanum* (Milan) to the west and to *Brixia* (Brescia), *Verona*, *Patavium* (Padua), and the Adriatic coast to the east. What would have impressed him were the narrow streets, the crowds, the shops, the displays of food, the tower houses of the wealthy, the churches at every few paces, and, in the huge open space at the centre of it all, a palace raised up on staunch columns and pointed arches, with the tallest tower he had ever seen standing guard over it, and just behind, a massive church big enough to hold the church of Saint-Matteo ten times over.

These varied sightings and impressions exist only in our imagination because we do not know whether Alberto has stopped off in the capital of his province; we know only that, visit or no visit, he continues some 75 km across the flattest land he has ever seen until he arrives before another unimaginable mirage of walls and towers, named Cremona. No majestic promontory here; this city is set on a flat surface. The walls are surrounded and occasionally undercut by canals that draw from what to him seems a surprisingly broad, slow-paced river, the Po, which passes close by the city on its south side.

Whether he had stopped at Bergamo and can now make comparisons or is seeing a city for the first time, Alberto finds Cremona busier and more exciting on every single day than all the feast days of Saint Matteo he has ever experienced put together. Everywhere he goes he sees more people, and is acutely aware he does not know any of them; there is some consolation in seeing that most of them seem not to know each other either. Street by street Alberto discovers for himself what listeners fortunate enough to hear Albert the Great preach in Augsburg in *c.* 1260 will hear, namely that while all cities have some areas with dark and menacing streets, nothing whatever can prepare one for the thrilling preview of paradise one gets upon entering, perhaps especially for the first time, into the main square.[3] The city, for all the ugliness it harbours and insecurities it engenders, can at its centre be strikingly beautiful.

Still, more his style is the sight of so many people working, although he has to admit he has no idea what many of them are doing. He of course knows how to do many things, to use many tools, to perform many tasks. One of these is to carry liquids in a *brenta*, a wooden vessel with shoulder straps like a backpack (see Figure 3). At home in the mountains there is nothing unusual about a man occasionally needing to carry a brenta, normally with either water or milk, nor about being skilled at pouring the liquid into smaller containers by leaning forward, the brenta still on his back, and pouring over one shoulder. He is astonished, though, to learn that in this city there are men who make their living by carrying a brenta all day long every day, and

Figure 3 A brenta of the typical sort found in the north Italian countryside. This one, called by some using a diminutive form *brentina*, holds 50 l.

what is more, their cargo is wine; they are called *brentatori* (wine porters).[4] Eventually Alberto got a job as one of them, and when, if ever, he got to see all the brentatori who worked in Cremona gathered in one place, he would have realised that they were as numerous as all the men of many a mountain village.

Amazing as this new world Alberto discovers in Cremona is, it would pale in comparison with his ultimate fate if he had any inkling of what that was to be, but of course there is no way he can. The notion is beyond anything he can imagine, namely that he is going to be one of these wine porters in Cremona for the rest of his life.

As for what comes after that, perhaps many people fantasise about the memories that others will have of them after they are gone, but some of the rich and powerful build monuments to themselves and strive mightily to control the fate of their reputations far into that abyss of time. Alberto, though, could not have comprehended even if the Virgin herself had revealed to him in a vision that his unexceptional life was merely the preface to five centuries of fame, honour, and service to his fellow workers that were to follow.

The other main characters number in the thousands and most of them to us remain anonymous, although they were no less important to the story for that. They were the men who over many generations carried wine in all of the larger northern Italian cities.

To come to the point: how did it happen that a humble worker in thirteenth-century Italy, a historical nobody, embarked immediately after his death upon an afterlife of fame and honour that gained him sainthood, not once but twice, and veneration at altars in several cities for between one and five centuries? And how, over the same half-millennium, did other mountain dwellers who migrated to the cities below – along with peasants from the plains, who moved into those cities where for their hard work they got little pay and much aggravation – how, one asks, did they establish solidarity, defend their interests, and keep their self-respect? One answer will make do for both questions: in a word, sainthood.

I

Alberto

It was said that he made many miracles and was called 'Saint Alberto'.

Annals of Piacenza, 1279

Thus it is that sinners or sick persons go badly astray by casting aside true saints and by praying to one [like Alberto] who cannot intercede for them.

Salimbene de Adam, *Chronicle, c.* 1285

1

The legend of Saint Alberto

Already at a tender age, little Alberto used to give away some of his food to beggars who came to the door of his parents' home, a clear indication that he was destined for spiritual greatness (see Figure 4). Thus begin many versions of Alberto's legend, most episodes of which were already in place from shortly after the time of his death. It continues with Alberto as an adolescent who, after having finished his daily work as a field hand, was accustomed to return home and kneel before a cross to say his prayers. Alberto's legend is a mix of significant and recurring forms of behaviour such as these two scenes show, together with specific, one-time episodes, which instead are all miracles. An example of the latter is the story of how some of his fellow workers, jealous of how much faster he was than they at cutting hay, hid an anvil in the section of the field where he was working. They watched with eager anticipation as he neared the anvil, only to see how effortlessly he sliced through it with his scythe. There is another scene in the legend that may shed light on Alberto's exceptional farming skills; in this one the future saint is digging in a field and right next to him stands a robust angel – presumably not visible to his fellow workers – wielding a shovel identical to his.

Alberto got married. Of course it was not his idea, but he agreed to do it out of respect for his parents and their desire that he do so. Married life brought little joy to Alberto, for his wife nagged him constantly. What provoked her ire more than anything else was his generosity with their belongings towards the poor. Worst of all was his profligacy with their food. Once when beggars came by just as she had put out a plate of steaming polenta and a bowl of milk, Alberto gave away their meal to these poor people.[1] This

ALBERTO FANCIULLO DI ANNI SETTE
DISTRIBUISCE IL PROPRIO CIBO AI POVERI

Figure 4 Alberto as a precociously holy boy gives away his dinner to the poor in this processional banner made in 1903.

sent his wife into a rage. She berated him, shouted insults at him, and threatened him. But Alberto? Alberto understood that all this was happening because God was testing him, and he knew that the correct response was patience. His tactic was to put up with her by remaining calm and silent. In this particular instance, after several minutes of her outburst, there appeared suddenly on their table another plate of polenta and two bowls of milk (see Figure 5).

Wife or no wife – she seems to drop out of the picture without any explanation of when or why as the legend progresses – Alberto maintained his charitable ways. This he did by caring for sick people in a hospital as well as by offering food and lodging to pilgrims in his home. He himself had the experience of being a pilgrim, for he went several times on the two most renowned pilgrimages in Europe, to Santiago de Compostela in northwestern Spain and to Rome, plus at least once to the Holy Land.

It was on his return from one of these jaunts that he arrived at the Po but lacked the money to pay for his passage across the river. He simply spread his pilgrim's cloak on the water, stepped on it, and floated across to the opposite bank. Two Augustinian friars witnessed this rather extraordinary scene but Alberto admonished them not to mention it to anyone.

In one rather charming episode Alberto assisted a woman who was distraught because an entire brenta full of her wine had fallen over and spilled out onto the ground. The legend does not assign blame for this accident to anyone, perhaps because the question of blame was soon moot; Alberto knelt down, scooped up the wine from the ground in his hands, and poured it back into the container (see Figure 6). That's not all: the wine tasted better after the spill than before.

Miraculous elements dominate in the telling of Alberto's death and burial in Cremona. As he lay on his deathbed awaiting the arrival of a priest, who after being summoned seemed to be taking an inordinately long time to arrive, a dove flew into the room where he lay and placed the communion wafer it carried in its beak upon his tongue (see Figure 7). Once Alberto was dead and his body was to be carried to the parish church of Saint-Mattia, all the church bells in the city started to ring at once, this without the intervention of any human bell-ringers. Thus a large crowd assembled at that church and witnessed still another prodigious

ALBERTO RIMPROVERATO DALLA MOGLIE PER AVER
DISPENSATO AI POVERI IL PREPARATO DESINARE
PREGA E TOSTO RICOMPARISCE SULLA TAVOLA IL CIBO

Figure 5 Alberto's wife berates him for giving away their dinner to the poor. The standard clerical view regarding marriage as incompatible with saintliness lay behind this misogynous theme, which is found in the legends of several lay saints. That this 1903 processional banner follows a centuries-old convention of depicting poor people as small suggests that the design was based on an earlier image of this scene, now lost.

ALBERTO
RACCOGLIE COLLE MANI IL VINO SPARSO IN TERRA
E NE RIEMPIE LA BRENTA

Figure 6 Although the legend does not blame any individual for spilling the wine, Alberto is shown in this processional banner of 1903 gathering it up from the ground in his hands and putting it back in the brenta.

ALBERTO MORIBONDO E COMUNICATO DA UNA COLOMBA

Figure 7 As the priest called to Alberto's deathbed does not arrive in time, the Holy Spirit in its standard guise as a dove carries a Eucharistic wafer directly to the dying holy man. In this processional banner made in 1903, the three objects on the far side of the bed refer to three kinds of work Alberto was said to have done: the brenta of a wine porter, the scythe of a field hand, and the comb of a wool carder.

act: the grave diggers were unable to penetrate the ground of the churchyard with their shovels but were instead directed to enter the church. There in the choir at the very place where Alberto had frequently prayed they found a tomb miraculously prepared to receive his corpse.

Every saint needs a legend. For a cult to become and remain vital, clerics and laypeople alike need to know and to be reminded why the holy person in question merits their devotion. All legends are to some extent kept alive by oral transmission, but many get written down sooner or later. Those that remain unwritten are more likely to have a relatively restricted geographic diffusion, and are more subject to change, if not eventual oblivion, with the passage of generations. Although the word *legend* carries for us the meaning of myth or of a tale at least partially fictitious, it simply derives from *legere*, meaning to read, more precisely from the gerundive form meaning something that is or ought to be read. If the faithful are to benefit spiritually from emulating the lives of saints, their pastors ought to read up on them to be able to instruct their charges in the meritorious deeds of those saints. The purpose of a *legenda* is thus to supply the priest with either a text to read to worshippers or material for the sermon he will preach to them in his own words on the saint's day. By preaching on the subject he is able through emphasis and interpretation to transform an old legend into a relevant message for his contemporaries.[2] Seen in this light, what are the Gospels after all, especially those by Matthew, Mark, and Luke, other than variants on the legend of Saint Jesus?

The legend of Saint Alberto came down in both written and visual form. The three earliest surviving written versions of the legend date from the sixteenth century, although their respective authors acknowledged having consulted earlier sources. A Bergamasque cleric named Marcantonio Benaglio wrote the first of these versions, and the source he cited was an 'old history' found at the church of Saint-Mattia. In Benaglio's telling, the fact of Alberto's birth having taken place in the mountains, a sure sign of low birth, necessitated his prettying-up of the narrative with the image of a rose amidst thorns or of gold emerging from lowly sand. On the other hand he found Alberto's parents to be acceptably 'notable' (*non obscuris*). This apparently meant that they were sufficiently well off to provide him with some possessions, for once he was 'out of his parents' hands' he began to distribute liberally his wealth and belongings to the poor. Then, that he not miss any occasions to be tested, in particular by the torments and bothers of marriage, he got married. With Benaglio's view of marriage so dismal, it is not surprising that his comment on Alberto's wife's complaints in regard to his alms-giving was that such behaviour by a woman was to be expected.[3]

The Alberto who emerges from Benaglio's version is not a poor worker but not a rich man either; he was a farmer with some land of his own and the capacity to hire field hands. In recounting the miracle of the anvil in the hay, he explains that Alberto did not have to work in the fields, but did so out of humility. The fact that in a given amount of time he got more work done than two field hands lay at the basis of the hidden-anvil episode.[4]

Because of other jealousies that arose, Alberto left home and went to Cremona, although Benaglio places him there one century too early. He went to visit the sacred sights at Rome and at Santiago. Upon returning to Cremona one time he crossed the Po in the miraculous fashion we have seen. There follow the miracle of the spilled wine that he picked up, his deathbed communion brought by the dove (understood of course to be the Holy Spirit), the church bells that rang out spontaneously, and the tomb prepared inside the church. Afterwards there is mention of 'innumerable' sick people who came asking to be cured, as well as of testimonies to cures received left in the form of images, messages, and ex-votos.

Finally, Benaglio reports that the good people of Villa d'Ogna, knowing of the fame of their native son, sent emissaries to Cremona to request the concession of some of his relics. After many supplications, in 1481 they obtained an arm of the most holy Alberto, which they brought back home (*in patria sua*) where it reposed for more than four centuries in an appropriate container in the parish church.

The main story line of Alberto's life from his birth in Villa d'Ogna to his death in Cremona carries over into the second version of the legend. Also the work of a cleric from Bergamo, Bartolomeo Pellegrini, this relatively brief version appeared in a printed book dated 1553. Gone are the notable parents, the substantial belongings for distribution to the poor, and the hired hands. Gone, too, is the notion that Alberto worked not out of necessity but as an affirmation of his humility. Pellegrini keeps Alberto's wife in the story, relating that Alberto worked hard as a peasant, kept that part of his earnings that met his and his wife's needs, and distributed the rest to the poor, the weak, widows, orphans, the sick, and pilgrims. Most unusual of all about this account by Pellegrini is his assertion, made without any explanation, that Alberto never belonged to a religious order of friars.[5]

The third version of the legend composed in the sixteenth century appears in the *Annals of Cremona* published in 1588 by Ludovico Cavitelli, a cleric from Cremona. These annals purport to cover the period from the year AD 15, 'when Jesus began to preach', to 1583. As no earlier edition of these annals is extant, one has to surmise what part of Cavitelli's entry for 1279 he took from earlier sources and what part is his own contribution. However, he says that for his entry for Alberto he consulted writings at Saint-Mattia, perhaps the same ones that Benaglio cited, from which he learned of the miracles of the replaced food, the spilled wine, the Po crossing, the deathbed communion, and the tomb inside the church. Concerning Alberto's pilgrimages he specified that the holy man went to Santiago eight times. That said, there are three noteworthy details in Cavitelli's text that are not present in either of those by Benaglio or Pellegrini: first that a dispute over land was what drove Alberto to abandon Villa d'Ogna, second that besides carrying wine he was a woollen-cloth maker, and third that in Cremona Alberto put on the habit of the Third Order of Saint Dominic. This last assertion directly contradicts Pellegrini's claim of thirty-five years earlier that Alberto did not belong to an order of friars, suggesting that this subject had already been a matter of contention back then. The Third Order of Saint Dominic, like its counterpart in the Order of Saint Francis, was an organisation of laypeople who, without abandoning either their family life or their work – the two defining characteristics that distinguished the laity from the clergy – sought to associate themselves with the lives of the friars by practising as many of the latters' devotions and observances as they could.[6]

Besides these three sixteenth-century versions of the legend, there were a few visual sources that call for attention. To be sure, representations of scenes from sacred history in both painting and sculpture had for centuries provided the principal subject matter for artistic expression, and second only to biblical themes in forming this repertory were the legends of saints. While individual paintings or sculpted capitals were able to show individual scenes, fresco was an ideal medium for portraying many different scenes in succession, making it possible to recite graphically whole legends, or portions thereof, across wide expanses of church walls. The kinetic effect of such art is supplied by the movement of observers as they walk along the wall reading each scene in succession, all in the narrative order chosen by the artist.[7]

The late thirteenth and early fourteenth centuries constituted the great age of fresco cycles, both because of the popularity of such saints as Francis and because of the consummate skill of such artists as Pietro Cavallini and Giotto. Of the two cycles of the Alberto legend that we know of, one in Saint-Mattia and the other at a small sanctuary down by the Serio at Villa d'Ogna, neither survived into the age of photography or even into the sketchbook of an artistically inclined traveller of the early modern era. No one imagines either of these to be major losses to the artistic patrimony of humanity. We do have eighteenth-century verbal descriptions of these cycles but they add nothing of note to what we know from the texts.[8]

What we are left with, however, is a collection of fifteen processional banners, four of which we have just seen. Local artisans made them at Villa d'Ogna in 1903. This was a moment of intense enthusiasm for the Alberto cult there because at long last the relics remaining in Cremona were finally released by the bishop of that city for removal to the saint's native village. Each of the banners has sewn into it a scene from the legend together with a caption at the bottom. They were made for use on the saint's day when viewers standing along the procession route are able to get a cumulative, cinematic effect from seeing these episodes of Alberto's life pass before them.[9]

That which we have been here referring to as a *legend* could just as well have been called a *vita*, meaning *life*. The two terms were used interchangeably in the titles of hagiographical works. In that context they mean the same thing. On the other hand, a saint's 'legend' and a modern 'life', in the sense of what we consider a biography, or a historical reconstruction of that life, are two quite different matters.

2

The life of Alberto

Alberto came from Villa d'Ogna, a village near the town of Clusone in the Serio River Valley, 33 km northeast of the city of Bergamo. He lived and worked as a wine porter in the city of Cremona. He died there in 1279 on 6 May, a Saturday to be precise, and was put to rest on the following day at the church of Saint-Mattia.[1] No other details of Alberto's life survive. None whatever.

The fact of his burial at Saint-Mattia indicates that Alberto had lived in that parish. Such an assumption would also be reasonable because Saint-Mattia was located in the newer section of the city, the *Città Nuova*, where people of relatively modest means such as lesser merchants, shop keepers, artisans, and manual labourers lived. It is no coincidence either that this was the section where people recently arrived from the countryside settled. Meanwhile the older, wealthier families, including those of the knights, judges, and leading merchants, had their residences in the *Città Vecchia*, close by the cathedral and the city's other major monuments.[2]

Yet the fact that we know even the little that we do know about Alberto raises the question of why any information at all about such a historically unexceptional person should have survived. We can eliminate the obvious hypotheses, namely parish records of births, communions, and deaths, or tax records or membership lists of guilds. None of these exist for the relevant places and times.

Instead of such archival sources, it is from the annals of four different cities that we glean our information about Alberto. The persons responsible for writing up the most notable happenings of a given year in the lives of their respective cities obviously chose to include events and persons that they considered exceptional or historically significant. They were carrying on a venerable tradition of historical writing with important precedents in Antiquity but also in times closer to them, namely in the monastic chronicles or annals that individual monks, some identified but most anonymous, kept adding to year-by-year through many generations. What merited mention of Alberto in the entries for 1279 in the annals of Reggio Emilia, Piacenza, Parma, and Cremona was, however, nothing that he had accomplished during his lifetime.[3]

3

The afterlife of Alberto

Alberto's transformation from historical non-person to celebrity began within a few days of his burial. What convinced the authors of the annals of cities near Cremona to take note of him was the flurry of reports of miracles that filled the air, and the fact that so many people from their respective cities were flocking there to see for themselves how true those reports were. As we have seen, even as Alberto's corpse was being borne to Saint-Mattia, the grave diggers' shovels bounced off the churchyard dirt as if it were solid rock, and that mystery led to the mystery of the tomb inside the church.

The *Annals of Piacenza*, where this account of Alberto's burial appeared, identified Alberto as a carrier not just of wine but of grain, too, calling him a 'good, God-fearing man' who was persistent in alms-giving and who made many pilgrimages to Rome. Should these details about how he lived and what he did be added to the bare-bones sketch of Alberto's life? We cannot declare any of them impossible, but except for the assertion that he was a carrier of wine (his carrying of wheat is not corroborated by any other source), there is a chance that such claims as his frequent praying in Saint-Mattia derived from, rather than preceded, the news of his healing miracles. It would be better to consider these details as factual accounts of his posthumous reputation, without prejudice to whatever reputation he had during his life.[1]

Word of Alberto's miraculous burial travelled fast, and the virtual certainty that this wondrous event signified that more miracles would be on the way brought the sick and needy from all over Cremona, and soon thereafter from the countryside beyond and from still other cities. As the claims of miracles proliferated, the numbers of persons seeking help swelled.

The crowds were too large for the parish church of Saint-Mattia, so the authorities set up an altar with a large canopy spread over it outside the church. Franciscan and Augustinian friars, priests of other religious orders, and priests from other parish churches lent a hand to the clergy of Saint-Mattia in saying masses. There were also priests assigned to gather the testimonies of persons claiming miraculous cures and to authenticate, or not, those claims. Then it was the turn of the notaries who were there to make a legal record of the authenticated miracles. A portion of this record still exists in a copy made two centuries later. It records twenty-one cases that involved fourteen females, half of whom were children, and seven males, two of whom were children. Their ailments included bone deformities (six cases), paralysis (also six), and in decreasing numbers gout, demonic possession, blindness, and a hunchback. All but two had suffered their afflictions for over a year, usually for three-to-five years, but in one case for thirty years. The supplicants and their witnesses came from Cremona and its surrounding territory, but also from Piacenza, Bergamo, Brescia, Mantua, and Parma. One witness, Ottolino Gualterio, ferried passengers on the Po between Casalmaggiore and Cremona. The twenty-one extant recorded cases may of course not be representative, for the list could well have been longer. They appear to have taken place within the first few months of Alberto's death, but in any case no evidence remains to indicate how long the fame and power of Alberto continued to draw large numbers of invalids in search of miraculous cures.[2]

Along with a reference to the death of Alberto, 'a porter in Cremona', a chronicler of Reggio Emilia included in his entry for 1279 mention of these miracles of 'Blessed Alberto' and added that they took place not just in Cremona but 'in many other cities and places'.[3] Although he failed to elaborate on what other places, the *Annals of Parma* provides precious information on this point. Like the other annals it reports that Alberto the wine porter had died in Cremona, and that many miracles were taking place at his tomb and attracting a multitude of pilgrims. But it goes on to say that certain wine porters of Parma went to check out what was happening in Cremona and were so enthusiastic about what they observed there that they sought to replicate it back at home. They had an image of Alberto painted on the outside wall of the church of Saint-Peter, which is located in Parma's communal square. Wonder of wonders: the image in Parma appeared to have the same thaumaturgical power as the relics in the tomb at Cremona. The 'whole city, the clergy and the people' (*tota civitas, clerus et populus*) came there. Invalids lay on the ground in the square and every day a mass was celebrated there. Members of all the professional and trade organisations, great and small, showed up in groups before the image, carrying banners and flags and bringing large sums of money. Enough funds were gathered to purchase a house that became the Hospice of Saint-Alberto for assistance to the poor.[4]

This story of the transfer of the Alberto cult from Cremona and a fuller account of the goings-on in Parma appear in the famous chronicle by the Franciscan writer Salimbene de Adam. As he was a native of Parma and writing at that very time – he died in 1288 – Salimbene had an obvious interest in this story, which he told in considerable detail. Moreover, he told it in an attention-getting tone, evident in the very opening sentence: 'In that same year (1279), there took place the phony miracles of a man from Cremona named Alberto, who had been a wine carrier [*portator vini*], at the same time a wine drinker [*potator vini*], and indeed also a sinner [*peccator*].' With this double Latin pun on 'porter', Salimbene disparaged Alberto himself, as well as all those who believed and participated in his cult.[5]

He offered no new information on the origins of the Alberto cult in Cremona, or on its extension to Parma, but he does inform us that it spread even further, from Parma to the city of Reggio Emilia (see Figure 8). There, he wrote, the wine porters affixed images to the wall of the baptistery, which stood right next to that city's market, and also to the wall of the venerable parish church of Saint-George one block away. Salimbene was unambiguous in pinning the initiation and propagation of this cult on the wine porters and claiming that it was they who benefited from it at every turn. He thus seems to corroborate the version in the Parma *Annals* that specified that the wine carriers of Parma had brought the cult back from Cremona following a visit there. While the *Annals* mention no other means of promoting the cult in Parma than the affixing of images of Alberto to a church wall, Salimbene makes the same point but adds that it was the presence also of relics of Alberto that attracted the crowds to the church of Saint-Peter. This mix of relics and images produced spectacular results.

Like the author of the *Annals*, Salimbene says that people brought donations, specifying purple cloth, samite (silk fabric interwoven

Figure 8 Alberto's world, from Villa d'Ogna to Cremona, and the main centres of his cult, from Villa d'Ogna to Reggio Emilia, are here shown superimposed on a detail of the NASA satellite image of northern Italy.

with gold or silver threads), canopies, and considerable sums of money, but in place of any mention of a hospice he says matter-of-factly that the wine porters divided up these donations among themselves. Still, nothing they did exercised Salimbene in the same way the misdeeds of clerics – i.e. of those who were supposed to know better – did. In the first place the Roman Church had not approved the cult of Alberto, so no cleric should have permitted or condoned it, let alone performed a mass as part of it. Furthermore, clerics were complicit in this false cult not just for failing to oppose the appending of images on church walls, but also for copying the same practice in their own churches. 'This is expressly contrary to church law', he wrote, 'because no one's relics are to be held in reverence unless the person in question be first approved by the Roman Church and inscribed in the register of saints, nor is anyone's image to be painted in the manner of a saint unless his or her canonisation has first been announced by the church'. Most reprehensible of all were the bishops who failed to discipline the offending priests over whom they had jurisdiction; they deserved to be deposed from their episcopal offices, but as there was no one willing to discipline them, they merit this curse from Zechariah 11:17: 'Woe to my worthless shepherd, who deserts the flock! May the sword strike his arm and his right eye; let his arm be all withered and his right eye utterly blinded.'

Salimbene's explanation for the success of this false cult first of all cited 'the large numbers of invalids who came there from Pavia and other parts of Lombardy' with hopes of being cured. Next he mentioned the curious, who were simply drawn to the spectacle, and then the clerics who were envious of the new religious orders – namely the Order of Preachers, i.e. the Dominicans, and of course his own Order of Friars Minor, the Franciscans. Without further mention of the wine porters, he listed the bishops and canons, those who made of this cult a money-making scheme. The final group of participants he included was that of political exiles, by which he meant members of factions who had been expelled and dispossessed by the ruling faction of the moment. Salimbene's take on the exiles was that they figured that their chances for amnesty and thus a peaceful return would be aided by these claims of new miracles, although he did not make clear just how that would work.

All of these parties to the cult suffered humiliation, to Salimbene's evident satisfaction, when word spread that another relic of Alberto, a toe, was about to arrive from Cremona in Parma. People of all ages and conditions from every part of the city streamed into the centre to join in a vast procession to accompany the toe to the cathedral. When the toe was placed on the main altar, Lord Anselm of San Vitale, a canon of the cathedral and the bishop's vicar, approached the altar and bent to kiss the relic. As he did so, though, he was made suspicious by a strange odour and quickly told this to the clerics standing about him. They gathered in close and leaned forward to examine the relic, only to find that they had been duped, for the 'toe' was nothing other than a clove of garlic. In Salimbene's view, this was God's way of showing how foolish they had all been. Thus it is, he concluded, that 'sinners or sick persons go badly astray by casting aside true saints and by praying to one who cannot intercede for them'.

Salimbene's charges were neither frivolous nor limited to him alone. On the other hand, we lack evidence that his book and opinions circulated widely or found sympathetic listeners among either clerics or laypeople. In any case his views had no perceptible impact on the development of the cult of Alberto in the cities that he wrote about. As at Cremona, no source tells us how long the initial burst of enthusiasm for the cult with its steady flow of miracles endured at either Parma or Reggio Emilia, but the simple truth is that it became well enough established to last for several centuries.

In the meantime, although at Bergamo no text tells us of either miracles or a cult of Alberto, there is a seventeenth-century inventory that lists a relic of 'Saint Alberto of Clusone, confessor' in the cathedral church.[6] A lone relic, though, does not a cult make. Far more significant than that relic is an entirely different kind of testimony found in Bergamo, namely a fresco on a church wall showing a full-length, albeit partially covered-up, portrait of Alberto (see Figure 9). He is here identified by name and dressed as a pilgrim. He is also shown about to receive the Eucharist from the beak of the dove. This is a curious juxtaposition of two elements of the legend, Alberto as pilgrim and Alberto receiving communion at the end of his life, even though here he is not on his deathbed but standing up and looking healthy.[7]

The fresco is located in the church of Saint-Michael-by-the-White-Well, which stands 100 m or so outside the twelfth-century city walls on one of the two busiest roads of access to and from the city, the one connecting with the Borgo Sant'Antonio below. Saint-

Figure 9 Alberto, dressed in a long cloak with a pilgrim's hat and staff, receives the viaticum from the Holy Spirit. This fresco, executed by the Master of Angera in the 1280s in the church of Saint-Michael-by-the-White-Well in Bergamo, was partially covered over in the fifteenth century by another fresco, and later on entirely covered over with white paint. Restorers uncovered both layers of fresco during the early 1940s.

Michael housed a parish confraternity that was founded in 1266, a voluntary organisation of laypeople particularly active in the life of the church. Nothing in its rule or other documents, though, any more than those concerning the church itself, mentions or makes a connection with Alberto.[8]

The date of the fresco, however, can tell us something. Seen in a purely local context, there would have been little hope of identifying the artist or of determining the date other than placing it after 1279, the death of Alberto. But when a team of art historians undertook in the 1980s a systematic survey of all paintings in Lombardy, they recognised the hand of the painter of this fresco as the same as that seen in certain works in the churches of Saint-Eustorgio and Saint-Leonard in Milan, and especially – because of a large-scale fresco cycle – in a castle at Angera near the southern end of Lake Maggiore. They were able to piece together many details of the career of this painter, still anonymous, but whom they named the 'Master of Angera'. And in reconstructing his itinerary, they placed him in Bergamo in the 1280s.[9]

Nothing whatever remains of the images of Alberto that Salimbene probably saw on the walls of Saint-Peter and of other churches in Parma, or of those he had heard of if not actually seen in Reggio Emilia. But at Saint-Michael in Bergamo we can see an example of just what got Salimbene so fired up: a fresco not far inside the church on the left wall showing the image of a man with a halo, confidently identified as 'S. Albertus'. The image dates from the decade following Alberto's death and preceding Salimbene's. One cannot help wondering who commissioned the Master of Angera to execute this image at Saint-Michael. We are not likely ever to find the answer, but it would be unreasonable not to wonder whether something was happening at Bergamo analogous to what Salimbene tells us so explicitly the wine porters were up to both at Parma and at Reggio.

In 1304 the bishop of Bergamo granted permission for founding a hospital of Saint-Alberto near the end of a bridge over the Serio at Villa d'Ogna. There was probably a sanctuary associated with this hospital from the start, but in any case a document dated 1332 mentions a church dedicated to Saint Alberto at this site, the same where frescos with a series of scenes from the legend were later executed. In 1426 the bishop of Bergamo decreed that 7 May, long since held to be the date of Alberto's death, was to be the saint's feast day for his diocese. Outside the city of Bergamo, the cult grew and remained strong in various communities in that part of the Serio Valley close to Villa d'Ogna. The nearby town of Nembro, for example, had its patrons and protectors, Saints Martin of Tours, Bernard of Clairvaux, and Rocco, move over to make room for their new co-patron, Saint Alberto.[10]

In 1471 the bishop of Bergamo approved the establishment of a confraternity, dedicated to Saint Alberto and named the Company of the Young People of Villa d'Ogna. Persons of any age could belong, but those over the age of twenty-five were not eligible to hold office. The seat of this organisation was in the complex of the church and hospice by the river. The confraternity rule obliged all members to make weekly contributions, plus a special contribution each year on 7 May, and all of the money raised went for the upkeep and support of the church on that site. All through the sixteenth century the reports of episcopal visitations record that the bishop went to the parish church in the village but then also to the hospice and church by the river, where notice was duly taken that the confraternity continued to be active. The same remained true in 1583 of the famously thorough visit and detailed report by the archbishop of Milan and future saint, Carlo Borromeo. In 1610 Franciscan friars took over the site by the river, where for nearly two centuries they maintained both the cult and the tradition of assistance to the needy.[11]

As in Bergamo, the bishop of Cremona decreed that the Feast of Saint Alberto was to be celebrated on 7 May in his diocese. During the 1470s the seat of the Alberto cult in Saint-Mattia underwent a major transformation, consisting firstly of a separate chapel built in the saint's honour, and secondly of having his remains taken out of the tomb in the choir floor and placed in an urn that was to be the centrepiece of the new chapel. The plan to move the saint's relics gave the people of Villa d'Ogna an occasion to press their request for a relic, which they did and which the bishop of Cremona granted. It was in 1481 that the new chapel was dedicated in Saint-Mattia of Cremona and the parish church of Villa d'Ogna got Alberto's right hand and forearm.[12]

A decade later, in 1493, the ecclesiastical authorities of Cremona went so far as to change the name of the church to Saints-Mattia-and-Alberto. Moreover, they consigned the chapel of Saint-Alberto to the wine porters of their city, meaning specifically that the latter were obligated to support the daily saying of a mass at its altar and supply the oil for a lamp that was to be kept lighted there at all hours of every day. The wine porters were the obvious choice for these responsibilities since they had chosen Alberto as the patron saint of their guild, and in their regulations set 7 May as the day on which, after attending the mass in honour of Saint Alberto, they elected their leaders for the year.[13]

The choice of a saint's death date to be the annual feast day on which the faithful were to honour his or her memory was in accordance with long-standing tradition. Usually one thinks of someone's death date as referring to the last day that person was alive. In the tradition of saint-lore, however, that same day is known as the saint's *dies natalis* or day of birth: the real birthday, the one that marks the passage, as Benaglio said of Alberto, 'not from life to death but rather … from death to eternal life', or in the humbler language of historians, from life to afterlife.[14]

Even though both of the dioceses in which Alberto had lived honoured his annual commemoration, they did so differently. In the case of Bergamo, the cult demonstrated greater vitality in the communities of the Serio Valley, whereas in that of Cremona it flourished mainly and perhaps even exclusively in the city. This distinction, if accurate, does after all reflect the two fundamentally different environments, or at least the two we know about, in which Alberto had lived.

The cult as extended to Reggio Emilia followed a still different pattern, for it does not seem that the bishop declared the feast day as valid for his entire diocese, but in any case the cult remained confined to the city. The same is true of the cult as it developed in Pavia, Piacenza, Parma, Bologna, and Ferrara, and yet in those places it was also transformed in a fundamental way that will bear scrutiny; furthermore, because of a special connection with the Dominican Order alluded to earlier, we shall find the cult also in at least three cities in Catalonia.[15] The story of the broadening-out of the cult just in the Po Valley plain, though, is so thoroughly entwined in the history of the wine porters that it becomes necessary at this point to ask who they were, where they came from, and what they did, in order to see how they were connected to the cult of Alberto.

II

The wine porters

The work done by wine porters is very useful for city-dwellers all year long.

Statutes of the wine porters' guild of Pavia, 1553

In our city one can really live well because everything needed to make life pleasant is at hand ... and any man, if he be worth his salt, can earn money and honour according to his status.

Bonvesin de la Riva, On the Marvels of Milan, c. 1288

Vile métiers are to noble ones like clouds to the sun; they make it shine more brilliantly.

Tomaso Garzoni, A Commonplace of All the Professions of the World, 1585

4

The brenta and the brentatori

Since *brentatore* (plural *brentatori*), the Italian term for a wine porter, derives from *brenta* (plural *brente*), the container for carrying
wine, any discussion of origins and meanings must begin with the
brenta itself. Archaeology, philology, and history all agree on defining the territory of the brenta as southern Switzerland and northern Italy, from the Alps to the Apennines, and from the region of
Piedmont in the west to the Adriatic coast in the east.

The origins of the term *brenta* lie in the remote past, in pre-
Roman times and therefore before Latin. The earliest among its
several meanings is demon or devil, followed by storm or wind or
rain, then flood or watercourse. The connections are that demons
were thought responsible for meteorological happenings, which
included torrential rains that in turn formed watercourses. From
there one gets to a man-made channel lined with wood and thence
to a wooden container for liquids.[1]

The River Brenta, which arises in the Trentino and cuts through
the Veneto to the Adriatic, derives its name from the meaning of
brenta as a watercourse, a point confirmed by several other uses of
Brenta as a toponym in northern Italy. It represents the elevation of
a quite common term to a proper noun in the same way that *arna*, an
archaic term for riverbed, gave Tuscany the name of the Arno River,
or that *ticino*, a term for rushing stream, became the name of the
river that flows down from the canton of that name in Switzerland
and passes Pavia (Roman *Ticinum*) just before joining the Po.

The evolution of meaning from a natural watercourse formed
by erosion thus led eventually to a particular kind of receptacle, the
brenta, just one among a vast array that included vats, barrels, buckets, pails, pitchers, bowls, and so on, all of them made of wood, that
were developed by Alpine dwellers. Those receptacles, specially made

Figure 10 A traditional gerla of the sort commonly found in the Italian countryside.

for transport as opposed to just storage, show a variety of solutions for carrying; an example would be the pair of milk pails that can be attached to the ends of a pole that is carried across the shoulders and the top of the back, and that the carrier steadies with his or her hands. But as anyone who has ever hiked, and especially hiked in mountains, knows, no method of carrying a burden works better than back-packing, which is less tiring and leaves one's arms and hands free for helping maintain balance. The ideal receptacle for carrying, say, kindling wood or mushrooms or chestnuts, is a basket carried on the back with shoulder straps. Such a basket, in Italian called a *gerla* (from Latin *gerere*, to carry), has a flat side that goes against the back (see Figure 10). The bottom measures about 20 cm across and rests against the lower back. The gerla flares outward towards the top, which reaches roughly to the top of the carrier's head and can be about as wide as the carrier's shoulders. At elevations hospitable to vineyards, the gerla was an ideal receptacle for harvesting grapes. The point of the funnel shape is to avoid making the centre of gravity so low as to place undue strain on the carrier's back.[2]

With this shape in mind, one can describe a brenta as a sort of gerla made for carrying liquids. While these two are similar in shape they differ markedly in construction, for a brenta has to be made far more like a barrel than a basket. The sides consist of wooden slats placed vertically; these had to be softened up and shaped in the same way that coopers did in making barrels. Indeed coopers probably did make brentas. Matters of weight and centre of gravity are far more urgent in the design of a brenta, which by itself, empty, weighs about 10 kg. If filled with 70 l of liquid, it would weigh 80 kg.

The term *brenta* came also to signify a unit of liquid measure, namely the amount that a brenta could hold. In the cities of the Po Valley plain, where brentas came to be used principally for wine – their having been first developed in the mountains for carrying water or milk – the unit of measure varied from one jurisdiction to another, ranging from a brenta of Turin (*brinda* in Piedmontese), which in metric terms equalled 49 l, to the brenta of Piacenza, equal to 75 l.[3]

To carry a fully loaded brenta one had obviously to be strong and steady. For a peasant living in the mountains it was presumably an occasional task, one among many that living in that environment entailed. The need to transport some water or milk was not an occasion for calling in a specialist. Yet in the cities of the valleys and the plain the division of labour so intensified that this very function, carrying a brenta – a brenta of wine – became the work of a specialist, known either as a *portator vini* (wine porter); or, by a derivation of *brenta*, in Latin a *brentator* (plural *brentatores*); or their Italian equivalents, which we have seen. In his version of Alberto's life and cult, Salimbene used both terms: *brentator*, the one more current in Parma in his day, and *portator vini*, the latter in order to get in his barbed pun against Alberto.[4]

All of the cities between the Alps and the Apennines had wine porters, but not all of these porters were brentatori.[5] Although the brenta, both as an object and as a term, was known throughout the countryside of this region, within cities of the lands bordering the Adriatic the preferred vessel for transporting wine was a *mastello* (in Latin *mastellum* or *solium*), which looked like a washtub that two persons could carry by passing a pole through two holes placed opposite one another near the rim (see Figure 11). The region of the brenta included Piedmont, Lombardy, Trentino,

Figure 11 The mastello, or soia, appears to be as much an invention of the flatlands as the brenta is of the mountains. Both saw use in carrying wine within northern Italian cities but the evidence indicates a vastly larger preference for the brenta when it came to the full-time job of delivering wine from the market to the residence or other site indicated by the buyer.

Emilia, and the western part of the Veneto, essentially Verona. The region of the mastello on the other hand was made up of the central and eastern part of the Veneto, the Po delta, and Romagna.[6] In the central façade of Saint-Mark's in Venice, one of the thirteenth-century sculpted panels groups together appropriately the city's purveyors of bread and wine. Between the bakers and a man drawing wine from a cask into a pitcher stand two men holding a mastello between them. No brenta is in sight.[7] There were, though, wine porters who used both types of containers in Mantua, Ferrara, Cremona, and perhaps other cities as well.[8] Brescia meanwhile offers a notable linguistic peculiarity, for even though the container used there was unmistakably the brenta, Brescians called it a *zerla*, their way of saying *gerla*, and called a man who carried wine in a zerla a *gerulatus* in Latin or, in the vernacular, *zerlotto*.[9]

One theory put forth to explain the peculiar geography of the brenta argues in favour of a Celtic origin, and hence involves going back to pre-Roman times when Celts dominated northern Italy, minus the Veneto but plus the Marches south of the Apennines. In that early period, Romagna and the Marches remained very much under Greek cultural influences, which included the use of terracotta amphorae. Later on, when wood took over from terracotta, Romagna adopted the mastello while the Marches opted for the Tuscan *bigoncia*, a small wooden cask. Even with these differences of terminology for both containers and carriers, the general term *portatori di vino* remained in use throughout northern Italy alongside whatever name local usage prescribed.[10]

Wine porters, however called, worked independently. They gathered at fixed places, as taxi drivers do at taxi stands in many modern cities, or as porters – non-specialised – have done for centuries and still do in Venice as well as in numerous other cities elsewhere in the world. The wine porters were to wait their turn to be hired by someone who was purchasing wine and needed to have it carried home or, in the case of a tavern keeper, to the cellar of the tavern. Their charge for this service increased with the distance they had to go.

This specialised *métier* of the wine porters was one of the countless effects of the series of economic and social changes experienced in Western Europe between the eleventh and fourteenth centuries, and called by some historians the 'Commercial Revolution'. The conscious borrowing from the phrase 'Industrial Revolution' serves to underscore the depth and long-lasting significance of those earlier, parallel changes felt throughout Europe, but felt precociously and most thoroughly in Italy. Where there had previously been a two-tiered economy with a relatively small class of warriors who engaged in pillage and gift-exchange while controlling a large mass of peasants who strove to maintain little better than a subsistence agriculture, there now emerged thriving centres of commerce, both local and long-distance; a vastly increased supply and use of money, along with the fundamentals of banking, credit, and insurance; and new urban elites that challenged the grip on power traditionally held by the leading aristocratic families. What had long been a stagnant population took off in the eleventh century and increased threefold by the onset of the great plague pandemic in 1347. Urban life, essentially moribund since the sixth century, flourished anew; where in those earlier centuries town dwellers occupied only a small proportion of the old Roman urban footprint and cultivated much of the otherwise unoccupied land within the old walls, people soon filled up all the spaces within the walls, and many cities went on to build two, and some even three, different sets of new walls within the three centuries starting in the early eleventh century in order to keep up with their expanding populations. The cathedral churches, baptisteries, bell towers, episcopal palaces, communal palaces, markets, public squares, and remnants of the various rings of walls remain today in city after city as testimonies to the combination of demographic growth, prosperity, and civic pride that characterised this extraordinary age. Moreover, climatologists refer to the age as 'the medieval anomaly', for their evidence demonstrates that it was favoured by exceptionally felicitous conditions of climate and ecology.[11]

In political terms this same period marked in northern and central Italy the age of the communes, when newly dominant groups of urban dwellers succeeded in revolting against their local lord, usually a count or a bishop, to take over control of their city. Councils made up of elected representatives governed the communes. Between the early 1100s and early 1300s over two hundred Italian cities gained and held onto their independence in this way. Each city had its unique set of circumstances and political vicissitudes, but there were general patterns to the communal movement. Relatively oligarchic in their early days, the communes gradually broadened their bases of political support by involving ever larger and more popular sectors of the population in the governing process. Hardly any city escaped the bitter experiences and feelings brought on by factional strife, which made violence or the threat of it the norm and civic tranquillity the exception. The usual response to this problem from about 1175 on was to hire an outsider for a year or even just a half year to administer the affairs of the city. Such a neutral leader, called a *podestà*, was to be trained in the law, was not to have relatives or financial interests in the city, and was not eligible for reappointment, at least not immediately. The pressures nonetheless exerted upon republican institutions by circumstances but even more so by individuals acting by design were relentless. Already in the second half of the thirteenth century some cities found themselves in the hands of princely rulers; within a few decades the age of the independent communes was over, with the lone exemption of Venice, which resisted external control until the arrival of French revolutionary armies in 1797.[12]

The new lords in the age of the *signoria* (lordship), which began in the fourteenth century, masked the abruptness of the change by retaining much of the republican vocabularies and forms they had taken over. There were still city councils made up of elected representatives, just as the bureaucratic structures put in place under the independent communes continued to function under the regime of the lords. Among the major concerns faced by communal authorities under either of these regimes was the regular provisioning of their communities with food. Most cities set up a government office to deal with these matters, placing officials in charge of it called in some cities 'judges of the food supply' (*giudici delle vettovaglie*). They regulated the entry of foodstuffs for sale within the city as these passed through the city's gates; they regulated the locations, days, and hours of markets; they regulated standards of sanitation and waste removal, for example in the work of butchers; and among still several other such concerns, they regulated prices as well as weights and measures.[13]

Given this active role of city governments in regulating the provisioning of food, the major and often earliest sources for learning about the work of wine porters include the statutes of the cities in which they worked. The communal statutes of Bergamo of 1248, for example, set the liquid measure of a brenta at an amount equivalent in metric terms to 64.14 l, and stipulated that every brentatore take an oath to measure wine 'correctly and fairly and in good faith' (*recte et juste et bona fide*), whether on behalf of the seller or of the buyer. Clearly these wine porters performed a public function by guaranteeing the quantity of wine in any transaction between a buyer and a seller. In fact in many instances wine porters were also referred to as 'measurers' (*misuratori*) as well as 'transferrers' or 'pourers' (*travasadori*), meaning those who transfer or pour wine from one container to another. Besides determining the quantitative definition of a brenta, the commune licensed the carrier's brenta to authenticate its size and specified that it also be marked to show the precise levels of a half- and of a quarter-brenta.

The communes assigned other tasks to wine porters that were entirely incidental to their wine-transporting labours. The most important of these was to serve as firemen. Since wood was then the predominant building material used and most urban buildings were packed in tightly along narrow streets, fires were not just frequent but also capable of destroying entire sections or neighbourhoods. To prevent fires, the city of Rovereto forbade bakers and others to carry a light or open flame through the streets on a windy night, and Modena ordered bakers to have a supply of water close by their ovens.[14] The reason that Venetian glass making is concentrated in Murano is that the city ordered all the glass makers to move there in 1291 as a fire-safety measure.[15] So as to contain fire damage in some cities, when the fire alarm sounded carpenters and masons had to present themselves prepared to knock down buildings in the path of the fire. But in all cities that had wine porters, they had to show up at a fire with their brentas filled with water and to remain there to help until the official in charge dismissed them. The statutes of Bologna and Brescia, to cite two early examples, contained such provisions by around 1250, Parma likewise in 1266, and most other cities of the region within the next few decades. Stiff fines awaited those who failed to show up for fire duty. In the case of Ferrara, brentatori and mastellari alike had to rush to the fire with their respective containers. The fire-fighting regulations of Modena reveal in passing that some wine porters, although consistently referred to as *brentatori*, at times worked in teams of two and carried a sort of mastello called a *quartaro*. This occurs in a passage ordering that, as it was impractical for brentatori to climb narrow stairs or go out on roof tops with their *quartari*, which were too large and could be carried only by two men, the Jewish community supply them with twenty good brentas when the occasion arose. Other burdens shouldered by wine porters included guard duty on the walls of Modena, washing the marketplaces of Piacenza and Brescia after the markets closed, distributing water to domiciles at Imola, and distributing food to plague victims at Cremona.

A commune was an association of individuals, at first of the 'law-worthy men' (*boni homines*) of a city, but soon of all that city's citizens; it was a sworn association in the sense that all its members, whether these were few or many, had to swear their allegiance to it. Within a few decades of the establishment of the communes, there began to take place an astonishing proliferation of smaller, internal associations. It is as if the communes by their example spawned these organisations, which brought together the town's inhabitants in a variety of groupings. There were neighbourhood associations, such as the Consortium of the Neighbourhood of San Pancrazio in Bergamo, from which we still have the minutes of the meetings held between 1283 and 1303.[16] There were parish associations such as the confraternities set up in nearly all parish churches, which have left extensive documentation including rules or statutes, membership lists, records of charitable donations and disbursements, etc. There were peace-keeping associations, such as the Consortium of Faith and Peace founded at Cremona in 1266. There were charitable associations, such as the many congregations for assisting the poor founded in Venice; in several places this sort of organisation was named a *misericordia*.[17] There were specialised charitable associations, such as the Consortium for Assisting Prisoners at Bergamo, and military associations, such as the Society of Fraternity and Arms at Modena. These all had their specific, stated purposes, which in many cases overlapped, but overall served a common function, just as taverns and religious festivals did, namely of integrating and socialising the city's inhabitants. People who live in villages all know one another, whereas those in cities of even just a few thousand inhabitants do not. In traditional societies the world over, villages are fully integrated. To state matters most simply, take the universal example of a death in a village: everyone takes part in the funeral. It is not so in cities, yet in almost every association founded within an Italian commune, no matter what its principal reason for being, there was a provision stating that when a member of that association died, all the other members had an obligation to attend the funeral.[18]

It is in this context of multiple, functionally overlapping associations that took root in the communal era that we turn to guilds, those other groupings of people by their line of work, such as goldsmiths or butchers or tailors. Most guilds combined some of the characteristics of both professional organisations and labour unions of more recent times, but permission to organise had to come from the communal government – or from the judges of the *vettovaglie* where food was involved – as did approval of the guild's statutes. The guild members, who came from various parts of the city, participated in meetings to discuss matters of mutual interest and to elect their officers. Nothing demonstrates better the division of urban labour than the long list of guilds found in most cities.

Guilds went by many names, mainly well-known Latin collective nouns such as *collegium* (college), *ministerium* (ministry), *ordo* (order), *schola* (school), *societas* (society), and *universitas* (university). The term generally favoured in Lombardy, namely *paraticum*, probably refers to the parades in which workers, usually dispersed, participated as groups. The favoured term in the Veneto was *schola*, although in Padua it was *frataglia*, a term that persists in the use of *brotherhood* in American union nomenclature. The term *ars* (art) is sometimes taken to signify a guild, but it normally refers instead to a profession or *métier*. As we shall see, an *ars brentatorum* (*métier* of brentatori) existed in most cities by the thirteenth century, but guilds of them for the most part came only later. Just one term, *collegium*, seemed mostly reserved for guilds of such professionals as judges, notaries, physicians, or, as at Brescia, masters of grammar. Still today, Italian auditors have their Collegio Nazionale dei Revisori dei Conti (National College of Auditors), just as chiefs of vascular surgery in hospitals have their Collegio dei Primari Ospedalieri di Chirurgia Vascolare. This tradition has also an echo in the name of the first organisation of medical professionals in America, the College of Physicians of Philadelphia, founded in 1787.[19]

The guilds of professionals, plus those of merchants, were among the first to be formed in the communes. Indeed they reflect the social elites that were instrumental in forming communes in the first place, and along with the expanding social and political base of the communes there took place a parallel expansion of concessions to form guilds. One economic sector to which most cities at first specifically denied the right to organise, however, was the one having to do with provisioning the community with food supplies. The statutes of Bologna of 1250 and as revised in 1288 sought to prevent textile workers and, among others, those such as the brentatori involved in feeding the city from forming any kind of association or choosing any leaders whatsoever.[20] That communal governments wished to keep tight control over these types of workers seems apparent, and one motive might have been to keep individuals considered of low social standing from gaining power by organising.

Treviso permitted the formation of a Scuola dei Portatori di Vino already in 1316, but nearly a century passed before other cities did something similar. These included Ferrara, which made exceptional use of *collegium* for an association of wine porters in 1402, the Collegium seu scolla brentatorum et mastellatorum; Bologna in 1407, which permitted the formation of the Compagnia dei brentadori; Verona in 1416, which approved the Statuta portitorum portantium vinum (Statutes of the porters carrying wine); Trent, which in 1426 approved the Capitoli di li Portadori di vino; Cremona in 1434, which approved the Paraticum artis brentatorum; or Brescia in 1436, with the Paraticum zerlottorum. The foundation dates continue in the sixteenth century: Reggio Emilia, 1503; Milan, 1531; Parma and also Pavia, 1553; Venice, 1568 (Scola dei Venditori (sellers) et Portadori de Vin); and Bergamo, 1598 (Paratico dei Brentatori e Facchini (porters)).

Given the distinct personalities, styles, tastes, pronunciation, and manners of speaking that distinguished and still distinguish these cities, the uniformity of the notarial culture they shared stands out. Starting with the communal statutes of the thirteenth century in one city after another, script, decorated capital letters, paragraph length, sentence structure, vocabulary, tone, and substance are all closely, and recognisably, related. They may begin with a brief religious invocation such as 'In the name of Almighty God and saint ...', but for the rest remain focused on the business at hand. They are the handiwork of notaries and the common source can be found in the law faculty of Bologna, specifically in books of templates such as the manuals prepared in about 1200 by Master Boncompagno da Signa, a Bolognese master of rhetoric.[21] To be sure, the statutes in some cities were undoubtedly influenced by those from other cities. For example, the introduction to the statutes of the brentatori of Modena, dated 1727, cites as sources the '*Arte de brentatori di Reggio* and the customary practice in this city of Modena'.

The multiple uniformities observed in communal statutes trickled down as it were to the myriad of neighbourhood associations, parish confraternities, charitable organisations, and indeed guilds, all of which had their own constitutions, or statutes or laws or regulations – essentially what in English one would call 'by-laws'. These were all drawn up by notaries, even those that governed the principally religious associations, whether devoted to a particular saint such as the Virgin Mary, or to a particular devotion such as the Eucharist, or more generally to the defence of orthodoxy. Behind these stood a long tradition of religious rules, a not irrelevant point given that confraternities were in significant ways heirs to the monastic tradition, projected via the new mendicant orders, the Franciscans and Dominicans especially, right into the heart of the urban scene to laypeople. But the rules of the orders of monks and friars, for all that they dealt with organisational, even domestic, details, are spiritual works, each bearing a new religious message for its time from an innovative and charismatic religious reformer. Not so the rules of confraternities, which, like those of other associations of the age, were made up of such sentences as 'In the first place all of the above-mentioned members of the above-mentioned consortium established and ordered that the said consortium have one head who be of the said consortium and faithful to the said consortium.' Another essential element these regulations shared was clarity about the consequences of disobedience, in keeping with Boncompagno's advice that statutes must specify the sanctions to be imposed for contravening the terms stated therein.

A brief listing of the contents of the statutes of the Bolognese brentatori of 1410 gives an idea of what such statutes generally contained. Following the invocation and a brief account of the founding of the guild, there comes the first of seventeen chapters or paragraphs; it states that anyone who performs the work of a wine porter in the city of Bologna must belong to the Company of Brentatori of Bologna, must observe all of its rules, and must obey its officers. The next paragraph deals with the election of the officers, followed by others that describe the officers' duties and their authority in disciplining disobedient members.

The fifth paragraph prohibits anyone from carrying wine on Sundays; Christmas Day; Easter Day; and the feast days of Saints Mark, Ambrose, and Petronius; as well as on those of all the Apostles and evangelists. The list adds to these the feast days of the Virgin and of Saints Lawrence, Anthony, Catherine, and Lucy. Such laws and regulations against working on Sundays, although very common, perhaps needed reinforcement, for in the fifteenth and sixteenth centuries there appeared a new devotional figure in northern Italy, namely the Sunday Christ (*il Cristo della domenica*), shown wounded by ordinary working tools such as hammers, rakes, ploughs, coins, casks, etc. instead of the usual instruments of the passion. A rare exception to such rules, brought to light at Lodi, was most likely imposed on the people of that small city by foreign occupiers. A 1759 copy of the rules of the wine porters' guild stated that each porter (the term there used was *brentore*) was obliged to report to one of the syndics within three days how many brentas of wine he had delivered on a feast day *al militare*, which in that precise context meant to the Spanish presidio that dominated the town.[22]

Next in the Bologna statutes come the obligation to assist in putting out fires, a prohibition against any wine porter interfering with the work or gain of a colleague, and then a paragraph that sets the entry fees for membership in this society. The text does not say but assumes that only men do this kind of work. For a resident of Bologna the fee was 15 pounds, while for an outsider it was 25 pounds. The son or grandson of a wine porter, however, paid only 2 pounds. Since the going rate for carrying a brenta of wine within the city was 1 *bolognino*, and 12 of these made 1 *soldo*, and in turn 20 *soldi* made 1 pound, the entry fee for the descendant of a wine porter was equivalent to transporting 480 brentas of wine. The next two provisions prohibit the use by anyone of someone else's brenta without express permission, and set the penalties for customs fraud and for carrying wine through the city gates without the permission of a customs official.

Paragraph 12 obliges the wine porters as a group to attend mass at the church of Bologna's patron, Saint Mark, on that saint's feast day, 25 April, and, along with the city's many other corporations, to make their guild's annual offering of candle wax. Furthermore, when any member of the society dies, all other members are obliged to attend his obsequies. Along with a prohibition against speaking badly of the guild officers, the remaining paragraphs set out detailed rules on such matters as not altering agreed-upon quantities or qualities of wine.

The statutes of the wine porters of Cremona of 1434 are rather more compact and coordinated than those of Bologna. They begin with three paragraphs on membership, then two on religious observances, two on the functioning of the guild, and a final two with admonitions to guild members about their work. One of these is that they do their work well and legally (*bene et legaliter*) and without fraud, while the other forbids them to carry wine for anyone who is a debtor of any other member of the guild. Prohibitions of another sort enter into the regulations for wine porters in both Reggio and Modena, namely that they not use their brentas to carry garbage, butcher's offal, or dead bodies, and that they have nothing to do with cleaning latrines or sewers (*canaletti*). On a pleasanter note, the Modenese carriers, like their colleagues in Cremona and Vicenza, were to cover the tops of their brentas or mastelli with clean white cloths when these had wine in them.

The invocation at the head of the first statutes of the Company of Brentatori of Bologna, set down in 1410, reads: 'To the praise, honor, and reverence of Almighty God' ('Ad laudem honorem et reverentiam omnipotentis dei').[23] Worked into the splendidly decorated initial letter *A* is the image of a wine porter (see Figure 12). He is slightly bent forward in order to balance the weight of the brenta

Figure 12 The original manuscript of the statutes of the Company of Wine Porters of Bologna, dated 1410, bears this elegantly illuminated initial letter 'A' with the image of a simple wine porter, plodding along under the weight of his liquid cargo. Other copies of the statutes are known to exist but none with this illuminated letter.

on his back; he holds a staff in his left hand – in fact an unfinished branch replete with the stubs of several smaller branches – and in his right hand he rather loosely holds a rope that is attached to the brenta. The staff served as a walking stick, giving the porter stability, especially on uneven surfaces, or on stairs, say, leading down into a cellar. But the staff also served another, quite different purpose, along with the rope, when the wine porter had to pour out the contents of his brenta into another receptacle. Without removing the brenta from his back and shoulders, he stood a metre or so in front of the receptacle, tilted his head slightly to one side, and poured the wine over his shoulder right into the receiving vessel. But to accomplish this, and in particular to keep control of the enormous – as well as shifting – weight of his liquid cargo, he spread

Figure 13 In this version of the marriage-banquet scene at Cana, a wine
porter gets to play a major role in sacred history. Andrea of Bologna
painted this fresco in the early fourteenth century at the Abbey of Pomposa.

his legs apart, and by leaning forward on his staff formed a tripod.
Then as he leaned forward and tilted his head to the side, he pulled
on the rope to guide the mouth of the brenta to the very point from
which he wanted the wine to flow out. To carry a full brenta, as
we have observed, required tremendous strength, but to pour out
its contents without a spill required skill in addition. One can only
imagine beginners practising with water. Fortunately there exists a
rare image of a wine porter performing this delicate task; it is in a
fresco painted by Andrea of Bologna in the early fourteenth century

at the Abbey of Pomposa, near Ravenna (see Figure 13). It shows a porter working at no less an occasion than the marriage feast at Cana. No known text explains how the wine porter performed this task but the Pomposa fresco makes clear that the key to pouring successfully was that stable tripod. No wonder the statutes of the wine porters' guild of Pavia warned its members not to carry a loaded brenta without also carrying a metal-tipped wooden staff for support, because anyone who failed to do so and suffered a spill had to pay for the wine. No wonder either that one of Alberto's miracles was his gathering up in his hands of wine that had spilled on the ground from a brenta and pouring it back – perfectly fit for drinking – into the brenta.

These earliest representations of brentatori at work show a form of the brenta significantly different from that of any brenta one sees today. Starting with the drawings and photographs of brentas reproduced in the books of late-nineteenth-century folklorists right through to the real thing that one can now find in the countryside (as seen earlier in Figure 3) or in displays of traditional agrarian tools in museums of folklore, the brenta is only slightly larger at the mouth or top than at the base, and the slats, while a bit wider at the top than at the bottom, are not curved. Yet the brentas depicted in these images from earlier centuries are mostly much larger at the top than at the bottom, and most of these, although not all, conform to the curve of the carrier's stooped back and loom over his head. One can, for example, see curved brentas, shaped almost like powder horns, in early-fourteenth-century manuscript images of market scenes; these occur in some of the extravagantly illuminated manuscripts of Roman legal texts produced at Bologna. Along with cloth merchants opening out bolts of cloth and men discussing the merits and value of a horse, in one of these there is a brentatore – not using a staff by the way – who pours wine into a terracotta vase while another man steadies the vase and three men look on. In another of these scenes, a brentatore fills his brenta from a great cask while a prospective client tastes wine from a glass and a person holding a flask, presumably the one who poured that glass of wine, stands by as if awaiting the taster's reaction (see Figure 14). From the mid-fifteenth century there is a splendid drawing by Jacopo Bellini that shows a wine porter standing, both hands on his staff, slightly bent under the weight of an immense brenta that is decidedly curved about as those of the Pomposa fresco or the Bolognese law manuscripts.[24]

Figure 14 Wine porters are here shown at work in a market in Bologna, *c.* 1345. This scene, painted by the so-called 'Master' of 1346, illustrates one of several such manuscript copies of Justinian's *Digests*.

The work of a wine porter began where wine was sold. In most of the cities between the Alps and the Apennines this meant the main square: the largest and most central place, and in several cases the only adequate space, for a market. Such cities were tightly packed, so that one could walk from one side to the other of many of them in a matter of fifteen or twenty minutes. The typical urban population ranged between about 10,000 and 30,000. After growing rapidly until the 1270s, and then either continuing to grow but at a declining rate of acceleration, or actually declining slightly until 1347, the size of most communities was severely set back by as much as one-third or one-half by *Yersinia pestis*, the disease commonly known as plague, and not just one time, for the dreaded disease made several return visits. These were quite frequent in the latter half of the fourteenth century and much of the fifteenth as well, but then erratically infrequent, but no less destructive, in the two centuries following, for example in 1576 or in 1630. The result was that the pre-plague population figures were not everywhere matched or exceeded until the eighteenth century, when the disease finally abandoned Europe.

In Reggio Emilia at the time of the commune, the cathedral, the baptistery, and the bishop's palace were free-standing buildings that effectively enclosed a small square. This square served as the site of the food market. Here is where the wine porters first worked, while somewhere close by, 'in the neighbourhood of the cathedral', they stored their brentas. When the episcopal palace expanded in the late fifteenth century to fill the space between the cathedral and baptistery, the market was squeezed right out into the communal square. Cremona had a separate space for the wine market, which was set in the bishop's court, and although it later transferred to another location, this information is noteworthy if only because it tells us where Alberto started out every workday. In Bergamo the market took place for a few centuries in the main square, in the shadow of episcopal and communal authority. Later on, though, well after the Venetians conquered the city in the 1420s, the new rulers moved most commercial activity from there to a new piazza in order to leave the old one to serve mainly as a centre for displaying power and staging ceremonies. In addition to a few small squares that hosted the fish, hay, and shoe markets, there were other markets still. Small as Bergamo's population of about 20,000 people was in 1300, and compact the area within its walls, the population of the city spilled down the hillside from the upper city to two quite populous neighbourhoods, the Borgo Sant'Antonio and especially the Borgo San Leonardo. Each had its own butcher's shop, and yet the sources have not, to date, revealed where specifically, or even whether, one could purchase wine in either one. Still, the Venetian diarist Marin Sanudo told of walking down the steps from San Domenico, where the San Giacomo Gate now is, to the Borgo San Leonardo – this was in 1483 – and finding it, with its walls and watercourses and streets and houses, the equivalent of a whole city. A century later, the Venetian governor of the time specified that the population of San Leonardo was 3,000 and its piazza had shops on all sides and stores with cloth and other merchandise of great value. It is hard to imagine, in other words, that wine was not sold and transported within these two extra-mural neighbourhoods. In any case, the regulations governing the wine porters' guild reflected this cityscape by calling for its members to vote each year for three syndics. One of these was to be from 'the city', referring to what is now called the 'Upper City' (*Città Alta*) and is contained within the walls, and one each was to be from these two populous neighbourhoods. The reason for this arrangement could be that the guild included members who lived in each of those three places, but a more likely explanation would be that it had wine porters stationed at markets in all three.[25]

Parma had two main squares, one truly the preserve of the bishop, for it contained his palace, his cathedral church, the baptistery, and the bell tower; and the other the *platea communis*, where both the seat of the communal government and the market were located. Built on the site of the Roman forum, right where the main north–south cross street intersected the Via Emilia, this latter square housed to one side the church of Saint-Peter where, according to Salimbene, the wine porters launched what he saw as the bogus cult of 'Saint' Alberto in Parma. The church now faces on the square, but in the thirteenth century the church was oriented in the opposite direction so it was the apse that fronted on the square. On the outside of the apse was a portico, and it was here that the wine porters were stationed, like taxi drivers, waiting their turn to be called to transport wine.[26]

The next cities up in size were those with populations that regularly exceeded 30,000: Brescia, Padua, and Verona. Brescia had a separate wine market one block south of the cathedral, its memory preserved through the early modern centuries in the name of the Piazza del Mercato del Vino. Through most of the early modern period Turin appeared unlikely ever to become a major city, but in the eighteenth century its numbers shot up to 80,000. Bologna instead had 45,000 people by 1300, and in the seventeenth and eighteenth centuries was more consistently in the 70,000–80,000 range. The Company of Brentatori in that city had its headquarters in the Via de' Pignatari (makers of pots and pans), just a few steps away from the façade of the cathedral church of Saint-Petronius, and thus close by the city's great main square. The local term in Bologna for a station where the wine carriers waited to be summoned was *trebbo*, and it is not surprising that a city of such size had more than one of these; indeed by the seventeenth century there were no fewer then eighteen *trebbi* spread throughout Bologna. Similarly Milan, from the start of the Commercial Revolution northern Italy's second-largest city, had multiple waiting stations for wine porters, as many as thirty-five of them in the seventeenth century when the population reached about 130,000. Finally, the largest city, namely

Venice, had already reached 150,000 in the sixteenth century. Plague cut that number to 100,000 in the epidemic of 1630, but within a few decades the population stood at 160,000. The main seat of the wine trade was, like the main market, close to the Rialto at the Fondamenta (canal embankment) or Riva (canal bank) del Vin. The distribution of wine also took place elsewhere in the city at subsidiary points where one finds these place names repeated or variants such as Campiello (Little Square) del Vin. Since 1505 there had been a guild of wine merchants (Scuola dei mercanti da vin) housed very near the Rialto at the church of Saint-Sylvester, and from 1568 a guild of vendors and porters of wine, located close by at the church of Saint-Bartholomew. These two groups merged in 1609.

How many porters did it take to keep a whole city population supplied with wine on the last leg of its journey from the producer to the consumer? Cities that set the maximum number of wine porters give helpful answers. Brescia, with a population of 43,000 in 1609 set that number at 80, but following the epidemic of 1630 and the population drop to 20,000, they reduced the number to 50. Mantua limited the number of wine porters to 30 in 1435, and raised it to 70 in 1548 by which time the population had risen to about 38,000. Also helpful are the guild records that have lists of members at a given time: Verona had 32 wine porters in 1430; Modena 12 in 1576 and 27 in 1730; Bergamo 57 in 1571, but these included both wine porters and generic porters (*facchini*); and Venice 156 in 1569 and 400 in 1773. At Cremona in 1742 69 wine porters signalled their presence in writing at their annual meeting. On the basis of these figures one gets a rough estimate of 1 wine carrier per 400–500 people.

The occasional membership lists of guilds fortunately provide us with names of some individual wine porters, thus freeing them from the anonymity that was the fate of most. Those who did this kind of work, although not wealthy or major players on their respective civic scenes, do appear now and then, identified by their occupation, in documents not directly connected with guild membership. One example that is nonetheless work-related comes from the trial of a wine merchant charged with (and convicted of) selling spoiled wine; this was in Bergamo in 1614 and the man who delivered the wine was called to testify. For the most part, though, such documentary appearances have to do with other matters entirely, such as witnessing a document, belonging to a confraternity, or receiving assistance from one. In Bologna there was a public official known as a *ministralis* at the level of the parish, elected for a one-year term, who was to oversee such matters as public order, sanitation, morality, or fire prevention. Some of those elected were prominent figures such as notaries, and yet most of them were quite ordinary citizens. The occupations of those elected in 1348 included butchers, smiths, shoemakers, and at least one brentator, named Bertolomeus. The study of Bolognese wills follows the expected social pattern by which people in lower-paid trades were far more likely to appear as witnesses, if at all, than as testators. Yet here, too, there stands out the case of one Gerardus, brentator, who made his will in 1340 in the peripheral parish of Saint-Isaiah.[27]

Age and age limits figure only rarely in documents on the wine-carrying trade, understandable enough given that the physical exertion it demanded limited its practice to the truly able-bodied. One of these rare mentions of age occurs in the paragraph on the porters' obligation to serve as firemen in the revised statutes of the guild in Bologna issued in 1614; it specifically exempts members under eighteen years of age and those who are sixty or older from this obligation.[28]

Any attempt to understand the world of wine porters has to give attention to the religious component of the guilds. Even though a guild's reason for existence was the organisation and control of one key element in the city's economy, its corporate identity derived largely from its participation in corporate worship and corporate charity, whether in concert with other associations or independently. One of the grand occasions that mobilised the entire city was the feast of *Corpus Domini* (the Body of the Lord), also known as *Corpus Christi*, an innovation dating from the lifetime of Alberto. This was a time of far-reaching changes in religious practice and attitudes, the start of something that in certain ways culminated some two-and-a-half centuries later in the Protestant Reformation. Such fundamentals of Christian worship as prayer and the sacrament of the Eucharist, or Communion, were being transformed.

To go back only as far as the ninth-to-twelfth centuries, religion in the Latin West of that time was largely about the observance of forms; was largely a matter that concerned a caste of full-time 'religious', i.e. monks and nuns; and thus for the laity was mainly a vicarious experience. Monks and nuns did the praying, and members of the land-controlling warrior class endowed monasteries, mainly with land, in the expectation that the religious would pray for them and their ancestors in perpetuity. The bishops and priests who ministered to laypeople did so mainly by performing rituals. The other 90-or-so per cent of the population laboured to stay alive and to feed these religious and fighting elites. How different were the urban populations of the Commercial Revolution and of the communes it spawned. The new religious orders established early in the thirteenth century, the Franciscans and Dominicans, did not live in monasteries out in the countryside but settled exclusively in cities, and nowhere were these orders of friars stronger or more influential than in the cities of central and northern Italy. Among the many revolutionary notions that they introduced was that laypeople could and should pray, instead of leaving the praying entirely to someone else; specifically they encouraged people to memorise and recite the Lord's Prayer. In the wake of the Crusades, the new orders demonstrated their interest in the Near East and beyond in introducing some religious practices that came from Indic culture. The Franciscan contribution was a new posture to assume when praying. The traditional way was to stand with arms extended in the air and palms facing forward; they now prayed and counselled others to pray with their hands joined together in the Hindu fashion, a practice that obviously caught on. The Dominicans for their part invented the rosary, adapting the eastern practice of multiple recitations of prayers and keeping track of them by fingering beads – another successful bit of acculturation.[29]

More revolutionary still was the movement to involve the laity in the sacrament of the Eucharist, the theology of which was worked out definitively only in the course of the eleventh and twelfth centuries. By legislation passed at the Fourth Lateran Council in Rome in 1215, each layperson was to go to confession and subsequently to take communion at least once a year. To get this new role in the religious life accepted by laypeople required a massive programme of instruction and persuasion over several decades. A key part of this programme was the institution of a holiday specifically to promote the new observance. According to a pious woman at Liège early in the thirteenth century, Jesus confided to her through visions his displeasure at the lack of an annual celebration specifically dedicated to honouring the sacrament of his body and blood. Her persistent efforts on behalf of this divine wish led to the establishment of such a day in the diocese of Liège. Subsequently an influential Dominican, Hugh of Saint-Cher, the first of his order to be named a cardinal, took up her cause and succeeded in convincing

Pope Urban IV, who happened to be a former archdeacon of Liège, to proclaim the new holy day, Corpus Domini, in 1264. The new observance took its place in the liturgical calendar on the Thursday following Trinity Sunday, which is the eighth Sunday after Easter, and so, depending on the date of Easter in a given year, it comes in late May or early June. Another grand occasion for processions in the liturgical calendar was Assumption Day, which commemorates the bodily flight of the Virgin Mary to heaven, a centuries-old tradition celebrated every 15 August.[30]

The communes worked out all the details of the year's major processions, which involved every corporate body in the city: where they were to assemble, the need for them to have their processional banner – the same one they would use on their respective saints' days – and of course the order of the procession, a sure indicator of status. The earliest such processional list known comes from the statutes of Padua of 1287; it consists of thirty-six *fratalie*. The list starts with notaries and then merchants, and concludes with wine porters, sawyers, weavers, and woollen workers. Bologna listed twenty-three *societates artium* in 1294, which started with money changers, merchants, and notaries, but, as we saw, the wine porters were among those not yet permitted to organise a guild and thus not able to march. The latter are also absent from the list in the Cremona statutes of 1313, which include fourteen *paratici*, starting with the least important, the tavern keepers and hoteliers, and ending with merchants, but then adds two *collegia*, one of judges and the other of notaries.[31]

Reggio Emilia listed twenty-two *métiers* in 1318, starting with judges, notaries, and merchants, and leaving the brentatori in twenty-sixth place just ahead of *calderai* (tinkers) and *rigatieri* (junk dealers). A list prepared at Ferrara in 1322 combined three *collegia* with twenty-two *universitates artium*, with, once again, the wine porters third from the end followed only by barbers and bakers. To cite just three more such lists: Como placed *portatori* seventeenth out of seventeen *paratici* in 1335; Brescia, after three *collegia*, placed the *zerlotti* twenty-first of twenty-five *paratici*; and Bergamo promulgated for Corpus Domini in 1692 a list of thirty-two groups to go 'in the traditional order'. Public officials made up the first group but the rest of the list, as at Cremona, is in ascending order of importance, starting with '*Facchini, Brentadori, Misuratori di Biade* [measurers of animal-feed]', and finishing with goldsmiths, spice dealers, and merchants.

The wine porters in some places had a greater role in these feast days than just marching along with everyone else. In addition to their other civic roles as fire fighters and street cleaners, they had the high obligation to transform secular into sacred space. Their statutes at Cremona and at Piacenza ordered that they clean the great piazza on the eve of the Assumption of the Virgin.[32]

In addition to these universally observed holidays, each city of course devoted one of the all-inclusive days of festivities to an obligatory procession to honour its own patron saint. The day's choreography specified the order in which professional organisations presented their ritual offerings, usually of wax or money, such as the offerings to Saint Mark at Bologna, as we saw, or to Saint Geminiano at Modena or to Saint Abbondio at Como. But the days on which the spotlights shone most brightly on these organisations were those devoted to their respective patrons – days that topped off an entire year's worth of support and devotion. As we noted about Cremona, the wine porters maintained an altar for their patron saint, Alberto; paid for masses to be said there; and also supplied the oil that kept a lamp burning there at all times. Clearly the culmination of all this effort came on each 7 May, when they processed together to Saints-Mattia-and-Alberto for the mass in honour of Alberto's feast day. In Reggio Emilia the wine porters celebrated his feast day by gathering near the cathedral and going in procession to the church of Saint-George to attend a sung mass at the altar of Alberto, which had a painted image, and to make their offering of candle wax. During his visitation to that church in 1593, the bishop of Reggio made note of the altar, 'whose care is administered by the wine porters'. To the Reggiani the saint was known, not unreasonably, as 'Saint Alberto of Cremona'.

In Parma and Piacenza, the wine porters must surely have fostered the development of the cult of Alberto, or so we can reasonably surmise. Some of them, as well as many of their fellow citizens, had been among the first to travel to his tomb in Cremona, and the role of the wine porters of Parma in launching the cult outside Cremona is well attested. Even so, in both of these cities near the source the cult took a very peculiar turn. The commune of Piacenza authorized the *brentori*, as they were called in that city, to organise a guild in 1627. The statutes they promulgated the following year include such usual clauses as those concerning the rules for membership, the elections and duties of the officers, and the obligation of all members to attend the funerals of fellow members. However, the clause concerning a saintly patron departs from the norm: 'The said *brentori*, knowing it to be impossible that the said guild could endure or govern itself for long without having a protector, ... have congregated and elected as their protector ... the Glorious Father Saint Alberto of the Carmelite Order; this they have established and also confirmed upon the advice of wise, intelligent, and prudent persons' (*persone savie intelligenti e prudente*). Furthermore, on their patron's feast day, which was and is 7 August, they were to gather in the morning at the seat of the guild and from there go in solemn procession to the church of the Fathers of the Madonna del Carmine for the mass in honour of the saint and to make an offering to him.[33]

This other Alberto was a somewhat younger contemporary of our Alberto: a Carmelite friar who lived in Trapani in Sicily and died in 1307; his name is often given as Alberico. The Carmelites were a late-twelfth-century spin-off of the Crusades in Palestine who gained official recognition as a religious order by the Roman Church early in the thirteenth century; they began to settle in Europe in 1238, first in Sicily, and from there they spread northwards. Alberto of Trapani became their first saint, venerated from the time of his death and canonised by the pope in 1476.[34]

Since the wine porters of Piacenza were not organised before 1627, it is difficult to know what ties if any they had had before then with the cult of Saint Alberto of Villa d'Ogna. What is in any case noteworthy about the account given in the statutes is that learned people advised these illiterate labourers to select Alberto of Trapani as their patron. It happens that in Parma also, probably by sometime in the seventeenth century, the wine porters were holding their corporate worship in the Carmelites' church. This was located just two short blocks from the main square, where they continued to assemble for work next to the church of Saint-Peter. As for the wine porters of Pavia, when they organised their guild in 1553 they chose Saint Augustine as their patron and celebrated his feast day, 28 August, at that saint's church. However, a century-and-a-quarter later they appear to have chosen Saint Alberto for that role, and since they celebrated his feast day in the Carmelites' church, we can surmise that they, too, venerated the Alberto from Sicily.[35]

The association of wine porters with Alberto of Trapani obviously signals the possibility of a confused identity between two saints who had the same name. Such confusion on the part of a religious order, however, would be highly unlikely. All orders had traditions of learning, some more than others to be sure, while all demonstrated strong interest in their respective histories and in the lives and miracles of their saintly founders. Workers' guilds on the other hand had no such strong interest in their corporate histories. Their patron saints of course served to help build and maintain their group identities, but their main concerns focused on their particular lines of work, whereas those of religious orders focused on fulfilling the spiritual visions of their founders. The perhaps anomalous case of Piacenza notwithstanding, the further away one gets from Cremona the more likely it is that the fame of Alberto of Villa d'Ogna faded.

The Bologna guild's statutes of 1410 make no mention of a patron saint. However, those of 1424 include along with the clause about the annual gift to Saint-Mark instructions for the members to go to the church of Saint-Alberto, located outside the walls on the Via San Vitale, on the feast day of Saint Alberto, i.e. 7 August – hence, once again, that of Alberto of Trapani. These instructions specify that they organise to go there in the same way that they do for Saint-Mark. Furthermore, those of 1614 add that following the sung mass for Saint Alberto on that day there should be a mass celebrated for the souls of the guild's founders.

Ferrara has the rare distinction of a cultural patrimony that includes to this day a chapel of the wine porters; it is the second chapel on the right in the church of Saint-Paul. This venerable church building, which dated from the tenth century, passed into the hands of the Carmelite Friars in 1295. The statutes of the College of Wine Porters of Ferrara, set down in 1402, start off with the porters' obligation to maintain an oil lamp, lit day and night, in Saint-Paul, 'where the ancient register of the wine porters is kept'. Thus the connection between the porters and Saint-Paul certainly reaches back into the fourteenth century. We know very little of that building because it suffered extreme damage in an earthquake in 1570, whereas the present church is the one rebuilt and enlarged in the decades immediately following the earthquake. In 1602 the Carmelite fathers and wine porters agreed that the latter would have a chapel in the new church – in fact the second chapel on the right, dedicated to Saint Alberto of Trapani, and still known as the Chapel of the Brentadori. The altarpiece showing the saint reviving a child with water he had blessed dates from the late eighteenth century.[36]

The cult of Alberto continued without interruption at Villa d'Ogna, but of course that had nothing to do with wine porters. Mountain villages did not have such guilds, let alone practitioners of that *métier*. That Alberto came from there was justification enough. What is odd, though, is that so little evidence of an Alberto cult, whether or not connected with wine porters, has come to light in the seat of his home diocese, the city of Bergamo. Even so, Alberto must at least have been the patron of the wine porters of Bergamo, for their processional banner, an eighteenth-century text so informs us, bore an image of Alberto. Furthermore, there is the fresco with a full-length portrait of Alberto in the church of Saint-Michael, even though it was covered up by another fresco in the fifteenth century.

To conclude with a particular charitable undertaking of the wine porters, we should recall that, according to the *Annals of Parma*, the wine porters of that city collected enough money, starting in 1279 from the crowds gathered in the communal square, to purchase a house where they founded a hospice and named it for Saint Alberto. Beyond their critical role as founders, though, no information remains about their subsequent involvement, if any, as patrons. Salimbene, of course, made no mention of this pious foundation and yet, as his account of the Alberto cult shows, he was particularly well informed about what went on in his native city. For him to acknowledge this act of charity would have justified both the cult and the wine porters' part in establishing it. Besides, such concern for the plight of the poor would most likely have appeared from his point of view as treading on Franciscan territory.

In spite of Salimbene's hostility, the hospice took root and grew. Over at least the next few decades, some well-off citizens of Parma included donations to the Hospital of Saint-Alberto in their wills.[37] This kind of charitable giving was characteristic in the cities of the new commercial age. Whereas the landed class of earlier centuries patronised mainly monasteries, the urban wealthy began by the late twelfth century to patronise various forms of assistance for the poor. Besides the confraternities founded in all cities to channel poor relief, donors founded or supported institutions variously referred to as 'hospital', 'hospice', or 'hostel'. Whatever the term used, such places were not like modern hospitals. Some did offer medical assistance to the ill, but for the most part they offered hospitality to pilgrims and other travellers, or shelter to local poor people, or comfort to the ill and dying. Overall the assistance offered was more spiritual than medical. In city after city such havens proliferated between the thirteenth and fifteenth centuries, and most of these were very small, with space available for perhaps only five or ten persons. As these small foundations continued to grow in number many bishops and communal authorities sought to consolidate them into larger institutions, which by the sixteenth century did in some ways start to resemble modern hospitals.[38]

The statutes of Cremona of 1339 ordered that the alms collected at Saint-Mattia on Assumption Day be given to that city's Hospital of Saint-Alberto provided that the rector of the church did not object. This hospital was located in the neighbourhood of the church, a connection that at least suggests a close association between the hospital and the wine porters. Documents from the 1430s and 1440s concerning property holdings of this hospital demonstrated its continued success, and then Cremona's version of the consolidation process took place. The general council of the city voted in favour of it in 1450. In the year following, Pope Nicholas V granted the citizens of Cremona permission to set up a hospital that would take the place of many 'pious foundations spread throughout Cremona and its province'. The new hospital bore the name of Santa Maria della Pietà, and one of the twelve institutions gathered into it was the Hospital of Saint-Alberto.[39]

The work that wine porters did day after day remained essentially unchanged in century after century. Like his counterparts of later times right up to the end of the Old Regime, when the Cremona wine market opened every morning – except on Sundays and feast days during the 1260s and 1270s – Alberto had to be there with his brenta ready to serve customers. The various urban annals of Lombardy and Emilia, plus Salimbene's *Chronicle*, all agree in reporting that Alberto was a wine porter. Even though the wine porters of Cremona, as in other cities, gained permission to form a corporation only much later, the vested interest of the commune had already determined many of the essential modalities of the trade by his time. As with all the trades involving the supply of victuals to the city, the commune kept careful track of those who did this kind of work and how they executed it, not least by certifying the capacity of the containers they carried. These considerations, plus the admiration shown by the Cremonese wine porters for their deceased co-worker Alberto, tell us that carrying wine was not a part-time job, one that just anyone could do or that anyone could move in and out of casually. Alberto was one of the wine porters of Cremona; he was one of them. Such was his identity: not that of an occasional worker, and surely not that of a wealthy man able to go off every now and then for months at a time to visit shrines in Spain, Italy, or Palestine, or to offer hospitality to pilgrims and beggars in his comfortable home. He was a poor worker.

What did change over the years was not what the wine porters did but the nature of their guilds, and not only of theirs. What happened to their guilds is part of the well-known history of virtually all European guilds of virtually all trades in the seventeenth and eighteenth centuries, namely tendencies towards ever-increasing restrictiveness with regard to membership and an all-consuming preoccupation with preserving, and if possible even extending, their privileges. Of all the *bêtes noires* of the Enlightenment, the privileged corporation was at or near the top of the list. Agents of Empress Maria Theresa decreed the suppression of the guilds of Cremona in 1776, while agents of her son, Joseph II, did the same in Milan a decade later. What the enlightened monarchs left undone in these matters was soon completed in Venice and elsewhere in the late 1790s by the regimes installed by the armies of revolutionary France.[40]

The guilds vanished quickly but the *métier* of the wine porters dragged on here and there for a few decades, or in some places for much or all of a century. In Mantua, the two-man teams that carried mastelli and wore the uniforms prescribed by Francesco Gonzaga in 1548 lasted long enough to be immortalised in photographs. The de-organised wine porters of Parma formed their own private association, which allowed them and their heirs to perpetuate the carrying of brentas for the distribution of wine in that city until 1910. But the loss of the wine porters' monopoly at the end of the Old Regime involved more than just making it legitimate for anyone to carry wine in a brenta for pay; henceforth the way was open to innovation, for example by letting buyers bring their own (small) vessels to market for the wine they bought, just as they brought their own baskets for carrying food. The use of glass bottles sealed with corks, which had its beginnings back in the seventeenth century, was now coming into wide use, thus radically altering the time-honoured practice of distributing wine from market to consumer in brentas. In such ways the liberalised marketing of foodstuffs in the nineteenth century brought the wine porters' *métier* to an end.[41]

5

Topography and migration

Why did Alberto leave the Val Seriana and why did he go to Cremona and take up a job there carrying wine? The legends advance two possible answers, first that his desire to make pilgrimages lured him away and second that a property dispute drove him away. But the lack of corroborating evidence demands that we suspend judgement on these matters, and turn instead to topography, plus the historical experience of several generations in Alberto's part of the world, to consider what these have to say, not specifically about Alberto's motives, but about the kind of move he made from a mountain village to a city in the plain.

The brenta itself had made a journey similar to Alberto's at least a century earlier. Philologists and archaeologists inform us that they located examples of this curious vessel, which they claim to be of Alpine origin, throughout most of the triangular territory formed by the Alps, the Apennines, and the Adriatic. The term *brentatore* on the other hand did not come down from the mountains with the brenta but originated, as we saw, in the lowland cities where the latter arrived. In use and without need of any explanation at the latest by the 1240s, *brentatore* and the specialised trade it designated originated in the twelfth-century explosive growth of urban population, commercial development, prosperity, and highly specialised labour markets.

The similarities between the trajectories of Alberto and the brenta call attention to the topography that these traversed. While the descent from mountain peaks to valley floor is of course a continuum, the human inhabitants of the region have obviously always been sensitive to the variants of terrain and climate that distinguish among the mountains, the plateaus or upper plains, and the plain or lower plain, which in Lombardy is called *la bassa*. Today as in the past, there are very few settlements higher than 1,500 m above sea level; mountain settlements tend instead to be found at elevations between 400 and 1,400 m, and tend to be small as well as located in or close to valleys. The intermediate zone of the plateaus, between roughly 150 and 350 m, appears throughout history to have been the most hospitable to human habitation. And while people in our times correctly consider the lower plain, the *bassa*, to be one of the most highly productive agricultural regions of the world, it was not always so.

Between some 6 million and 3 million years ago the entire valley up to what is now about 300 m above sea level was, as mentioned at the outset, under water; it constituted one vast bay or gulf of the Adriatic Sea. Among the many reminders of this aquatic past are the spiral-shaped marine fossils in the pink marble of Verona, which has been used over many centuries for such monuments as the Roman arena in Verona, the twelfth-century south-portal steps of Modena cathedral, or the post-Second World War Verona Porta Nuova train station. When the sea eventually receded, it left behind a soggy terrain. Henceforth the discipline that mountain valleys imposed on rivers dissipated as the water reached the lower plain and slowly spread out on the spongy and uneven old seabed, creating a watery landscape of stagnant pools, malarial swamps and ponds, shifting stream beds, and rivers prone to reckless flooding. A rich variety of fauna flourished there but human beings preferred the greater safety afforded by higher ground.[1]

The transformation of this former seabed into the productive plain we see today required centuries of arduous human labour. The Romans began the task of taming this wildly unpredictable terrain by clearing and draining land and channelling water. In the second century BC they built the Via Emilia on the southern edge of the plain parallel to the Apennines and established colonies along it in a string of cities that include Bologna (once Etruscan Felsina), Modena, Reggio Emilia, Parma, and Piacenza.[2] The fate of Modena shows, though, how much the Romans left undone, for a fifth-century flood so buried that town in mud that the site did not attract settlers again until the eleventh century. Even so, until the eighteenth century the reborn town remained essentially an island, where the dukes paraded themselves on canals and made their grand entrances into and exits from the city on a state barge in the manner of the Venetian doges.[3] Out near the centre of the plain, the city of Mantua at 19 m above sea level remains even today very nearly an island, set beside the Mincio River where it opens out into three lakes.

The other major cities established out in the plain in Antiquity included Cremona and Ferrara, essential ports on the Po for several centuries, plus, further south than the outlet of the Po, Ravenna, the major port on the Adriatic for the entire valley. The shifting course of the Po has, though, long since abandoned both Cremona and Ferrara, and silting has pushed the Adriatic coastline about 10 km further out from Ravenna.[4]

Most of the rest of the Po Valley cities are found skirting the edge of the old seabed, those on the north side fed by the broader, deeper, and faster-moving rivers of the Alps, the others by their less imposing counterparts on the side of the Apennines. These cities were once crossed by streams, or more especially canals, most of which have been either filled in or covered over by streets in more recent times. Here and there one can still encounter street names that evoke memories of these watercourses, such as the Corso Canal Grande of Modena, the Via Riva di Reno (Bank of the Reno) of Bologna, or the Via Ripagrande (Great Riverbank) of Ferrara.

When the work of clearing, draining, and channelling that had been abandoned in late Roman times began again in the eleventh century, the initiative could of course no longer come from a powerful, imperial government intent upon controlling and exploiting an entire region. This time instead it had to be the multifarious, independent, fractious, and competing cities of the region that undertook these projects. The story of this renewed initiative is an integral chapter in the history of the Commercial Revolution.[5]

The threefold increase of the European population between the early eleventh century and the advent of the Black Death in the mid-fourteenth involved far more complex developments than a simple quantitative increase. The most notable as well as long-lasting of these developments was the growth of cities throughout Europe, although as noted earlier this was more the case in Italy than elsewhere. The mostly uninhabited shells of former Roman cities began to fill up again and eventually could no longer contain their expanding populations. Their growth was more on the order of a sixfold or even as much as a tenfold increase.[6] In addition to the repopulating of old urban centres, the same age witnessed the establishment of new towns in all parts of Europe, some easily identified by such names as Newport, Villeneuve, Villanova, Neustadt, or Novgorod; one new city without this type of generic name was Alessandria in Piedmont, founded in 1168 and named for Pope Alexander III, who sided with this and many other northern cities that were allied against Emperor Frederick Barbarossa.[7]

Landlords all over Europe pressed the workers they controlled to transform forests into arable fields, to clear up log-jammed rivers, and to drain swamps. In the Lowlands during this same period such projects included the earliest construction of polders for reclaiming land from the sea. In Lombardy in the 1170s work began on bringing the waters of the Ticino to Milan, a project that lasted three-quarters of a century and ended up as the 50-km-long *Naviglio grande*; as it was large enough to be navigable, it served the needs of commerce as well as of irrigation. Without such a massive intervention of labour, there is no way that this city, Roman *Mediolanum*, could have become a metropolis of 100,000 people by the late thirteenth century; moreover, in the fifteenth century another project brought also the waters of the Adda to Milan, this one via a canal that is 30 km long.[8] As for feeding such a population, that, too, would have been unthinkable without transforming vast stretches of swampland to Milan's west and south into productive land, which in the fifteenth century was further transformed into rice fields. The East Asian gift of rice production first to Sicily and then to Lombardy and Piedmont has been reciprocated in Milan's gift of risotto to the world.[9]

When workers from the countryside flocked into towns in search of the jobs these had to offer, many of them were simultaneously seeking to free themselves of servile obligations. For their part many communes responded with statutes that granted both of these desires.[10] The common interests of labour markets and of motivated workers are established elements for understanding the growth of urban populations, yet not sufficient for explaining it entirely. Early statistical studies in historical demography beginning in the middle years of the twentieth century revealed a crucial characteristic of the pre-industrial European city; not only could the population of that city, as a type, not expand without a constant infusion of new inhabitants from the outside, it could not even maintain itself in a steady, or zero-growth, state.[11] Another crucial characteristic, but one that was plainly visible from the earliest days and thus in no need of modern studies, was that these cities did not produce their own food. Of course there were small plots of cultivated land here and there within city walls, but virtually all of every city's food supply had to be imported. Thus it is no exaggeration to say that, given their needs for people and for food, towns were doubly dependent on the countryside.

The case of Bologna exemplifies most of these generalities albeit with a share of its unique variants. Its placement at the intersection of a major trans-Apennine route and the Via Emilia undoubtedly facilitated the development of the leading feature of its uniqueness, namely Europe's first university. 'What made Bologna unusual was the university, which attracted a high number of scholars and professors, making it the fifth or sixth largest city in Europe.' This observation came at the start of a book by the economic and social historian Antonio Ivan Pini titled, significantly, *The Bolognese Countryside: The Agrarian Roots of a Medieval Metropolis*. And the follow-up sentence reads: 'The university in turn was made possible – for people to come there in the first place and then stay – because of the fertile and fruitful countryside capable of assuring an abundant and constant supply of victuals for the thousands and thousands of university students.' Pini pinpointed this critical connection between food supply and universities by citing the attempts of certain other cities to lure students to their own, newly established universities, as when Frederick II urged students from his realm to abandon Bologna for the university that he founded at Naples in 1224 by stressing the abundance there of grain, meat, and fish. Vercelli sought to shake students loose from Padua to enter its new university in 1228 and Toulouse tried to do the same to Paris in 1229, both touting their ready availability of inexpensive wine, bread, meat, and fish. So it was that in this, Bologna's first great era of expansion, the twelfth and thirteenth centuries, precisely when the university and its various sub-cultures, e.g. rooming houses, taverns, stationers, book sellers, etc., took root, the owners of the land outside the city – who for the most part dwelled within the city – rationalized the use of that land to maximize its productivity and, obviously, its profitability.[12]

Bologna stood midway between two rivers, the Reno to its west and the Sàvena to its east, which flow at right angles to the Via Emilia about 6 km apart. In the 1170s and 1180s the commune tapped into both of these with canals that brought water into the city; within a century, some thirty-two mills lined one of these canals and fifty mills the other. The fact of Bologna having thirty bridges in spite of not being placed on a large river testifies to the extensive network of canals that hydrated, powered, and cleansed it and its people.[13]

Migration from the countryside into Bologna, beginning back in the tenth century, was specially intense and continuous all through the twelfth century and first half of the thirteenth. In this earlier phase migration was essentially spontaneous and unregulated. However, by 1246 the commune felt a need to address the disequilibrium between the overcrowded city and the undermanned countryside, and henceforth for a quarter-century followed a demographic policy that limited or impeded immigration, together with resettling some persons in the nearby countryside. From 1274 to 1347 there was a period of quite stable population, which at times called for minimal adjustments of attraction or repulsion as appropriate to the moment. With the advent of the plague epidemic and a 35 per cent drop of population from 35,000 to 24,750 in a year, plus recurrences of plague in 1381, 1383, 1389, 1393, and 1399, the community needed to encourage not just immigration from countryside to the city, but migration from outside Bolognese territory into its countryside, in order to keep the city itself alive.

The attractive pull of the cities reached well up into the mountains, so that the human as well as topographical connections that tied the mountains, the plateaus, and the plain need to be considered. Those connections, as well as the differences, were among the salient points in the magisterial work of Fernand Braudel on the entire Mediterranean basin, first published in 1949. Braudel founded his historical investigation upon the comparative topography of the lands bordering that sea, starting with the observation that from Palestine moving clockwise around to Tunisia the desert comes right to the coast, whereas from Tunisia to Lebanon it is the mountains that come astonishingly close to the seaside. Where else, Braudel pointed out, did the fine art of making ice cream develop but along the latter coastlines, where on sweltering summer days snow and ice could be brought down from the mountains on a regular basis?[14]

The principal insight of Braudel in this connection was to tie the cities' insatiable need for human labour together with the mountains' incapacity to support their populations. Numerous studies had shown that life in the mountains was rough, that the valleys were for the most part very narrow, and that the growing season was brief. The difficulties of travel imposed self-sufficiency, thus depriving mountain dwellers of the benefits of specialisation. The lands above 1,500 m were essentially unproductive, and although those further down could yield wheat and grapes and olives and, starting in the sixteenth century, maize, they did so reluctantly and in small quantities. And whatever the size of the yield, the labour required to get it was disproportionately long and hard. The one abundant staple was the chestnut, and when the stores of grain, if they had any to begin with, ran out, people turned to using chestnut flour to make bread. They also had goats and cows, indeed shared quarters with them, but the number of these animals they could keep was limited by the fact that the growing season lasted long enough for only one crop of hay, thus in turn limiting the quantity of fresh milk and cheese the animals could provide.[15]

No matter how hard people worked or how favourable conditions were in a given year, the danger of starvation always lurked in the mountains in the late winter and early spring.[16] The towns were hardly impervious to this danger but their situations were not so consistently precarious. The well-organised provisioning of towns included careful storing of foodstuffs for the non-growing season. Moreover, the activities of some of the civic charitable organisations founded in the thirteenth century included maintaining storehouses of grain and wine for distribution to the poor when needed.[17] On the western edge of Bergamo in the Valley of Astino, the Abbey of the Holy Sepulchre, established in 1103, undertook early in Lent of each year to distribute bread to poor people. The notion of giving up any food for Lent is truly at odds with the essential fact of rural life at this time, namely that Lent coincided with the low point of the year for the availability of food. The problem for much of the population back in Alberto's time and right through the early modern centuries was trying to make what little they had last through that very season.[18]

For sheep and their shepherds the solution was transhumance. The flocks that summered in the vast high plain of Asiago north of Vicenza spread out when they came down in the fall to grazing lands in the regions of Vicenza itself, Treviso, Padua, Verona, and even Mantua. This springtime climb to graze in mountain pastures for the summer followed by the autumnal descent has remained a reliable fixture of the Mediterranean calendar for centuries. The trek in each direction took a month or more and the sojourns at the highest altitudes lasted at least three months. The contracts between those who rented out winter pastures in the region of Lodi on the west side of the Adda (*i fituali*) and their seasonal tenants from the Bergamasque valleys (*i Bergamín*) set as the departure date from the plain Saint George's Day, 23 April.[19] The appearance of shepherds playing their bagpipes in lowland cities to raise money during the Christmas season reminds city dwellers of their annual sojourn in the plain but also of course of the prominent role that their counterparts in ancient Palestine had played in the Nativity story.[20]

For many mountain dwellers, the solution was migration, whether as temporary and regular as the pattern of transhumance or more permanent. However, there are many variants in the ways that people found to deal with the realities of life in the mountains.[21] One is that of going down to the plain long enough to sell chestnuts in the city streets and then returning home. Another involved movement from one mountainous area to another in accordance with shifting needs of the labour market. Still another emerged from the personal experience of the historian William H. McNeill, who served as a soldier in Greece during the Second World War and later returned with an assignment to write a report on Greek politics. While trying to understand the radical shifts in the political views and behaviour of mountain people, he came to understand that since they were able to raise food that lasted them through only half of the non-growing season, they had to come down to the plains each year to get food, either by earning it as migrant labourers or by seizing it forcibly from plains dwellers. If the latter, they justified this brigandage by whatever political ideology was handy at the time, but hunger, he came to understand, was what they were about, not ideology.[22] In fact fighting for pay by bands of mercenaries from mountain communities was yet another widely used strategy for survival. The most famous and perhaps most long-lasting example of such a band is that of the Swiss Guards, who began serving the papacy in the 1400s and on a regular basis in 1506; to this day they have never completely left home.[23]

The mountain dwellers' safety valve of migration meshed well with the nearly continuous need for labourers in the plateaus and the plains, i.e. in towns to be sure but also in their respective countrysides, which fed the towns. This migration of labourers from the mountains to the plains of northern Italy in the later Middle Ages and the early modern era shares in the key elements of all migration history: there have to be compelling reasons to leave home; there has to be a perceived promise of better conditions elsewhere; and as migration is inevitably an alienating experience, people prefer to travel together with, or at least resettle among, people of their own language and culture.

At Bologna, which is in Romagna, a Company of Lombards took shape and gained official recognition in 1256. Within a few years it had 550 members, and although we are not told where in Lombardy these people originated we do know the professions of half of them. They worked in sectors that were left for the most part in the hands of outsiders (*forestieri* or foreigners), the largest sub-groups by profession including the 25 tavern keepers and 11 wine porters. As these sectors were not permitted to form guilds, at least at such an early date, membership in this company served to some extent as a substitute for belonging to a guild. In the same years Bologna also had a Company of Tuscans for workers from the other side of the Apennines.[24]

In Piedmont, particular valleys exported people to particular areas, such as from the Arroscia and the Tanaro valleys to the high plains of Cuneo, or from the valleys of Susa, Sambuco, Brella, and Chivasso to Turin. The guilds at Turin grouped their members into *nationes* (nations, i.e. by the places where the workers were born), and thus we know that in 1626 the city had 60 wine porters from the Valsesia. The city, as noted earlier, increased in size and importance rapidly in the eighteenth century; one sees both this new size and the old modes of labour organisation in the report of 1746 showing that Turin had 203 brentatori from the Valley of Viù and 223 porters of all sorts, including wine carriers, from Varallo in the Valsesia.[25]

Mantua has no nearby mountains to back it up, yet a goodly number of heavy lifters came there from the mountains of the Trentino. In the Mantuan census of 1658, of the 427 immigrants from that region 269 were listed as porters. Over the course of several decades in the seventeenth century, the marriage declarations listed 290 Trentini males of whom 187 were porters. This work was the speciality of immigrants from the Rendena Valley, which lies to the west of Trent. Another valley in the same area, the Val di Sole, supplied Mantua especially with butchers and tripe makers. After the Trentino, the next largest groups of immigrant labourers in

Mantua came from Piedmont and Lombardy. In general the immigrants to that city held jobs that they could do in the streets, and hence rarely worked inside shops. Yet another example shows that they completely dominated the work of the *garaveni*, the stevedores of Mantua's port. An expert on Mantuan immigration concluded that these outsiders did work that most of the local people would not accept to do because it was so strenuous, so humble, and indeed so degrading.[26]

The upper plain around Bergamo and particularly to its south attracted many new settlers when the population boom of the eleventh and twelfth centuries got under way. The most promising lands were of course the first to go, and soon people were pushing on further south and into the plain. Of particular interest is the peopling of the 20-km-wide corridor between the Adda and Oglio rivers that goes from Bergamo to Cremona and a bit beyond to where the Oglio joins the Po.[27] The story includes the foundation, half-way between the two cities, of a new town, Crema, first mentioned in a document of 1074.[28] François Menant shows how familiar the trek back and forth in this corridor was to shepherds who spent the summers with their flocks in the Val Seriana at such places as Vall'Alta, Vertova, Leffe, Gandino, Clusone, or Castrone, or in the Val Brembana at Valdimagna, Zogna, Endema, or Valleve. Their winter stations stretched from Martinengo, on the Serio just southeast of Bergamo, past the lands around Soncino and Crema, all the way to a vast pasturage on the south side of the Po directly across from Cremona.[29] Commercial traffic as well as these flocks moved back and forth freely between Bergamo and Cremona, as guaranteed in the 1248 statutes of Bergamo or assured in a contract of 1308 concerning the transport of salt from Cremona to Bergamo either by the road through Castellone and Crema or by the one through Soncino.[30]

The mountains above Bergamo sent many of their people down the valleys in search of work. To be sure, some went no further than the city of Bergamo itself, like the porters in Bergamo from the Val Brembana or the chimney sweeps from the Valdimagna.[31] In the late fourteenth and early fifteenth centuries roughly one-third of the immigrants in Brescia had come from Bergamo's territory, many to work as porters or wine carriers.[32] In the thirteenth century the Milanese had need of workers skilled in the building trades for such projects as canals and walls, some of whom they recruited in Como and Lugano; for less skilled workers, including porters, they took men from the mountains of Bergamo, Brescia, and Italian Switzerland.[33]

Two peculiar variants stand out in this history of Bergamasque émigrés who worked elsewhere as porters. One is that a small market town in the Bergamasque *bassa*, Urgnano, supplied porters over many generations not just to Milan but also to the ports of Pisa and Livorno, meaning that they had to cross over the Apennines and continue south to get there.[34] The other concerns the monopoly of men from the Val Brembana on the work of stevedores in the port of Genoa. By 1340 they had their own organisation, the Company of the Caravana, which fought doggedly to get and preserve its members' privileged monopoly right until the middle of the nineteenth century.[35]

The one remaining place that attracted great numbers of Bergamaschi was Venice. The conquest of the Terrafirma by the Republic of Saint-Mark proceeded inexorably through the late fourteenth century and early fifteenth until 1426 when it absorbed Bergamo. Venice thereby landed practically at the doorstep of its great rival, Milan; it fortified and held on to Bergamo as its westernmost outpost until 1797. Traffic on the roads connecting the two cities included government officials, soldiers, merchants, scholars (mainly to and from Padua), artists (Lorenzo Lotto being the most famous of them), the couriers of the Venetian postal service, and unemployed labourers in search of jobs.[36] A Venetian diarist, Girolamo Priuli, wrote in the early sixteenth century: 'The city of Venice is truly full of Bergamaschi at all times, and they are called *fachini*' (a new word for porter at the time).[37] Towards the end of that century, the Venetian governor of Bergamo and its territory, Giovanni da Lezze, wrote in his official report that 'as the region of Bergamo is sterile, it is barely able to maintain its people for four months', and for that same reason 'a large proportion of the people from those valleys lives in Venice'.[38] The workers from Bergamo did not get a stranglehold on the *métier* of stevedore in Venice the way their compatriots did in Genoa, but so numerous were they in the port and around the Riva del Vin and as porters throughout the city that the prevailing view was that all workers who carried heavy loads came from the mountains of Bergamo.[39]

Even though we cannot establish with certainty why Alberto emigrated from the Val Seriana, we can at least now add another possible motive for his leaving, namely famine. Besides the usual lack of food in the mountains in late winter, a detailed demographic study of Bergamasque territory points – for just the middle years of the thirteenth century, which was when Alberto most likely moved – to 1244, 1256, and 1260 as years of particularly severe famine.[40] In any case there was certainly nothing unusual about his leaving his native village and migrating to the lands below to work. Neither can we claim to know why, specifically, it was in Cremona that he stopped, but here again there was nothing unusual about someone from Bergamo crossing the well-travelled plain between the Adda and the Oglio. We can at least safely exclude going to Venice as a likely option, something that became common practice for people from Bergamo as we have seen, but only after the Venetian conquest of 1426. Finally, as to why Alberto became a wine carrier, which we cannot explain specifically as against his doing some other heavy labour, it is clear that Cremona, like all cities of the Po Valley plain, needed to import workers in the thirteenth century – Braudel called them 'indispensable immigrants' – and that the kinds of jobs these unskilled outsiders got were typically the most onerous, humble, and looked-down upon of all.[41]

6

Porters of the imagination

The wily swindler Cingar needs to settle a score with simple-minded Zambello, so he fills a brenta nearly to the top from a latrine, leaving room for a thick layer of honey on the top. He meets up with Zambello and convinces him to come witness a sure-fire scheme for making money. 'Selling bee-shit' is the way he puts it, except that Zambello doesn't hear the 'bee'. Cingar gets Zambello to carry the brenta and they head to an apothecary's shop to make a sale. After dipping his finger in the honey and tasting it, the apothecary agrees to buy the load for three scudos. Cingar says he'll stop by later to pick up the container and hurries off with the money. Zambello, who fails to pick up the more subtle aspects of Cingar's ruse, goes away determined to work full-time at selling excrement. The next day he carries a steaming brenta through the market hawking his load of 'really good shit, freshly-pooped'. The apothecary spots him pass by his shop, quickly puts down his pestle and takes up a big stick. Once he's within reach of his prey he lifts the stick high over his head and with one blow smashes the brenta, breaking its hoops and splintering its staves so that 'the broth of nauseating liquid' spills all over Zambello (see Figure 15).[1]

Welcome to the scatological imagination of Teofilo Folengo and the wild adventures he recounts in his lengthy macaronic poem *Baldus*. It is from such works in the literary and also visual arts of the sixteenth and seventeenth centuries that we get a glimpse of how porters and particularly wine porters were perceived by others. Before then, the Pomposa fresco of the marriage at Cana, the Bolognese legal manuscripts showing wine porters at work in markets, and the decorated initial letter of the statutes of the brentatori of Bologna are wonderfully informative and at the same time remarkably free of judgement. However, once testimonies to

Figure 15 Scatological slapstick, sixteenth-century style: Zambello, having filled his brenta from a latrine, hawks his pungent, steamy load in the city streets. The apothecary, upon whom he had the day before played a dirty trick (albeit unwittingly), sees Zambello pass by and is here getting his revenge. This woodcut appeared in the 1521 edition of *The Adventures of Baldo* by Teofilo Folengo.

imagined wine porters started to proliferate in the sixteenth century, these took on a significance that was quite other than the purely descriptive. Something new was afoot that went way beyond the centuries-old clichés spoken by city dwellers about rustics, country bumpkins, those who still smell of the barnyard, and the like.

Folengo (1491–1540), born into a wealthy family of merchants and notaries in Mantua, was a Benedictine monk of prodigious learning. While a master of Hebrew, Greek, Latin, patristics, theology, and philosophy, he replied to writers who argued over which languages were the most refined by placing Bergamasco and the slang of chimney sweeps on a par with the ancient literary languages. The language of his *Baldus* poem, which first appeared in Venice in 1518, is a playful mix of Latin, Italian, various dialects, puns, and neologisms.[2]

Already in the poem's opening line Folengo shows off his coarse humour in claiming that the fame and name of Baldus will make the earth tremble and the underworld defecate all over itself. The misuse of a brenta for a slapstick scene featuring crap may tell us obliquely of Folengo's view of wine carriers, but Baldus's departure for a sea voyage occasions a head-on exposé of his take on all sorts of porters. Baldus and his companions ride to the port of Chioggia on the Adriatic and secure passage on a merchant ship then being prepared for departure to Turkey.

> Here you could see a thousand porters compete to carry donkey loads for a measly six marks; such greed for gain makes them crazy. For the most part, porters are Bergamaschi. I don't mean the inhabitants of the city of Bergamo, whose great wisdom shines forth, but men fed on chestnuts and bread pudding, whom the mountain above Clusone sends throughout the world ... How much stuff they can pile on their robust shoulders! They are short, stocky men with big hind-quarters; their chests and stomachs are always covered with thick hair.

As for being able to defend their own interests: 'one curse from the mouth of a Bergamasco is worth more than a hundred blatherings of a Florentine'. Folengo eventually wanders back to the story from this digression.

> There is no country that is not full of porters. Just as there are flies everywhere and friars clogging along, so also do you run into porters everywhere. No other people weary themselves in this toting art; porters come only from Bergamasque stock ... Therefore here too, the porters diligently load the ship and ferry bales that a camel could scarcely carry.[3]

A near contemporary of Folengo was Angelo Beolco (*c.* 1498–1542), a playwright who took the name Ruzzante from one of his own characters.[4] His father came from the branch of a Milanese noble family that had moved in the 1450s to Padua, where Ruzzante was born. His family and the people they associated with were wealthy and cultivated, so Ruzzante grew up with a refined literary education. He founded a theatrical company in about 1520 and is known to have staged a rustic comedy, the *Pastoral*, in Venice at that time. He restricted his many plays to one area, centred on Padua and extending as far as Venice and Ferrara, in which the local dialect was understood. In ways that recall Folengo, Ruzzante selected a mix of literary Tuscan Italian and the low-status dialect, *Pavan*, spoken in the countryside. He included some Bergamasco as well. The title of one of his most admired plays, *La moschetta*, refers to the mishmash spoken by people trying to express themselves in proper Italian but making mistakes unwittingly by slipping in elements of grammar, syntax, or diction from their dialects.

Ruzzante's characters are often either peasants or else urban workers uprooted from peasant origins and corrupted by the experience of living in an urban environment. He could make them funny and make fun of some of them, but he had no overriding intention to ridicule them. On the contrary Ruzzante was deeply sensitive to the misery and suffering of the poor, the awful costs of warfare they bore, the persistent pangs of hunger they felt, and the spectres of famine and infectious diseases they faced. He understood how such experiences sharpened their survival skills, astuteness above all others. There were, though, other characters, such as the Bergamasque medical doctor to whom Ruzzante attributed great scientific learning and a scornful, derisive realism. But when he has two poor soldiers – his character Ruzzante and a Bergamasco named Tonin – argue over which of them is the better soldier, Tonin calls Ruzzante a peasant, but Ruzzante insults Tonin back by calling him and his ancestors porters. Whereas Folengo is relentless in ridiculing porters, Ruzzante, who holds a key place in the formation of the Commedia dell'Arte, neither ridiculed nor romanticises labourers but shows a sympathetic understanding of the conditions in which they lived.

An encyclopedic collection listing, describing, and commenting upon more than five hundred *métiers*, professions, or conditions that first appeared in Venice in 1585 became one of the great publishing feats of its time. The work of Tomaso Garzoni (1549–89),

*A Commonplace of All the Professions of the World, Both Noble
and Lowly* (*La piazza universale di tutte le professioni del mondo, e
nobili et ignobili*) went through at least twenty-five printings in less
than a century, including one in Spanish in 1615, four in German
between 1619 and 1649, and one in Latin – published in Germany –
in 1624.[5] Garzoni came from Bagnacavallo, near Ravenna, went to
schools in Ravenna and Imola, and studied law and philosophy at
Ferrara and Siena. He entered the Congregation of Lateran Canons
and got assignments to teach sacred scripture and to preach. These
he carried out for over two decades in Treviso, Venice, Padua,
Ferrara, and Mantua. Not a particularly original or creative writer,
Garzoni was an encyclopedist, skilled at gathering and putting in
order vast amounts of written materials on particular subjects.

La piazza universale contains 155 chapters, which, because they
start with (1) lords or princes and tyrants, (2) governors, and (3) religious, may seem to be arranged in some sort of hierarchical order.
Moreover, Garzoni did specify in the title that he was including
all professions, both noble and ignoble, or lowly. Yet the order of
chapters does not conform to any such scheme of values. Surgeons
and butchers, both held in low esteem because of the handling of
blood their labours entailed, fall within the first sixteen chapters;
judges on the other hand come near the end. However, it is within
chapters that one frequently finds mixed evaluations, starting with
the very first one, which contains examples of both admirable rulers
and detestable tyrants. In his chapter on farming, Garzoni pays due
homage to the utility and essential goodness of the work farmers
do, largely by citing the standard classical texts on the subject, but
then he pours out invective against the present-day peasant, who
keeps his hat on while talking with a gentleman, lies to and steals
from the landlord, puts his animals in the neighbour's pasture to
graze, fornicates with the neighbour's wife, makes a joke of going to
confession and doing penance, and 'in a word, lives like a beast'.

Chapter 114 is titled 'On Porters [*facchini*] in General, and in
Particular on Brentadori and Coal Deliverymen, Carters, and
Basket Carriers'.[6] One finds porters, says Garzoni, especially in
large cities like Venice, where some work at the Arsenale, some at
the Customs House, some at the market of course, and still other
places. Some carry brentas around the city and others containers of
coal. 'In speech they are like magpies; in fact their language is such
that actors who play ridiculous fools have adopted it for the laughs

it gets them.' Their gestures are lazy, their comportment gross, and their way of behaving could not be dumber. They are so loud, in part because they do little else other than fight among themselves. Anyone familiar with Venice will agree with Garzoni that when they're loaded up and on the move through that city's narrow streets, one has to get out of the way fast when they shout 'Make way, make way.' But then he adds: 'they get from one end of the city to the other with ease; a mule could do no better'.

Along with this only partial list of porters' faults Garzoni introduces a change of tone. Porters are so lowly and vile, he claims, that:

> one can hardly find any way to praise them, except to say that for the most part they are rather simple and good-natured if uncouth men, born in the Bergamasque mountains where like so many caged animals they are set free and sent down from the valleys to the benefit of all mankind, who in turn use them as asses or mules now and then as needed.

He concedes their utility, because 'they'll taste the wine for you to say whether it's good, and they'll carry it for little cost to you and little gain for them'. Even so, Garzoni stresses that the wine porters are vile, and explains that the reason is that they come from the mountains.

Twice in writing of porters Garzoni goes beyond this tolerant, patronising stance to express something closer to compassion. One comes where he relates what happens to porters at Carnival time in Bologna and Ferrara: some of them become amusements for cultivated people when they take part in a popular event in which, blind-folded, wearing helmets, and armed with sticks, they are supposed to kill a wild pig. What actually happens of course is that they end up clubbing each other, to the delight of the spectators. The second such passage concerns their long-range goals. Many of them suffer through years of work, he says, so as not to suffer later in life, saving as much of their earnings as they can to enjoy their old age back in their home valleys. Yet not all of these achieve even that modest goal, for some die early from all this hard work and self-deprivation and others while on their way home encounter robbers who leave them without anything.[7]

In the course of his lengthy book, Garzoni did not give a definition of its main subject, *profession*. The title simply announces that he will treat of all professions, noble and ignoble. However, he appears to have raised – very subtly – the question of whether there even exists such a thing as an ignoble profession, for in the book's second edition he simply dropped from the title the words *noble and ignoble*. For the text itself, there was little to change, because from the beginning he had used terms such as *arte* (trade, craft) and *mestiere* (*métier*) but not *professione* in writing about manual labourers and the mechanical arts. He saved *professione* for those who did work that was considered dignified and worthy of gentle folk.[8]

Just five years after Garzoni first published his book on all kinds of work, Cesare Vecellio (1521–1601) published, also in Venice, what in some ways can be seen as a companion-piece to the *Piazza universale*, namely a book on the clothing and costumes worn by various groups and stations of people, ancient and modern, from 'various parts of the world'. The book contains 418 full-page woodcuts, most of them full-length images of either a man or a woman. The accompanying texts focus mainly on descriptions of clothing, but some of these include passages based on – or lifted from – Garzoni. The paragraph on porters differs on one point of interest in saying that 'for the most part they are Bergamaschi, they come from the valleys near Trento, or they are Bresciani'. But beyond that difference of detail with its confused geography, the interest of this book is that it supplies a fuller description of what a basket carrier does.[9]

Cestaroli were porters in the city of Venice who stood in certain places near the fish market of Rialto, or similarly near butchers' shops. At the call of someone who was buying food in the market and wished to have it carried home, they presented themselves with a large, round, flat-bottomed basket, and they had a piece of cloth to cover the food that they were given to carry. From this description, one can readily see that *cestaroli* offered a service that paralleled that of the wine porters, albeit one that buyers were free to use or not, and that the commune did not exploit for controlling market standards. Moreover, no round, flat-bottomed basket loaded with food could match the weight of the loads carried by wine porters.

Turning now to a different medium, the finest drawing, or image of any sort, of a wine porter is the work of Annibale Carracci. It is part of a series that in turn is part of an entirely new phase of artistic interest and accomplishment. Carracci (1560–1609) owes his reputation as a major figure in High Renaissance Italian art not to his drawing of a wine porter but to the stupendous frescos with which he decorated the gallery walls and ceiling of the Farnese Palace in Rome.[10] Between 1595 and 1604 he created vivid renditions there of stories and figures from classical mythology. He had previously done work in a similar vein in palaces in his native Bologna, work that apparently prepared him for and won him the Farnese commission in Rome. But his earlier accomplishments amounted to far more than an apprenticeship for entering the big time. In addition to producing palace frescos, altarpieces, other religious paintings, portraits, and landscapes, he was in the forefront of genre painting, just then taking root in northern Italy.

Annibale's father and uncle, respectively a tailor and a butcher, had moved to Bologna from Cremona. Three of their sons became painters and they frequently collaborated on projects: Annibale, his older brother Agostino, and his cousin Ludovico. The leading Bolognese painters at the time these cousins were getting started were Bartolomeo Passerotti and Prospero Fontana. Ludovico worked for a while in their fathers' native city of Cremona, which, together with Parma, because of the connections established through the international banking interests of some of their most prominent families, had become ports of entry into Italy for Flemish genre painting. This import had spawned an Italian school of genre painters, including perhaps most notably Vincenzo Campi at Cremona but also Passerotti at Bologna. Annibale certainly knew Passerotti's works, possibly even as an apprentice in the latter's studio, but almost as surely knew Campi's, for he is thought to have worked with Ludovico on one of the latter's projects in Cremona; in any case he showed more than a passing familiarity with Campi's paintings. Typical of these early Italian genre paintings, like the northern paintings that inspired them, were their depictions of simple, poor people displaying fish, poultry, meat, or fruits and vegetables for sale on market stalls.

Passerotti and Carracci each made paintings of a butcher's shop, with all the stark realities of sharp cutting instruments, meat hooks, blood, and body parts on display. Passerotti made his butchers noticeably crude, as if to insist that the viewer notice the similarities between the human labourers and the beastly carcasses they were working on. Carracci made no such confusion; after all, his cousins, Ludovico's younger brothers, were carrying on their father's – his uncle's – trade.

Carracci showed a similar restraint when it came to that genre staple of simple people eating, whereas Campi depicted fish vendors eating in scenes with raucous smiling and finger-pointing that suggest some crude joke was going on. The same is true of Campi's

Cheese Eaters, one of whom, to the great amusement of his companions, is so stuffing himself with fresh cheese that he seems about to vomit. In Carracci's *Bean Eater*, however, a simple man is having a simple meal. The man is seated at a small table facing the viewer; he is wearing an open-necked shirt with a loose-fitting vest. He has his straw hat tilted slightly back on his head and he has dirty fingernails. He is using a spoon to eat from the bowl of white beans before him. The rest of his meal consists of a bunch of scallions, a flat pie made with greens (perhaps chard), some dark bread, and a glass of red wine. The scene has none of the coarse behaviour or erotic suggestiveness found in Passerotti's and Campi's work, and the bean eater himself is neither a buffoon nor an idiot.

Close examination of the specific contents of the bean eater's simple meal, as well as of the meals depicted in other genre paintings of the time, has revealed a complicated nexus of cultural codes, prejudices, and justificatory explanations concerning social stratification. Discussions of the social as well as medical significance of food had long been very much in fashion, but recent research has concentrated attention on a new book in Carracci's time, the *Examen de ingenios* published in 1575 at Baega in southern Spain by a physician named Juan Huarte de San Juan (*c.* 1529–88). This was a phenomenally successful book, with twenty-five editions in Spanish. There were also twenty-five in French starting in 1580; one in English under the title *The Examination of Men's Wits* in 1594; and, among still others, seven Italian editions starting with the one published by Aldus at Venice in 1582.[11]

Huarte's book is in the form of a handbook on how to beget and raise an intelligent child. Although he had very specific recommendations to make, and made them with unqualified self-assurance, he warned readers that these did not serve to produce any effect in female children. Females were simply not capable, in his estimation, of being smart. The book's English title would perhaps have greater meaning in our time were we to substitute *A Study of Men's Intelligence* for *The Examination of Men's Wits*; however else one would like to translate it, 'Men's' is just right as it is, and above all should not be turned into 'Man's' or 'Mankind's' or 'Human', precisely because Huarte is really only writing about male offspring.

The secret of success in Huarte's scheme of things lies entirely in diet. He demonstrates this by eliminating what we would call genetics and also upbringing as relevant factors, to wit: given that wise parents can have foolish children, vicious parents can have virtuous children, white parents brown children and vice versa, and given that that there can be much variety among children born of the same couple, it stands to reason that variations in diet are what cause the differences. In his words, 'hence I gather that there is no child born who does not partake of the qualities and temperatures of that meat that his parents fed upon a day before he was begotten'.[12] For parents at the time of engendering and for the child himself as he grows up, only noble foods can guarantee favourable results, and these include poultry, fish, white bread, and fruit. White wine is the drink of choice, although heavily watered for a child and then less and less so as he matures. The foods considered coarse include leeks, garlic, onions, beans, lettuce, barley or any kind of dark bread, cheese, red wine, vinegar, and fatty meats.

Coarse food leads to coarse behaviour, hence the promiscuous sexuality of the poor; it leads as well to their brute strength, their unthinking heads, their hot tempers, and still other traits that bring out more of their animal nature. Proof of the different consequences of different diets are readily available, according to Huarte, for all to see:

> Hence it is that among country people [*entro los hombres del campo*] it is a miracle if one turns out to have a sharp intelligence and a gift for learning. They're all born dim-witted and crude for having been made [*hecho*] out of foods of gross and evil substance. It is the contrary with city people, whose children we see have more wits and talents.

These same contrasts are present in the market scenes of Passerotti and Campi with their abundant displays of refined or 'noble' victuals, whereas the humble persons there to sell these goods are depicted slurping their usual grub.

The theories of the differences in intelligence and abilities that result from consuming different diets are of course more complex than arguing that a single pair of alternative actions leads to only one alternative pair of consequences: i.e. eating noble or coarse foods leads respectively to being either intelligent or stupid. Even so, the numerous variations on combinations of foods proposed in this period, each of them purporting to produce quite distinct capacities and character traits, while displaying their authors' vivid imaginations, do nothing to diminish the compelling force of the belief that one who consumes a peasant's diet ends up dull-witted.

Notably absent from nearly all of these writings on the social and intellectual implications of diet was discussion of the possible differences of cost there might have been between noble and vile foods. One who at least acknowledged cost as a factor in diet was a Bolognese priest, Giovanni Battista Segni, who published a treatise in 1602 on famine and hunger.[13] In his chapter on remedies for hunger, Segni proposes two quite separate strategies for the rich and the poor. 'There being a severe shortage of grain, such that the rich cannot always have bread made from refined white flour, they should use only the bran or else the whole wheat.' He also counsels the mixing of rice with wheat, as is done widely in the East, particularly India and Japan. If bread is lacking, he recommends that they make polenta (in fact the mountain dwellers' main staple), which they should saturate with milk of any animal, or with a broth thickened with any sort of flour, or with vegetables, or with chestnuts flavoured with fresh butter. As for the poor and miserable, who, Segni is quick to point out, suffer from a famine of all things including money, they should go for goat cheese, bran, and couch grass (a weed that infests fields). He also suggests that they could make bread out of sawdust from young trees, especially pear, apple, and cherry. The sawdust should be dried in an oven and made into fine powder. When well baked, the resulting bread, the author assures readers, will sustain the poor. We can grant Segni a charitable impulse in seeking to help poor people survive in difficult times and in recognising their 'famine of money', but there is an element of self-interest in his argument as well. Segni is explicit in expressing fear of the poor who, if lacking work and food, are likely to go on a rampage of looting.

Another theme, present in Ruzzante's plays and fundamental in folklore but that remained below the surface of Huarte's work and of those who translated, copied, and embellished his ideas, is the cleverness of the very same people who eat coarse food and are supposed to be so ignorant, so dense, so dim-witted. Where, after all, would the humour and charm of Arlecchino be if he were not so clever? This Bergamasque character, invented in the 1570s, who not incidentally was always hungry, was a (supposedly) dim-witted servant who outwitted his (supposedly) intelligent masters, a simple man who prospered by devising complex stratagems.

Another such character was Bertoldo, a deformed and ugly peasant whose lack of good looks was matched by the liveliness of his mind and the speed of his repartee. The creation of Giulio Cesare Croce (1550–1609), he gets summoned to an imaginary royal court at Verona to face off against the king in Croce's *Most Subtle Astuteness of Bertoldo*, first published in 1609.[14] The king is bored by the obsequiousness that surrounds him at court and so seeks to amuse himself at the expense of a country bumpkin by putting to test this common person's supposed wisdom. Their encounters start off as an enjoyable game, to which the king soon admits the queen and the courtiers. But the attraction of the game fades as the king never succeeds in making Bertoldo into a buffoon, while Bertoldo's consistent cleverness could not fail to be seen as chipping away at the king's prestige and authority. Eventually, though, Bertoldo proves himself to be so wise that the king decides that he cannot make do without his counsel, and thus arranges for Bertoldo to remain at court. The king has him treated with all the care and comforts due a distinguished royal visitor. However, after a lengthy period of experiencing the luxury of court life, Bertoldo falls gravely ill. Failing fast yet ever astute, he knows that it is the refined food that is killing him, so he begs the royal physicians to order for him a bowl of beans with onions. Alas for him they persist in treating him as they would a gentleman or a knight of the court, thus condemning him unintentionally but inevitably to death. In the end, the aggrieved king granted that this ugly yet extraordinarily intelligent peasant died for the lack of a plate of turnips and beans.

Croce was a close contemporary as well as an acquaintance of Annibale Carracci. Born the son of a blacksmith in a village close to Bologna, Croce received a bookish schooling at his father's insistence. Still, after his father died and he came under the care of an uncle, he soon had to learn the family trade. For a few years he worked on a large estate where he observed the contrasting ways of life of the peasants and of the masters they served. As a young man he moved on to the city with his peculiar cultural mix of an artisan and man of letters. He became a poet and storyteller – a street entertainer with a violin, a gift with words, and finely tuned powers of observation. He knew the social scale from top to bottom and never abandoned those on its lowest rungs.

Croce and Carracci for all their differences held quite similar social values. Carracci's butchers did their work with skill and dignity; indeed he emphasised the point by making their customers rather foolish-looking. In the world he experienced, the sons of tailors and butchers could and did become professional artists, just as the son of a blacksmith whom he knew became a writer.

Shortly before moving on to Rome, Carracci made another major venture into genre images that was very different from his paintings, namely a series of seventy-five drawings of street vendors and craftsmen who were familiar figures in the streets of Bologna. For whatever reason, he never had these transformed into prints for sale, as artists frequently did at the time, either individually as broadsides or gathered into a book. Few of his drawings have survived but plates made from them did make it into book form well after his death.[15]

In one of these drawings, a river-water vendor draws water into a wooden bucket from a large barrel that rests on the back of a donkey cart. Another water vendor with a pole over his shoulder that has buckets suspended from either end walks in the street with the aid of a staff; his water is specified as being from the Reno River. No worker in the collection bears a heavier load than the *Brendator da Vino* (see Figure 16). The top of the brenta he carries on his back flares outward and looms high over his head. Near the edge of the image on one side we see the hind legs and the tail of a dog and are left to wonder whether the man and dog are companions or strangers. These street vendors and carriers are standard characters in the daily drama of urban life, each with a precisely defined role in making the town's economy function.

A sub-genre of depicting market people and street vendors had begun in the years around 1500 in France, for which reason it goes by the name *cris de Paris*.[16] Works in this category, whether broadsides or pamphlets, tended to be inexpensively produced and to reach large audiences. As with other genre images, some artists introduced a comical element into their work, usually by making their subjects look silly and not very bright. But here as elsewhere, Annibale Carracci stands out for not belittling his subjects. Moreover, the four-decade gap between his death and the publication of two vastly different versions of his drawings in print form reveals significant differences.

The two bound volumes made from Carracci's drawings both appeared in Rome and in the same year, 1646; they had little else in common. One was a lavish production with an elegant frontispiece by a noted artist, a lengthy introductory essay on theory, and a remarkable title: *Diverse figures ... drawn with pen in the hours*

Figure 16 *Brendator da vino* is one of about seventy-five drawings made by Annibale Carracci in the early 1580s of the street vendors and delivery men who were familiar figures in the streets of Bologna. In striking contrast to one of the major canons of genre painting, recently imported from the Lowlands, Carracci portrayed his humble subjects as persons with great dignity.

of recreation by Annibale Carracci ... for the use of all virtuosi and those who aspire to the profession of painting and design. All of these elements indicate that the publisher had in mind a clientele of upscale, learned amateurs. Nothing about the book suggested a connection with the *cris de Paris* tradition. Moreover, the great painter of the Farnese gallery had made these drawings, according to the book's title, in his spare time, as models for aspiring artists. The author of the theoretical introduction, in keeping with prevailing notions that artists' figures were intended to be idealised, ran into difficulty in making simple street vendors out to represent ideal types of beauty; his solution was instead to regard them as ideal types of deformity, a device that permitted him and his well-heeled audience to admire Carracci's talent but at the same time to look down upon the lowly creatures he depicted. By way of contrast, many modern commentators have been puzzled by the application of this notion of ideal types of deformity to figures that anyone can see are not disfigured, because what Carracci actually did was to give his street people the posture and poses that artists routinely used to depict nobles.[17]

The other, more modestly produced volume of engravings included no discussion of theory and bore the straightforward title of *The Trades of Bologna* (*Le arti di Bologna*). It was clearly cast in the *cris de Paris* vein and spawned various imitations and variations that mostly increased the emphasis on the base conditions and appearance of the workers. An artist from Bologna, Giuseppe Mitelli, published a number of these in the late seventeenth century, using Carracci's name and the title *Le arti di Bologna*, even though many of the images he published did not come from Carracci's pen at all. Unlike Carracci, who was content to let his drawings and paintings speak for him, Mitelli paired with each image a few lines of rhyming text that reinforced the stereotypical view of workers held by those higher up on the social ladder. In the words of a leading expert on the art and society of this age: 'Mitelli gave his tradesmen and vendors speech in order that they might tell us that they are the broken, the stupid, the starving.'[18] The disdain for manual labour, once the preserve of noble birth, only strengthened in the course of becoming the province as well of educated urban professionals, who increasingly included artists.

Having evoked works of the literary and visual arts by a few individuals, we turn to an academy made up of artists (broadly defined) that came together in 1560 at Milan. This was the Academy of the Blenio Valley, named for one of the alpine valleys of Italian Switzerland (see Figure 2), at the time part of Upper Lombardy. Its membership included painters, sculptors, poets, essayists, composers, musicians, architects, and various artisans such as gem cutters, embroiderers, and armorers.

Much of the programmatic direction and tone of this organisation came from Giovanni Paolo Lomazzo (1538–92), probably one of its founding members, who came to be elected its head for life in 1568.[19] Lomazzo was a man of many talents, having been schooled in writing, painting, design, and music; he became a poet and essayist as well as a painter. He took a peculiar sort of Grand Tour by travelling through Italy as far south as Messina but also by heading north to see contemporary art in Flanders and Holland. Even while becoming so cosmopolitan Lomazzo developed a strong interest in local culture and tradition. One of his earliest works was a copy of the 'Last Supper' by Leonardo, who was considered a local given the fact that he had worked for the Sforza from 1482 to1499. Another early work was a biography of the leading heir to Leonardo's work in Milan, which Lomazzo intended as his first step towards doing for Milanese art history what Vasari was then doing in Florence.[20] Within just four years of his election to be head of the academy, Lomazzo became totally blind and henceforth had to limit all of his production to writing.

The main source for our understanding of the academy and its programme is a book by Lomazzo published at Milan in 1589 under the title *Rabisch*.[21] This word means 'arabesque' in the Lombard dialect, a painting term for intertwining leaves, flowers, fruits, and animals. In searching for a language to adopt as their own, Lomazzo and company settled on one form of Lombard speech often heard in the streets and public spaces of Milan, namely that of the city's several hundreds of porters, many of whom had migrated there from the Blenio Valley, whence the name of the academy. The language of these people was particularly harsh or gruff; in the ears of cultivated urbanites, it sounded rustic, barbaric even, and, of course, comical. The academy members spoke it or more likely wove some of it into their improvised mix of Milanese and Italian. They called themselves and each other 'porters' and even dressed up as such, just as Lomazzo himself appeared in his self-portrait, now in the Brera Gallery in Milan, wearing a wide-brimmed straw hat with a garland of vine leaves and a cloak of coarse fur. With his left hand he holds onto a staff, the symbol of his authority as 'abbot' (*abate*) of the academy, the term having long been in use for the head of a Milanese guild or corporation, itself called an 'abbey' (*badia*). The academy's divine patron was Bacchus, to whom they found it convenient to offer their devotion when they held their private gatherings in one or another of the city's renowned taverns.

This behaviour, with the dressing up, the virtually secret language, the drinking, and raucous conviviality, could appear superficial to an observer, indicating simply that the whole enterprise was nothing more than a drinking club, but it could also be seen as a screen, meant somehow to disguise the group's deep, serious reason for being. These people were serious all right, but their goliardic comportment, far from being either an end in itself or from disguising an opposite disposition, instead gave vivid expression to the very ideals they sought to realise.

These academicians stood for a wide-open conception of art, whether as concerned with the medium, the method, the message, the subject matter, or the liberty of the artist; they favoured disorder and the variety and changeableness of things, culture, customs, and language (Lomazzo, we note, cited Folengo's *Baldus* favorably in his book). They were for the exaltation of spontaneity and immediateness, of inspiration and caprice, which they allowed the cult of Bacchus to encourage; and for close observance and acceptance of nature, including the needs, desires and passions integral to their human nature. In marching under the banner of the arabesque, expressed in dialect and implying marginality, they were associating themselves with the peripheral and the lowly. In line with this they vigorously opposed hierarchies, whether social or intellectual; formal structures and systems of ideas; and the disciplining of reason, expression, or passion. Their work demonstrated their opposition to the separation of art from nature, just as the inclusive membership in their academy exemplified their opposition to the separation of artists from artisans.

Several of these ideals found their fullest expression in the development of the grotesque style, especially in the paintings of Giuseppe Arcimbaldo (1526–93).[22] His best known works depict convincingly human-looking heads composed entirely of, say, fish, fruits, vegetables, or, in his portrait of a librarian, books. He was familiar with similarly constructed images pioneered by Hieronymus Bosch and he also found inspiration in Leonardo's drawings of grotesque heads and faces. However much this work was in tune with the ideas of Lomazzo and company, Arcimbaldo almost certainly never belonged to the Blenio Valley Academy. A native of Milan, he often worked early in his career on projects related to the generations-long construction of the city's cathedral. These included designing the staging for some of the ceremonies in which corporations presented their annual contributions to the church's building fund. He surely had knowledge of both wine carriers and porters because the ceremonies he worked on in the 1550s included those for these particular workers' organisations. However, he left Milan in 1562, thus shortly after the founding of the Blenio Valley Academy, to go to work at the court of Emperor Maximilian II, dividing his time mainly between Vienna and Prague for the next quarter-century.

Arcimboldo's work evidently pleased his aristocratic patrons, and while he also had admirers back at home, these were artists, including Lomazzo and others of his circle, but decidedly not the dominant elite of his native city. Milan, along with most of western Lombardy, was under Spanish control from 1535 to 1706. The archbishop of Milan starting in 1565 was Carlo Borromeo (1538–84); named a cardinal deacon already at age twenty-three by his uncle, Pius IV, he became a major figure in the deliberations of the final phase of the Council of Trent, which concluded in 1563.[23] He dedicated his tenure in Milan to implementing and enforcing the reform programme of the council by preaching, writing, making episcopal visitations, and holding diocesan and provincial synods. The court, the nobility, and the wealthiest of the city's merchants and bankers declared their wealth and status by the not very original means of lavish expenditure on clothing, entertainments, and the decoration of their grand residences. This wealthy establishment, which of course included the Borromeo family and much of the senior clergy, especially supported those Tridentine reforms that were to do with artistic representation and taste.

The iconoclasm of the Protestants had created a dilemma for the Roman Church. How could Catholic thinkers defend the long and glorious tradition of Christian art while at the same time weeding out the aspects of that tradition that had occasioned so much criticism and fed so much of Reformation polemics? In justifying images of saints and especially their cultic use, the council fathers at Trent maintained that:

due honour and reverence are owed to them, not because some divinity or power is believed to lie within them as reason for the cult or because anything is to be expected from them, or because confidence should be placed in images as was done by the pagans of old, but because the honour showed to them refers to the original that they represent.

In more positive terms the council fathers decreed that through images the people could receive the means to recall and to meditate assiduously upon the articles of the faith. Indeed through the saints the eyes of the faithful could see the marvels and salutary examples of God, so as to be thankful and model their lives and behaviour by imitating the saints. Given the eminently religious purpose of sacred images, all abuses of them must be eschewed: every superstition, every indecency, and every excessive depiction of beauty, all of these were to be avoided.[24]

A close associate of Borromeo in formulating and propagating these principles was the cardinal archbishop of Bologna, Gabriele Paleotti (1522–97), whose *Discourse on Sacred and Profane Images* of 1582 contains one of the fullest statements of Counter-Reformation views on art.[25] When Paleotti gets to defining what kinds of works are unacceptable, he devotes entire chapters to paintings of each of the following sorts: those that are false and mendacious; that are improbable; that are indecorous; that lack proportion; that are imperfect; that are useless and vain, or ridiculous, or with unusual and new subjects, or with obscure meanings; that are imprecise, crude and frightening, or monstrous; plus no fewer than six chapters on 'so-called grotesque paintings'.

Paleotti clarifies that by 'grotesque' he does not refer to works or those parts of works with leaves, festoons, arabesques, frills, or similar 'reasonable ornaments', but rather those images of men or animals or objects that exist made in a way that they are not and never could have been or could be. He gives as examples of such works images of chandeliers holding not candles but human faces that spout flames; rivers that flow from sea shells; or trees formed of serpents and the faces of men, lions, and fish all jumbled together. In sum,

if each of the defects that we have discussed in several chapters in this treatise debases the dignity of the pictorial art, what is one to make of grotesque paintings, the majority of which, if not all, contain the full range of errors, such that they cannot be called paintings, unless they be qualified as lying, inert, vain, imperfect, improbable, out of proportion, obscure, and eccentric[?][26]

Here then was an iconographic manifesto that not only expressed a set of preferences but actually declared certain kinds of works as acceptable and certain others not so. The categorical judgements and confident tone of this text would have seemed excessive, if not absurd, were they not backed up by commensurate power to impose sanctions. Instructions went out to bishops to assemble the artists in their dioceses to inform them of the conciliar decrees. No commissions for artistic projects were to be granted without episcopal approval of the artists' sketches or plans or drafts. As things turned out in Milan, none of the artists associated with the Academy of the Blenio Valley received commissions; in fact some of them got in trouble – for example the painter Aurelio Luini was censured and even for a few months forbidden to paint by the cardinal archbishop. Theatrical performances, games, and many traditional public celebrations fell under the axe of this puritanical regime. Any such activities that were associated with religious holidays – the case with many of them – were especially vulnerable to the charge of profaning sacred times. Musical instruments other than the organ were thought to profane the sacred space of churches. The wearing of masks was banned because they profaned the face that God gave to men and women. That the duchy itself was becoming holy territory follows from the banning from its precincts of comedians and clowns, and also people known to hang out in taverns. The Borromeo programme went far and wide and it had teeth.[27]

For an example of this programme in operation, consider the festivities of 3 August, when Milan's more than one hundred guilds made their annual gift to the on-going construction of the city's massive cathedral. This was the *festa del mosgètt*, named for a container that held five bushels of grain and that for the occasion was enveloped in myrtle branches and tinsel. The porters' guild, as tradition had it, carried the *mosgètt* loaded with the offerings in a procession that wove through many of the city's principal streets to the Duomo. It was the porters' annual moment of glory, in which the procession was but the prelude to great feasting and drinking in the vast square in front of the church. The future saint's way of dealing with this colourful occasion was to suppress those profane festivities but to make certain that the annual 'donations' continued to flow in all the same. Thus the porters in a way shared in the fate of the academicians who imitated them.[28]

The balanced restraint shown by Carracci and Lomazzo, and to some extent as well by Croce, in depicting the workers they saw about them each day, modifies the view of an out-and-out class division characterised everywhere by disdain, contempt, and ridicule on the part of those who dominated society towards those whom they regarded as their inferiors. The stereotypes present in so many of these works are absurd in the same way as those assigned to supposedly characteristic national traits. Bergamasco, the dialect of one province, was clearly not the language spoken by all uneducated labourers in northern Italy. It is, to be sure, generally regarded as one of the Italian dialects least understandable to outsiders, which renders it even less likely to have been adopted commonly elsewhere. The linguistic stereotype, though, was a combination of mainly Bergamasco and Venetian invented by writers as the language of stock comic characters, supposedly peasants or mountain dwellers from Bergamo, who came to flourishing urban centres in search of work, bringing a mix of muscle and simple-mindedness tempered by rustic cleverness. Just as with their language, so also with their origins: it is not true, as we have seen, that all porters came from Bergamo any more than that they all came from the mountains.[29]

As social stereotypes never truly coincide with social realities, even if there are occasional overlaps, there does exist just as one would expect evidence of anti-social behaviour on the part of porters: some of them were loud and foul-mouthed in public, some did get into fights, and some did drink too much. To be sure, for at least as long as the wine porters had guilds, they supposedly had an obligation to monitor their own behaviour. The provisions of their statutes included prohibitions against 'injurious and uncivil language and behaviour' (Piacenza); against 'fighting among themselves for customers' (Reggio Emilia); or against 'saying indecent words to anyone', against 'speaking nastily to another wine porter', and against 'those who curse and commit sacrilege' (Parma).[30]

In a series of interesting public complaints in Cremona, observation of actual behaviour could well have been involved but if so it came mixed with a good measure of pre-judgement. In 1544 the commune sought to move the city's wine market away from the episcopal palace to a square not far away, and somewhat later sought to allow the selling of wine in yet an additional public space.

Both of these plans brought forth complaints of two types from those living close to the proposed sites. The first concerned the disruption and inconvenience caused by the additional traffic and the space taken up by the wine sellers' carts. The second stated that even if the inhabitants could tolerate such inconvenience, although not without great difficulty, what they found intolerable was that 'their women, especially the nubile ones, could not appear there, or indeed not continue to live there decently at all, because of the foul language and filth of the peasants and the wine porters'.[31]

In Modena the earliest surviving document in which the term *brentator* appears is a court judgement of 1439 against Guglielmo Patinato and Boldrino da Padova, *brentatores*, for a clamorous altercation that created public scandal by their use of vituperative language (*verba vituperosa*).[32] In Venice, too, these workers could get on each other's nerves, sometimes with tragic consequences. In 1352 two wine porters from Friuli came to blows at the Riva del Vin during a dice game that left one of them dead. Twelve years later there was another 'homicide among wine porters'.[33]

From time to time other outbreaks of violence occurred that stemmed not from personal disputes but from workplace competition. All guild statutes in spite of their many differences were alike in claiming for their members a monopoly on the particular kind of work they did. These statutes also tended to favour descendants of present or former members as well as favouring local inhabitants over outsiders. However, guilds never could have afforded to exclude outsiders categorically, particularly where the most onerous and least remunerative forms of labour were involved, and given the demographic realities of the time. Here on this underside of the economy one can nearly always find tension if not violence between legitimate or licensed and clandestine or undocumented workers. All of this is familiar to anyone who has seen words and fists fly between licensed and unlicensed taxi drivers.[34] An edict promulgated by the duke of Milan in 1670 refers to just such scrapes as 'evil disorders' (*mali disordini*) among both porters and wine porters at many of their work stations throughout the city. The claim is that illegitimate workers are trying to butt in and take a share of the work and the pay, and yet the document does not qualify them as illegitimate but only and repeatedly as outsiders, and uses an insulting epithet to rub in the point. These troubles, which arise continually, are, it continues, 'the fault of *brugnoni* wine porters and

Figure 17 Piero, a wine porter nicknamed 'the drunkard', in one of two
drawings made in 1525 in Modena.

porters, who are not of this state ... and who cause grave harm and
damage to the wine porters and porters who were born in and are
inhabitants of this duchy and state'. An early-nineteenth-century
dictionary of the Milanese dialect defines *brugnón* as 'an insulting
name given to tavern keepers, chestnut vendors, and wine sellers
who hereabouts are nearly all foreigners'.[35]

As for drinking, one could say, as Garzoni suggested, that it was
included in a wine porter's job description, for clients did occasionally ask them to taste whether a wine was good or not. In a less official way, though, there were ample occasions in which a wine porter
might have been offered a little taste of wine. Still, just two images
of a wine porter drinking have come to hand – actually two quite
similar drawings made at Modena in 1525 and 1527.[36] The subject
in both is one Piero, shown in profile with his brenta on his back,
his staff in one hand, and a glass in the other (see Figure 17). Poor

Piero; he is identified by his nickname, which everyone in town surely knew: Piero Imbriago (the Drunkard). Perhaps he could not resist the temptation to lift a glass. Perhaps, too, observers of the urban scene could not resist the temptation to draw the obvious connection between drinking and lower-class workers whose job entailed carrying around large open containers of wine. Perhaps it was also too strong a temptation for Fra Salimbene of Parma to resist associating Alberto the wine porter with drinking. Being one himself who kept an eye out for good wine, and not above enjoying a bit of word play now and then either, what harm was there in Salimbene's making a little joke about 'this Alberto' (*iste Albertus*), whom he of course had never known, being as much a *potator* as a *portator*?[37]

Salimbene's witticism failed not surprisingly to enter the canon of the Alberto legend. What were implanted there, however, by the sixteenth century at the latest, but became problematic only somewhat later, were the circumstances and in particular the place of Alberto's birth. We noted earlier that to the wine porters of Reggio Emilia he was known as Alberto of Cremona. To those in Cremona he was known as Alberto of Bergamo, while to those in Bergamo he was variously known as Alberto of Clusone or Alberto of Villa d'Ogna. By either of the latter designations, at least the locals knew perfectly well that he was from up in the mountains of the Serio River Valley.

To Mario Mozzi, a chaplain of Santa-Maria-Maggiore in Bergamo who included a version of the life of Alberto in his *Sacra Historia di Bergamo* (1615), Alberto's origins constituted a problem to be dealt with. His telling of the legend derives from the various versions of it written in the previous century, in particular by lifting the image with which Marcantonio Benaglio had begun his life of Alberto – that of comparing the sweet-smelling roses that bloom among thorns and the shiny gold that one finds in the sand with Alberto's birth amidst the rocks and high mountains of Bergamo's hinterland. Benaglio's efforts to ennoble Alberto we can now appreciate as in step with the determination of other sixteenth-century writers to establish a new nobility based on urban, professional status – one that was as distant from the countryside, mountains especially, and from manual labour, as they could make it. Still, where Benaglio had Alberto born of 'not obscure' parents, Mozzi follows most other versions of the legend in not suppressing or distorting

Alberto's modest origins. Instead, after appropriating and elaborating upon Benaglio's opening image, he wove it into a theological explanation for the problematic circumstances of those origins.

> If from wretched thorns we see come forth graceful roses dispensing sweet odours, if out of lowly sand comes precious gold, and from black shells are born white pearls, and God does these and other marvels of the natural realm in the service of mankind, why should we not expect that he would also do the same and even more for his glory in the spiritual realm?

With this rhetorical question posed, Mozzi launches into the subject at hand, namely *The Life of Blessed Alberto of Villa d'Ogna*.

> This, then, is precisely what we see in the case, among others, of Blessed Alberto, who was born of vile peasants amidst the horrid mountains of Villa d'Ogna, in the land of the Serio Valley. He was no less dear to God because of this, such that it pleased his divine majesty to work through him on behalf of many and to make of him an example for us of great wonders.

And so we have the word of a seventeenth-century Bergamasque cleric that Alberto was pleasing in the eyes of God in spite of the harsh facts that he was born of humble parents and born in a mountain valley above Bergamo.[38]

III

Sainthood

The power to canonise saints is reserved solely to that one who is both the successor of Saint Peter and the Vicar of Christ.

Pope Innocent III, 1200

Here begins the life of the most holy Facio whose body rests in the cathedral of Cremona. As for it being all right to call him a saint, you should know that the Church is twofold: there is the Church Militant, which is made up of us, and the Church Triumphant, made up of the saints. Even if he is not canonised in the Church Militant, that is, down here, he is canonised up above in the Church Triumphant.

A canon of the cathedral of Cremona,
Life of Saint Facio, 1272

7

Making saints

In the spring of 1748 Pope Benedict XIV signed a decree announcing the canonisation of Alberto of Villa d'Ogna. The procedures
followed at that time in the Roman Church have with few exceptions remained basically unchanged ever since. Both the procedures
and even many of the fundamental concepts of sainthood in play
in the 1740s differed in a number of essentials, however, from what
they had been back in Alberto's time. What is more, even by his
time canonisation had already had a long, evolving history. In all
ages canonisation, no matter how inflexible or adaptable at given
moments, has had to respond to changing conditions within society
at large as well as within existing ecclesiastical structures.[1]

The very notion of singling out exemplary holy people for veneration ante-dated Christianity, and thus not surprisingly a model
Christian came to be described by an adjective meaning 'holy' or
'blessed', respectively *sanctus* and *beatus* in Latin.[2] These terms
could be and were put to use also as nouns, and were moreover
used interchangeably to mean 'a saint'. The various phases of sainthood's long history, starting right with that of the martyrs of the
first three Christian centuries, far from being obliterated as they
were superseded, all left significant vestiges that have survived to
the present. The earliest Christians venerated the martyrs among
them for, to put matters simply, imitating what Jesus had done.
They willingly submitted to the death penalty at the hands of a persecuting authority for the offence of refusing to renounce their pro-
fessed beliefs. The public nature of martyrdom obviated the need
for authentication, and thus canonisation was a spontaneous act on
the part of the local community of believers. The cult that followed
took place on the martyrdom site and/or place of burial, while the
most intense remembrances of the martyrs' sacrifices occurred on
the anniversaries of their respective deaths.

At times when the authorities moderated their zeal in persecuting, the response of some zealous believers was one of frustration. The famous holy man of the Egyptian desert, Anthony, returned once to Alexandria in search of martyrdom, and accordingly made something of a display of himself in public. Ultimately the humiliation of being ignored forced him to retreat once again to his life in the desert. In a similar vein, when in the 250s an epidemic of some still unidentified infectious disease took an alarmingly high number of lives in Carthage, some Christians there complained that they were being deprived of the opportunity to become martyrs, whereas their bishop, Cyprian, urged them to appreciate that the disease offered them a still speedier departure for the eternal bliss of the next life.[3]

With the conversion of Emperor Constantine, the issuance in 312 of his edict extending toleration to Christians, and the consequent collapse of opportunities for martyrdom, the new model of Christian spiritual hero, designated *confessor*, was a person who, in the face of adversity and sometimes official opprobrium, even if not martyrdom, nonetheless remained steadfast in the faith. Chief among these were the hermits and monks who abandoned society for deserted lands; some went quietly but others issued scathing criticisms of the compromises that the mass conversions following that of the emperor had entailed. Some of these 'Desert Fathers', and perhaps some of the women among them who disguised themselves as men, developed a justification of their way of life by claiming to engage in a living martyrdom, a martyrdom that lasted not just for a few minutes in the arena but day after day and year after year in the desert. The disciples of the specially wise and experienced holy men of the desert kept alive the memories and teachings of these masters and venerated them after death just as their ancestors had venerated the martyrs.[4]

The category of the confessors also embraced teachers and scholars (Jerome, Augustine), prelates (Bishop Ambrose of Milan, Pope Gregory the Great); monastic founders (Benedict of Nursia, Queen Radegund); monk-missionaries (Denis in Gaul, Patrick in Ireland, Columba in Scotland, Columbanus in Frankish Gaul and Lombard Italy, Augustine of Canterbury in England, and Wynfried-Boniface in Germany); and, among still others, those kings such as Ethelbert of the Anglo-Saxons, Stephen of the Hungarians, or Olaf of the Norwegians, who were the first of their peoples to convert to Christianity. While the model of sainthood had shifted, the designation of someone as worthy of veneration and hence of emulation remained the spontaneous act of a community, whether that community were a monastery, a city, a diocese, a kingdom, or a people in the sense of an entire ethnic or tribal group. The fame of many – perhaps most – saints, regardless of the size of the communities they came from, remained close to home, making it reasonable to think that untold numbers of saints' cults came and went in the distant past without leaving traces. The most efficacious way of attaining fame far and wide for one's spiritual hero was to produce a book relating the saint's life and miracles, which could in turn create an extended, virtual community of readers; a list of well-known examples would include those influential *legendae* or *vitae* written by Athanasius about Anthony, by Sulpicius Severus about Martin, or by Gregory the Great about Benedict.[5]

While popular consensus within the holy person's community appears to have been the key mechanism, the operative criterion was that he or she had died with a reputation for holiness, or what was sometimes called 'in the odour of sanctity'. Still, this procedure could not remain totally 'popular'. The intervention of ecclesiastical authorities in these matters began not so much as a way to wrest control of naming saints from communities of believers as it was to keep a lookout for and if necessary investigate cults of suspicious origin, and to quash those found to be inauthentic. The main issue was not necessarily the designation of someone as *sanctus*, but rather the ritual veneration by the living that took place at the departed one's burial site. One example of such a conscientious bishop in sixth-century Frankish Gaul was Gregory of Tours, who kept an eye out for false prophets. The latter usually appeared in the guise of itinerant, unauthorised, or self-styled Christian preachers. They had much in common with some of the more flamboyant revivalist preachers of recent times, for example those charismatic figures that drew large crowds to the tents they set up on the edges of American towns, or the still more recent television evangelists. To Gregory, just as to later pastors of stable congregations, such visitors were unwelcome because of the potential danger these represented for their flocks and of the certain challenge these posed to their own authority. Gregory described vividly a particularly colourful character that he labelled the 'bogus Christ of Bourges' and recounted with satisfaction how the bishop of Le Puy had him killed. Gregory added that he had seen a number of these men with their entourages of 'foolish women' whom they had deceived into becoming their followers and to proclaiming them to be saints. What disturbed him most was that 'these men acquired great influence over the common people'.[6]

All in all the relatively informal practice of popular acclaim followed by formal episcopal approval lasted for roughly a millennium and apparently suited the spiritual needs of the communities that observed it, even if it occasionally ran into problems. Sometimes there were disagreements between ecclesiastical officials jealous of their authority and the faithful whom they considered reckless in their enthusiasms; in other cases it was among the authorities themselves that disagreements arose concerning the authenticity of some individual's saintliness. In spite of all the complex machinery that canon law has erected in succeeding generations, the potential for canonisation becoming a political matter has remained one of the constants of the history of sainthood.[7]

Popes were of course involved in making saints but largely in their capacity as bishops, just as other bishops were. The verb *canonizare*, meaning to inscribe a name in the canon or list of saints of the Roman Church, made its appearance in the early eleventh century but did not signify a fundamental change in the way saints were made.[8] Besides, in spite of this specific meaning, the term has often been taken to mean simply 'to make someone a saint'. A bishop who was persuaded of the genuineness of reports of miraculous responses by a purported saint to believers' appeals to intercede on their behalf was supposed to elevate the remains of the holy person to a more dignified burial place (the elevation); subsequently, in the translation, the remains took their place near, before, under, or inside an altar, which henceforth took the name of the person venerated. In some cases the bishop rededicated the church where this translation took place to include the name of the new saint, which we have seen was the case at Saint-Mattia of Cremona in 1493.

The list of saints proclaimed in Western Europe between the ninth and twelfth centuries demonstrates clearly that its membership was drawn almost exclusively from the minuscule proportion of the population at the very pinnacle of society: royal families, noble families, and high-ranking ecclesiastical officials.[9] The prevailing model of the Christian life in those centuries was monastic. Monastic authors had formulated a social theory based on a description of their society as made up of three major groups defined by function: those who pray, those who fight, and those who work.[10] This triad was both hierarchic and exclusive. Not only did the clergy, and especially the religious as distinguished from the secular clergy – i.e. monks and nuns – fulfil the highest function, that of praying, but they were religious specialists who performed the eminently social function of doing the praying for everyone else. Similarly the warriors, from kings on down to the lowliest of knights, did the fighting for all of society, while the remaining 90-plus per cent of the population toiled mainly to support their social betters while also striving to survive. The more monastic the spiritual life led by kings and queens and dukes and even bishops, the more likely were they to be regarded as holy – indeed the more likely were they themselves convinced that they would be saved, so dominant was the monastic model in thinking about the good life. And although this triad may appear to be about three social classes, that is not the case, because most of those in the upper tiers of the clerical order came from families of the fighting order. The bishops as well as the abbots and abbesses who headed religious houses were virtually all siblings or close relatives of kings and queens, counts and countesses, and so on. Indeed some abbots and abbesses proclaimed proudly that in their monastic communities there were no members who did not come from noble families. Meanwhile most priests were peasants who had a smattering of Latin.[11]

Kings stood apart for the fact that they shared in some of the key attributes of both the first two orders. Even while being the chief warriors and secular rulers of their subjects, kings had never completely lost the divine heritage that they inherited from their pre-Christian forebears, and that had once provided their ancestors with legitimacy. In theory, baptism ought to have sufficed to cancel this heritage, for claiming descent from pagan gods, whether a source of political legitimacy or not, was hardly consistent with professing the Christian faith. What in fact replaced that old claim was a Christian coronation rite – administered by bishops – of anointment with holy oil. Based upon the rite for consecrating a bishop, this coronation rite, newly minted in the eighth century, made of a king someone considered to be 'anointed of the Lord' (*christus domini*). According to scholars of the time, this new ceremony had been prefigured in the anointing of the kings of ancient Israel and in the person of the priest-king Melchizedek. Kings were thus not priests in the sense that they performed liturgical rites, but just as surely they neither were, nor thought of themselves as, mere laymen.[12]

Monasteries had been well established in the West since the sixth century and still existed in order to carry out ritual, regularly and in perpetuity. Monastic religion, the heart of monastic life, was ritual, specifically the seven offices conducted during the day plus the night office, all of which consisted principally of reciting Psalms; the rules provided punishments for monks who made mistakes in word order and pronunciation. The inspiration for this relatively archaic type of religiosity, in which form triumphed over substance, came from the earlier parts of the Hebrew Bible. It was a religiosity of the sort that Jesus had denounced so vigorously and yet it worked well for the eighth-through-eleventh centuries, when attacks by external enemies combined with subsistence economies, weakened governments, and unreliable institutions of justice to create an atmosphere of unrelieved insecurity. It was a coherent religiosity, with notions of a sainthood effectively reserved for lords and ladies that were consistent with all of its other manifestations.[13]

The extraordinary wealth, social prestige, and political clout that this monastic establishment had accumulated by the twelfth century gave its version of Christianity an aura of solidity and permanence worthy of an institution that offered guarantees of spiritual comfort to the end of time. The most visible incarnation of this power was the Abbey of Cluny, a monastery that had at most 460 monks and whose new church, dedicated by Pope Innocent II in 1130, was the largest church, indeed the largest building of any kind, capable of accommodating several thousand persons, in all of Europe. Yet more extraordinary still is the dramatic return to prominence of the Gospels in an astonishing proliferation of religious initiatives that sprouted in the twelfth century.[14] The adherents to these initiatives shared an antipathy towards traditional monasticism, whether for its formal religion, its aristocratic snobbery, or its wealth, and they strove to live in what they believed to be greater conformity with the lives of Jesus and the Apostles.[15] As one would expect of any such major reform movement, which one leading historian of the religious life has called the 'Reformation of the Twelfth Century', its participants ran the gamut from very moderate to very radical.[16]

The context for this reformation that preceded *the* Reformation by four centuries was the series of social and economic transformations that we have been referring to as the 'Commercial Revolution'. Some of the new religious initiatives began in the countryside and others in cities, and yet all of them, rural and urban, were in some degree responses to the rapidly expanding commercial economy and urban society. Among the innovators, clerics, especially men who had direct personal experience of the monastic life, dominated at first but laypeople eventually took on more and more of that role. The earliest ones shared the notion that the monastic life was not fundamentally wrong but that its current manifestation had wandered too far from the heroic early days of the hermits and monks in the Egyptian desert. They emphasised the need for a much simpler life and for disengagement from the affairs of the world. One of the early reformers was Stephen of Muret, who lived as a hermit in west central France at the end of the eleventh century and the start of the twelfth. In scenes that appear to imitate the stories about the Egyptian Desert Fathers, persons who had heard of Stephen sought him out for advice and wrote down his sayings. They were curious when they learned that he did not adhere to a particular religious rule and asked for his guidance should they wish to organise a monastery of their own. He acknowledged the existence of several monastic rules but taught them that there is really only 'one first rule of faith and salvation, one rule of rules, from which all others flow, namely the holy Gospel'. This simple reply carried a radical message that was to have significant reverberations over the decades following, starting with one of his own immediate followers who wrote that any persons, including those who are married, who live by the Gospel, are living the religious life.[17]

Another approach was to stay with Benedictine monasticism but to purge it of its many accretions since the time of Benedict, the solution offered by the Cistercians, whose most articulate spokesman was Bernard of Clairvaux. Bernard's denunciations of the excesses of monastic churches and liturgical trappings were delivered with all the passion of an Old Testament prophet. At the same time he emerged as an avant-garde prophet in his sensitive articulation of major new themes such as the love of God; the tender and comprehending Mary; and the suffering, deeply human Jesus, best seen perhaps in contrast to the distant, severe, regal judge that God had been depicted as in the immediately preceding centuries. The nearly four hundred Cistercian monasteries founded in Europe in the twelfth century, all in the countryside, testify to the success of this new programme, especially as articulated in Bernard's persuasive rhetoric.[18] But Bernard turned these same weapons against the social developments he saw going on about him. When he preached to students at Paris in the 1140s he railed against the existence even of these city schools where the masters were paid, where students had to purchase books, where religious texts were subjected to critical questioning and argued over indecorously in the street amidst vagabonds and pimps; in fact he railed against these young students being in Paris at all, a lurid Babylon that could only distract and corrupt them. The place for them, he declared, was really Jerusalem, the heavenly city, by which he meant a monastery like his, set in the quiet countryside, where they could read sacred scripture respectfully and ruminate upon it prayerfully, all the while learning from their 'books' – that is, the trees and rocks and watercourses.[19] What is significant in these tirades is that he put his finger precisely on what he saw as wrong and evil – put simply: cities, commerce, money – and the only solution he had to offer was to turn his back on them and flee. Within a generation or two of Bernard's death, his order had stumbled unwittingly into great wealth along with all the problematic entanglements that that involved. By occupying lands that were marginally productive for agriculture, the English Cistercians, for example, turned to raising sheep and started to sell their surplus raw wool to the growing Flemish textile industry, and soon ended up awash in money by becoming its principal supplier; their Italian counterparts were in the forefront of building the extensive irrigation system in parts of Lombardy and Piedmont mentioned earlier, a project that greatly expanded agricultural production at the very moment of a population explosion. The Cistercians continued to exist in the thirteenth century and beyond, just as the older Benedictine monasteries did, but their capacity for intellectual and spiritual innovation and relevance had rapidly dissipated.

Instead of the students whom Bernard admonished fleeing cities, it was the intellectual life itself that fled the monasteries, and headed to those newly vibrant centres. These densely packed communities and the easy flow of strangers among and in and out of them made of the city square a perfect theatre, with a ready-made audience included, for all sorts of entertainments and preachings. These last two categories were not always easily distinguished. Urban audiences heard messages their ancestors had almost certainly never heard in the countryside. The Gospels were being talked about as frequently in the squares as in churches. Whether or not preachers articulated explicitly the contrasts between an evangelical life and the life led by many clerics at the time, these contrasts were readily apparent. Of course there were clerics who were as enthusiastic about preaching and the new evangelism as any laypeople were, but many clerics, most tellingly those who occupied positions of authority (and large palaces), felt threatened and reacted accordingly. These last focused upon what they saw as two fundamentally different but inevitably related problems: the authority to preach, and the content of what got preached. Both matters fell within the purview of episcopal authority. Many city people sought ways to reform their lives, but not necessarily in the standard and traditional way of joining a religious community. Instead they remained in the city and continued to be married and to work, all the while trying to live their lives more in accordance with what they seemed to be learning for the first time was the way taught by Jesus in the Gospels. This evangelical wave gained momentum in the latter half of the twelfth century at the same time that an utterly new awareness of poverty and of concern for the plight of the poor (*pauperes*), especially urban poverty and the urban poor, manifested itself throughout Latin Christendom in tracts and wills and pious foundations intended to ameliorate these conditions.[20]

One of the earliest of a new breed of saints dates from this time. Born the son of a wealthy merchant, Ranieri of Pisa started to work in his father's business and yet was moved to become deeply religious when he learned of and subsequently met a very rich man who had distributed all of his wealth to the poor and become a hermit. At a certain point Ranieri went to the Holy Land on business, 'for the sake of merchandise and gain', and while there had a still deeper conversion to live in poverty. After several years of visiting and worshipping at the various sites associated with the life of Jesus, he returned to Pisa where he lived in poverty and did good works among the poor. Well known and greatly admired in his native city, Ranieri was already regarded as a saint before his death in 1160.[21]

Many groups of laypeople organised themselves spontaneously to live in the manner of the Apostles. Their very lack of formal institutional organisation make many of them barely visible to historians; only those who in some way were perceived to be encroaching upon the territory and prerogatives of the clergy and who as a result were branded as heretics are better known to us, but almost entirely through the distorted lenses of their persecutors.[22] The Waldensians, i.e. followers of Waldo of Lyons, came about as close to imitating the Apostles as possible given the circumstances of their place and times; they travelled mainly through Provence and Lombardy, although in some cases far beyond, in pairs and in poverty, to preach the Gospel. In several different dioceses they fell afoul of the authorities virtually always over the question of their right to preach, which they saw not simply as a right so much as a duty. Many more groups, though, were manoeuvred into unorthodox opinions that left them open to charges of heresy, the punishments for which escalated in vicious cruelty during the final decades of the twelfth century.[23]

What had smouldered for decades as sporadic and disorganised was becoming an all-out systematic, legally and theologically justified war, which can be seen as part of the formation of an all-powerful papal monarchy. Indeed the rise of the papacy from a central Italian lordship to commanding heights of power and prestige throughout Western Europe was yet another accompaniment to the economic, social, and religious transformations under discussion. It is truly one of the great success stories of the eleventh-through-thirteenth centuries, a story whose main theme is centralisation of power. Among the battles engaged in by several generations of popes was the one fought for control of the ecclesiastical hierarchy itself against the bishops. One way to gauge progress made on that front is to note that in the early eleventh century all bishops were chosen locally, whether by a king, a count or other high-ranking noble, nearby bishops or abbots, or even popular acclaim, whereas by 1300 the papacy already controlled about half of all episcopal appointments, a proportion that eventually arrived at 100 per cent. In addition to controlling these appointments, though, the continuing papal policy aimed at absorbing many of the most crucial episcopal prerogatives, and over time it was highly successful.[24]

There may be no simple way to explain this success, but one can easily identify the principal tool employed by the popes in pursuing their common goal – to wit, the law. The extension of the papal reach to the furthest corners of Europe went hand-in-hand with the revival of Roman law. Renewed interest in Roman law in eleventh- and twelfth-century Italy; the gathering of a school of law at the heart of Europe's oldest university, in Bologna; and the formation of a parallel discipline and system, namely canon or ecclesiastical law, were all instrumental in strengthening the papacy. Legal training became the favoured way to career advancement, and bureaucratic order and practices became the favoured means of assuring legal consistency. Proof of dramatic increases in the quantity of documents, which we are aware of because of the concomitant increases in careful record-keeping, can be demonstrated for governments virtually everywhere in Europe, but always with the papacy in the lead.[25] No one knew this better than the petitioners who came to the papal court from far away, like those proctors sent by the archbishop of Canterbury who had to cool their heels – and survive – in Rome, sometimes for several months at a time, while waiting to get an answer or make the right contact to get the privilege or clarification or settlement they had been sent to get.[26]

In the course of the eleventh century, one of the basic claims of papal authority underwent a major change. With little fanfare but great implications, the popes altered their claim to be the successors to the first bishop of Rome, i.e. to be Vicars of Saint Peter, to become instead Vicars of Christ.[27] From such high ground they were able to drive home their campaign to sharpen all possible distinctions that could be imagined between the clergy and the laity. This included insisting on clerical celibacy while simultaneously resisting any royal claims to ecclesiastical privilege that some kings might have thought derived from their anointment with holy oil. In the century following, another significant change, but of a wholly different sort, took place. In 1159, with the accession of Alexander III, the papacy passed for the first time to a professionally trained canon lawyer. For the next century-and-a-half, nearly all the most important of his successors were trained lawyers, including several professors of law. Little wonder that the principal exception, Celestine V, a deeply pious hermit, resigned from the papacy after just a few months on the job. His posthumous consolation was sainthood, an honour that eluded all the lawyer-popes. The latter, though, left their mark on all subsequent papal history, for if popes after 1303 again came from a variety of intellectual and professional backgrounds, the papal bureaucracy had become sufficiently immunised against the dangers of any non-legal-minded or overly impetuous or enthusiastic successor to the throne of Peter.[28]

Among the characteristic manifestations of this trend to centralise ecclesiastical authority in Rome were such practices as expanding

those types of judicial matters that could be appealed from episcopal courts to the papal court, or even reserving certain judicial matters exclusively to the papal court. In line with these practices, and
particularly how they affected the matter of canonisation, there is a
noteworthy statement by Alexander III in 1171 prohibiting any rite
of veneration not authorised by a pope.[29]

Thus at the end of the twelfth century, while the evangelical or
apostolic aspirations of laypeople were continuing to mount, the
papacy – indeed Latin Christendom itself – was approaching a critical moment in its history. As the institution had arrived at a level
of control over the Western Church that the mid-eleventh-century
popes could only dream about, their successors were now going to
have to distinguish those ideas and practices that were not doctri-
nally acceptable and thus in need of elimination from those that
were acceptable and thus worthy of emulation. Weightier still were
their subsequent responsibilities to call for all-out war against those
who held to the former, as well as to promote to sainthood those
who most outstandingly epitomised the latter. In January 1198
Innocent III assumed these daunting powers at the age of thirty-
seven. Formally schooled in theology but with a decade of experience in the legal-minded Roman curia, he showed no signs of being
daunted by his responsibilities. Innocent had been in office for
barely a year, when Sicard, a man of formidable learning who had
been the bishop of Cremona already for fifteen years, asked him to
undertake consideration as a candidate for canonisation a recently
deceased man from Cremona who had been a tailor, a husband,
and a father.

8

Sainthood by community

No more theatrical an urban space could be wished for than the main square, the Piazza del Comune, of Cremona. Construction of the vast Romanesque cathedral, built of brick but with marble facing on the front, lasted through most of the twelfth century; to one side stands its correspondingly vast baptistery, built of the same materials and completed in the 1160s; to the other its bell tower, begun a century later and once completed the tallest in Italy at the time. On the side of the square opposite this imposing manifestation of ecclesiastical power rise up two grand structures in brick that represent secular power, the communal palace and the so-called loggia of the knights. Alberto would surely have seen the bell tower and the loggia under construction in the third quarter of the thirteenth century, whereas the rest of these monuments would probably have looked to him as if they had always been there.[1]

Cremona like Bergamo was a Celtic settlement; its Roman phase, like that of nearby Piacenza, began in 218 BC as a defensive measure against the invasion by the Carthaginian army under Hannibal in the Second Punic War. Few traces of Roman structures remain visible in the modern city although much of the standard rectilinear street grid survives. The Po connected Cremona to the rest of the world, facilitated its prosperous commerce, and of course supplied its inhabitants with fish. Already in the ninth century salt from Comacchio and luxury goods from Venice were coming upstream, some of which continued on to Pavia and Milan, while raw materials were sent back downstream. In the same period the Carolingian rulers invested the bishop of Cremona as a count with effective political authority over the city and its hinterland. In addition to extensive land holdings, the count-bishop had lucrative rights to collect tolls, fees, and taxes from traffic on the Po, dockings at the city's port, and sales made at markets in and near the city. The bishops came from the knightly class, whose wealth also lay in land holding and privileges within their respective domains. This cosy concentration of power in the hands of very few persons faced intense challenges due to increases in both population and commerce in the eleventh and twelfth centuries. The challenges came from city dwellers, mainly merchants (*negotiatores*), who of course felt the sting of those tolls and other forms of taxation. Push led to shove already at the start of the eleventh century when they succeeded in driving the bishop out of the city and destroying much of his property. Such resort to all-out violence made frequent returns to the city's perennially tense social and political scene. Reference to a commune first appeared in a document of 1098, soon followed by mentions of an assembly of all citizens and of the election of consuls.[2]

While the oldest and wealthiest families of Cremona lived within the confines of the old Roman city close to the river bank, the newer arrivals were settling in 'suburbs' to the north and west. The fact that these together really constituted a single urban agglomeration gained acknowledgement in the 1170s and 1180s when the commune had new walls built to enclose both the 'city' and the 'suburbs'. But even within the united city inside its one set of walls the old divisions persisted. The knights (*milites*), who lived in the *Città Vecchia* with the judges, the leading merchants, and of course the person they considered *their* bishop, claimed to be the only legitimate political body; these were contested at every step by the *popoli*, the new people of the *Città Nuova* made up of lesser merchants, shop keepers, professionals, artisans, and labourers, all pushing for a greater say in the conduct of public affairs. The *milites* and the *popoli* each set up separate associations and secured space (that of the knights was the loggia in the piazza) for holding assemblies and storing weapons.[3]

This still very small but highly volatile community was well served for thirty years, 1185–1215, by Bishop Sicard. He had studied at Bologna, had gone on to teach canon law and theology at Paris and Mainz, and had written major works on law, liturgy, and history. His main political objective was creation of a stable political order in his city, which he worked at persistently.[4] The timing of his appeal to the new pope in 1198 to undertake the canonisation of a citizen of his city was not casual. Just one year earlier the *popoli* had revolted against the nobles for their continuing unwillingness to share control of the communal government; they expressed sympathy for their counterparts at Brescia who had succeeded at driving the nobles out of their city; they had not gone that far in Cremona but they did set up a parallel communal structure with their own *podestà* in the *Città Nuova*. Bishop Sicard, always in quest of internal peace, may well have seen in the canonisation of a tailor – although he preferred to refer to him always as a merchant – a gesture towards the *popoli* of openness and inclusion in the civic sphere, of which religious matters were always an integral part. Meanwhile for his part, Innocent III was busy in the first months of his pontificate seeking ways to extend his political influence in northern Italy in the wake of the Emperor Henry VI's sudden death in 1197, in addition of course to grappling with the issue of how to confront the numerous and burgeoning currents of religious initiatives on the part of laypeople. Both of these prelates found in the candidate for sainthood, a man named Homobono, a layman whom they could safely put forward as a model for lay believers to emulate.[5]

In this the first canonisation bull of his pontificate, Innocent spelled out for the people and clergy of Cremona his understanding of the requirements for sainthood: 'two things, namely the virtue of life and the virtue of signs, that is, works of piety in life and miracles after death, are required for someone to be reputed a saint in the Church Militant'. His reason that miracles during one's life are not valid indicators is that the devil can deceive people by having a person of reprehensible life impress others favourably with what seem to be good works. 'Neither works nor miracles alone suffice, but when the latter follow the former, they provide us with a true indication of sanctity.' God thus confirms the genuineness of a person's life of virtue by signs in the form of posthumous miracles.[6]

Turning to the specific case of 'the life and deeds and manner of dying' of Homobono, the pope cites as his source of information not a written text but the exposition made in his presence by Bishop Sicard, accompanied by several clerics and other honourable persons of his diocese. He states that Homobono meditated upon the law of God day and night; attended mass and the canonical hours regularly; prayed assiduously – indeed whatever he was doing his lips seemed to move continually in prayer; showed concern for peacemaking throughout the city; zealously performed works of charity for the poor that included giving food, shelter, and proper burial; spurned heretics; and showed his obedience by doing far more than what was asked of him in the way of vigils and other acts of penance. As the delegation from Cremona included the priest who had been Homobono's confessor at the church of Saint-Egidio for over twenty years (and most likely Sicard's chief source of information on Homobono), the pope had him give sworn testimony to the accuracy of all that had been said of the candidate. And still to foster confidence in the seriousness of these deliberations, he says that he discussed this case at length with a group of bishops and archbishops whom he summoned for this purpose to his council.

Sicard's view of this case is in all likelihood faithfully mirrored in the pope's bull. The only work now extant that speaks to the matter and is also attributed to Sicard is a liturgical text for the celebration of Homobono's feast day, probably prepared in between the canonisation and the translation of Homobono's relics from Saint-Egidio to the cathedral in 1202. The main difference in content between it and the bull is that Sicard identifies Homobono as a merchant, one moreover who made for himself a good deal by abandoning commerce in worldly goods in favour of commerce in spiritual goods, and who renounced 'perverse and wretched merchandising' (*perversa et misera negotiato*). The papal bull makes no mention whatever of Homobono's work or even any aspect of his social status and life. Another difference between the versions of this matter recounted by bishop and pope came in reference to Homobono's miracles. Sicard reported on several miracles that occurred at Homobono's tomb but the pope mentioned just one of these. Even so, the latter gloated somewhat triumphantly that 'the perversity of the heretics will be confounded when they see wonders multiplying at the tombs of Catholics'.[7]

In the end it should be said that Innocent did not really canonise a merchant. He and Bishop Sicard were exceptionally intelligent men, both very well schooled, able at administration, and astute in politics; they were also, in social terms, very conservative aristocrats, with their station's traditional disdain for anyone who had to do with commerce. In the shared views of these men, Homobono was no merchant who became a saint; he qualified for sainthood in their estimation, just as Sicard put it so precisely, because he gave up being a merchant. In other terms, he was canonised in spite of the fact that he had once been a merchant. None of this necessarily detracted from the political value these prelates hoped to gain by pleasing a critically important new sector of the north Italian populace.

There is no denying, in any case, that Homobono was a layman, for he surely was never consecrated as a priest or took monastic vows. That said, the image we get is of a somewhat clericalised layman. Lay status was usually characterised by marriage and by occupation; since the clergy came under the heading of those who pray, members of the laity came within the category of either those who fight or those who work. In Homobono's case, as presented by the bishop and officially disposed of by the pope, both his marriage and his work, which we learn about in some detail from later sources, were decidedly downplayed if not wilfully suppressed.

In 1200 Innocent affirmed explicitly his view that the power to canonise saints is reserved solely to that one who is both the successor of Saint Peter and the Vicar of Christ. This came in the canonisation bull for the wife of Emperor Henry II, Cunegund, who had died in 1040.[8] Subsequently the prelates assembled at the Fourth Lateran Council in 1215 repeated a four-hundred-year-old-decree outlawing the veneration of relics without the authorisation of the prince. The term *prince* at the time that decree was drawn up of course meant 'king', but the Council Fathers in 1215 chose to interpret *prince* as meaning the Roman pontiff. All of these rulings were then incorporated into a major revision of canon law carried out by Gregory IX in 1234.[9]

After accepting the reality of the diversion of a crusade away from an assault on Palestine by way of Egypt to attack instead the Greek Christian city of Constantinople in 1204, Pope Innocent declared a crusade at home in Latin Christendom against the so-called 'Albigensian heretics' in 1209. At precisely the same time and as a counterpoint to this declaration of war, the pope gave his approval to various evangelical groups of laypeople on condition of their subjection to the clergy. The most famous of these was the small band gathered about Francis of Assisi, and just a few years later there came along another such group led by Dominic of Guzman. The spectacular growth and historic importance of the two great religious orders, Francis's Order of Friars Minor and Dominic's Order of Preachers, which developed out of these modest beginnings, testify both to the widespread and strongly felt desire for change in the spiritual life of urban society and to the immense power wielded by the papacy, which thereby succeeded in domesticating a spontaneous and multi-faceted as well as utterly unpredictable social and religious reform movement.

Innocent III and his successors to the end of the thirteenth century undertook a total of forty-nine canonisation cases, twenty-four or half of which resulted in the naming of new saints. These included some well-known historical figures: Saint Francis of Assisi; Saint Dominic; Saint Clare; and, in 1297, King Louis IX of France – Saint Louis.[10] In the course of that century, various popes moved to translate the legal principle of papal canonisation into a workable set of procedures with clear assignments of responsibility and an equally clear sequence of steps to be taken. The bishop of the place where the candidate died was usually the one expected to initiate the process by gathering whatever information he thought relevant for making the case, as the bishop of Cremona had done in 1199, and sending it on to Rome. If the pope found this material sufficiently persuasive, he ordered the official opening of a canonisation process. First off he named commissioners to conduct inquests in those places of the candidate's birth, career, and death. All of the testimonies gathered, duly notarised, were to be sent to Rome along with a *vita* of the candidate and copies of each of his or her writings. The pope named three cardinals to prepare summaries of all the material submitted, and these were subsequently sifted through a series of meetings until the pope, alone, announced his final decision in favour of or against the canonisation. Besides the improvisations and slight modifications in procedure introduced here and there, there does seem to have been a consistent effort over time to set the standards increasingly high in order to avoid inflating the currency of sainthood.[11]

These new procedures, however, left out a certain matter that one could well have expected to find included, namely sanctions. If we consider the work of theologians and canonists to define and explicate doctrine, and thereby distinguish orthodoxy from heterodoxy or heresy, we find that it usually had as a sequel such specified sanctions as excommunication or even anathema.[12] In 1209 extermination was, as we have seen, the sanction chosen. In 1233 Pope Gregory IX placed the administration of sanctions for heresy largely in the hands of the Dominican Order in an institution whose name, *inquisition*, simply took over a standard bureaucratic term for an official inquiry or investigation. But in the matter of canonisation, given especially the unambiguous claims made for exclusive papal authority, no such attempts to challenge or quash the traditional modes of naming saints are known to have taken place. To be sure, Salimbene was not shy in defending the papal claim to exclusive authority, but he was just one friar, not a pope. As a result, canonisations by popular acclamation, by bishops or by the heads of religious houses and of religious orders, or by other groups, were able to continue on as before. As against the 24 saints proclaimed by the papacy in the thirteenth century, the older method yielded at least 270 new saints in the same period.[13]

Following the canonisation of Homobono in 1199, the typology of the papacy's 23 other thirteenth-century saints was strictly traditional, made up of 18 ecclesiastics and 5 laypeople. The latter all belonged to royal families: the king and the empress previously mentioned, another queen, and two duchesses. Therefore the canonisation of Homobono the tailor, obviously a layman associated with the new urban society, was exceptional. Meanwhile, the typology of the saints named in the traditional manner of communal consensus turned revolutionary. Of those roughly 270 saints named in communities all across Europe in the thirteenth century, at least 40 belonged to the laity. The newness appears not in the numbers or the proportions so much as in the makeup of the category of lay saints that emerged in urban Italy. With a few earlier exceptions such as that of Ranieri of Pisa in 1160, the number of the new kind of saints really took off at the start of the new century. Nearly always the dates of the person's death and the start of the cult coincide; the new breed of saints included Raymond Palmeiro of Piacenza, a cobbler, 1200; Giovanni of Lodi, 1205; Gerard Tintori of Monza, a dyer, 1207; Walter of Lodi, 1224; Gerald of Cologne, a pilgrim who died at Cremona, 1241; Giovanni Buono of Mantua, a minstrel turned lay hermit, 1249; Andrea Galleriani of Siena, a soldier, 1251; Amato Ronconi of Saludeccio (near Rimini), 1256; Anthony the Pilgrim, Padua, 1267; Armanno Pungilupo of Ferrara, 1267; Facio of Verona and Cremona, gold- and silversmith, 1272; and Zita of Lucca, domestic, 1278.[14] With such a list in mind, the reader of one of the urban annals of Lombardy or Emilia would not be startled to discover that at Cremona in 1279 a wine porter named Alberto had died and healing miracles began to be reported soon afterwards at his tomb. The story of Alberto fits comfortably into the social and religious context of late-thirteenth-century northern Italy, especially Cremona.

Through the intervention of Frederick I, Bishop Sicard gained independence for his city from its predatory neighbours Milan and Brescia, and he had those imperial privileges confirmed by Frederick II. His attempts at peacemaking yielded a few temporary respites from civic strife. Perhaps equally important was his build-up of an administrative structure that involved careful record keeping, which in the ensuing century, with tensions remaining always high and frequent irruptions of extreme violence that included confiscations and expulsions, nonetheless provided an element of continuity.[15]

The local factions of knights and *popoli* came to be associated respectively, although informally and inconsistently, with the pro-imperial or Ghibelline forces and the pro-papal or Guelf forces that divided loyalties all through central and northern Italy. Between the 1210s and 1250 Cremona was an imperial city; Frederick II had his northern headquarters there, thus bringing the city considerable prestige, order, and occasional prosperity (but with occasional intervals bringing debt as well). When he died his supporters came under attack and lost, but then quickly regained, control of the city. From 1250 to 1266 a Ghibelline leader named Oberto Pallavicino remained in power, while the *popoli* were becoming more intensely pro-Guelf. The regime built up a principality that included Piacenza, Pavia, and Crema, and gained a reputation for being friendly to opponents of the Church, so that many people accused of heresy and exiled for it from their own cities, as well as some Cathars from southern France, found refuge in Cremona. However, after Pallavicino's death, even though another Ghibelline took over, these recent immigrants were no longer welcome. With papal support a Consortium of Faith and Peace took form and launched a fierce witch hunt against suspected heretics; the Cathars from beyond the Alps were sent back home in chains. By 1270 the Guelfs took full control in a frenzy of violence that saw many Ghibelline deaths, expulsions, and expropriations. Thus began a forty-year period of Guelf hegemony in the city's public life.[16]

The church of Cremona could not but be affected by these twists and turns in urban politics. Following Sicard's thirty-year tenure as bishop, his successor, one of the cathedral canons named Omobono, held that office for thirty-three years, 1216–48. At some points in the earliest years of his episcopacy both the Franciscan and the Dominican Orders arrived and got settled. By the time Omobono died, the friars were solidly established, just as they had become in most Italian cities. Factional politics, however, were interfering with the stability of the episcopal office, and to the benefit of the friars as it turned out. Ghibelline families so dominated Cremona's cathedral chapter that none of the candidates for bishop elected by the chapter were able to gain papal approval, whereas those who were chosen and consecrated by the pope were prevented from entering the city and assuming control of their diocese. The result was that from 1248 to 1284 there was no bishop regularly in residence in Cremona, and chief among those who filled the void, along with the cathedral canons, were the Dominicans and Franciscans. This situation continued even after the long period of Ghibelline hegemony came to an end around 1266, when the friars were unleashed upon the 'heretics', both native and foreign, many of whom they ordered arrested and burned alive. Perhaps of greater significance was the practice observed in the Guelf years by which each official act of the city's political life had to gain the approval of the respective heads of the friars' convents. In the same period, moreover, the authority of inquisitors was superior to that of any local officials.[17]

All through this tumultuous period the economic and social transformations begun a century and more earlier continued apace. Traffic and trade on the Po increased; maintenance and improvements of the city walls and of the embankments that disciplined the Po, the Adda, and the Oglio continued; the growing of flax and making of linen cloth as well as the fustian industry, which made an inexpensive cloth by combining cotton imported from Egypt or southern Italy with locally grown and woven wool, expanded; the production of woad and madder and their use in the cloth-dying industry also grew; and all the while the population, fed by immigrants from the upper plains and the Bergamasque valleys, kept on course towards its pre-plague maximum of perhaps 35,000.[18]

This review of political, ecclesiastical, and socio-economic goings-on in Cremona constitutes the context for that part of Alberto's life that he spent there. Although we know practically nothing about his time in the city except for his *métier*, we can, once more, surmise from his burial in Saint-Mattia that he had lived in that parish, which, as we have noted, was located in the *Città Nuova*, and from what happened after his burial that he was well enough known among his fellow workers to make it probable that he had been resident in Cremona through at least most of the third quarter of the century. Sparing as the use we can make of this information about Cremona in relation to Alberto himself may be, the same information, if we fold into it some details about the lay saints from among the *popoli* who preceded Alberto, can be immensely helpful in decoding the relatively abundant sources that recount the birth and development of his cult.

To pick up the story of Homobono as it evolved in the thirteenth century, two other versions of his life, very different from what the bull of canonisation told us, eventually emerged. The earlier one, an anonymous work of the first third of the century, claims to fill in information left out of previous writings. This includes a description of Homobono as a man tall and thin, soberly dressed; an accounting of his eighty-year life as divided between fifty years in worldly pursuits and fifteen in spiritual ones (the earliest fifteen were presumably spent in growing up); mention of his regular practice of self-flagellation in his vineyard where he went to pray; revelations not only that he was married and had children but that his wife and heirs objected strenuously to his generous alms-giving; and finally a clarification about his trade, namely that Homobono made and sold clothes. He was a tailor.

The later view of Homobono, again anonymous, brings many of these disparate elements together with still other details in a more coherent portrait that dates from the second half of the thirteenth century. As in most biographies the story begins with the subject's family background. Already a few generations back Homobono's ancestors had settled in what became the *Città Nuova* near the church of Saint-Egidio. They had practised various trades and become generally well off as artisans and shop keepers, his father following in one of these trades – that of making and selling clothes. Homobono followed his father in this line of work and inherited from him, just as the latter had inherited from his father, both the house in town and the land outside the walls that supplied them with wine and some of their food. As a young man, so went the legend, he was honest and equitable in his dealings with others and obedient to his parents' wishes, including that he marry. Only once his father died – so frequently the crucial moment for the emergence of the true person in traditional patriarchal societies – did Homobono begin to show greater concern for the welfare of the poor than he did for his work. And again we read that his generosity infuriated his wife.[19]

The real difference in this telling of the story, however, is the absence of strong prejudice against the subject's occupation, with the result that there was no need to introduce a sharp turning point or conversion. His priorities surely did evolve and his wife did accuse him of abandoning his trade, which may or may not have been literally true, but he still had a house in which to offer hospitality to those without shelter and abundant supplies of food to dispense to the hungry. Two miracle stories, one about bread, the other about wine, confirm the point. 'One day during a time of famine, the baker delivered a quantity of bread, as usual, to the holy man's house.' Poor people followed the baker, and then begged Homobono to give some of it to them. As his wife was momentarily absent, he consented. Later, at the time of their next meal, when his wife went to the cupboard to get the bread, she found 'loaves of incomparable fineness and quality, as many in number as he had given away'. He acted as surprised as she, although he knew this to be God's work, but instructed the housemaid, who had seen what happened, not to say anything. As for the wine story, it tells of one day when he was carrying a jug of wine to his vineyard for the refreshment of the men he had working there. On the way some poor people entreated him to give them some wine, and once he had agreed they drank all of it. At this point he did not want to return home and face the certain reproaches of his wife, so he filled the jug with water and made the sign of the cross over it. 'He took it to the workmen, whom he found very thirsty. When they tasted it, they found it to be a most delightful and exquisite wine; they had never tasted any wine so good.' Homobono thought they were making fun of him, but a taste convinced him that this, too, was the work of God, to whom he offered abundant thanks.

The predominant theme of this version of the Homobono story from the later thirteenth century was not of someone who had changed his ways radically but of a well-off person who was loved and admired for being *pater pauperum* – the father of the poor. Such views of Homobono that emerged during the course of the thirteenth century, and that are so at variance with the one we get from the ranking prelates back just before the century began, appear to be signalling significant changes in social attitudes. The anonymous authors were still very likely to be clerics, but that in no way implies that they necessarily came from the highest ranks of society. Young men, more than likely younger sons, from families engaged in the relatively new mercantile and professional sectors of urban economies, were among those who were entering the priesthood and the mendicant orders in the thirteenth century. There may be significance also in the responses to these later versions of this saint's story, which included making him the patron and protector of guilds of tailors and even more generally of artisans and other workers, as well as of merchants, in many different cities within but also beyond the borders of Italy. In Cremona itself, the cult of Homobono at the cathedral, the church not of a neighbourhood but of the entire city, began in earnest in 1202 with the translation of some of his relics there from his parish church. The cult lagged somewhat after the death of Bishop Sicard in 1215 but regained vitality during and perhaps because of the Guelf takeover in the 1270s. In the same period the mixing of Homobono into the commune's identity became manifest with a fresco bearing his likeness on the walls of the communal palace alongside that of Saint Imerio, already for several centuries Cremona's patron and protector. In 1298 a diocesan synod decreed obligatory the daily commemoration of Saint Homobono along with that of Saint Imerio in all of the diocese's churches, while towards the middle of the following century Homobono had definitively taken his place as one of the city's co-protectors.[20]

Raymond Palmeiro, one of the new breed of popular saints, lived not far from Cremona in Piacenza and died in 1200, just three years later than Homobono. The main source for his life is a biography that his son asked Master Rufino, a priest who had known his father, to write; a later version exists but it differs in few details. We learn that Raymond came from modest circumstances, worked as a shoemaker, was married, and had five children. His work, which he practised in order to feed himself and his family, 'distracted him', as Rufino put it, 'from his spiritual practices'. Raymond became increasingly preoccupied with living a holy life and devoted his time away from work to informing himself about the teachings of scripture and then to transmitting what he had learned to his fellow workers. Rufino then explains that getting married had not been Raymond's idea in the first place but that God had allowed him to be persuaded by his relatives to get married so that 'his [God's] saint should experience what trials those joined in marriage undergo, in feeding and bringing up children and looking after a household'. After Raymond had gotten enough of this experience, the benign Creator of all things, as He knew that His servant could not devote himself with all his heart to the pursuit of the spiritual life while he was bound to servitude by the conjugal yoke and the care of children, took pity on him and decided to give him some liberty; He took all the children from this life within a year.[21]

Although Raymond then opted for continence, his wife did not agree and so they had a sixth child, a male. Raymond took the child secretly to a church and prayed before a crucifix that the Lord not separate this child from his siblings. The divine response was instead to take the life of his wife, so at least he would engender no new children and his son could grow up to join the religious life. Raymond handed the child over to his in-laws and took off on what he thought was henceforth his true vocation, namely a pilgrimage junket to Santiago in Spain, the Magdalene in Provence, Saint-Anthony in Padua, and then Rome, whence he planned to go to the Holy Land. But one night while he slept with other poor pilgrims under a portico of Saint-Peter's, Jesus appeared to him with news of a radical change of direction for his life. Because he so approved of Raymond's prayers and pious desire for pilgrimage, Jesus said: 'I freed you from the slavery of wife and children.'[22]

To this point, Rufino's biography is so exaggerated a pastiche of traditional clerical disdain for marriage and the family as to verge on caricature. Certainly no brief for or on behalf of lay sanctity, still it becomes a brief for a new form of sanctity.

> 'I do not want you to wander around the world anymore', Jesus told Raymond, 'but to return to your homeland, Piacenza, where there are so many poor people, so many abandoned widows, so many persons sick and overcome by various misfortunes who call upon my mercy, and there is no one to help them. You shall go, and I will be with you, and I shall give you grace to lead the rich to alms-giving, the unquiet to peace, and erring and sinful women to a right way of living.' Jesus then spells out the details of this mission, including promises to provide him a place where he could help the poor in Piacenza, to give great force to his words so that none could contradict him, and to make the bishop of that city favourably disposed to him. Jesus then sent him on his way: 'Go now, get started, leave Rome, where you are wasting your time and energy, and set out for your homeland.'[23]

All went according to plan. Raymond returned to Piacenza and went to see the bishop, who indeed received him favourably. The canons of the church of the Twelve Apostles granted him a space where he could store alms and set up a hospice catering specifically to pilgrims and the sick. In seeking donations all across the city he so inspired the good and generous and so terrified with menaces the avaricious that he obtained alms from all of them. He urged his listeners not just to support his work but to assist the city's many poor and hungry beggars directly.

Raymond took up the cause of the poor, who claimed to be unjustly oppressed, by speaking personally not just to the bishop but also to judges and other civic authorities; none of these dignitaries intimidated him. Making and keeping peace was also on his agenda so that when Piacenza and Cremona were about to go to war, he appealed successfully to his fellow citizens to seek a settlement, but when he got to Cremona he quickly found himself thrown in prison. Still, when Raymond's saintly reputation got through to people in Cremona, they sent him home because they feared God's vengeance for how they had treated him.

When Raymond died, 'the whole city flocked to see his holy body'. The leading men of the city, the nobles, and the worthy matrons rushed to venerate him, while the poor he had so tirelessly assisted bemoaned the loss of their protector. The bishop and the civic officials decreed that he should be buried in the church of the Twelve Apostles and that the hospice he had established be named the Hospital of Saint-Raymond. Once he was laid to rest, the crowds came there from all around, including many Cremonese. They were not disappointed for there was no lack of miracles. An amazing abundance of objects, coins, and images poured in every day, which the city's officers made sure went to support the hospital. At this point of the narrative Rufino interjected that someone recalled Raymond saying, not long before he died, that he would be of more assistance to his poor when he was dead than when alive.

Back in Cremona, the routine activities in that city came to an abrupt halt on an October day in 1241 when all the church bells in the city started to ring at once. The source is a sixteenth-century *Life of Saint Gerald*, which claims to be based in turn on a thirteenth-century original. Its description of the ensuing chaos makes it easy to imagine people rushing out into the street – or even, as it specifies, puzzled sacristans climbing their bell towers – all wondering what was happening, and the speculations that got launched, elaborated upon, and diffused. What the bells were announcing was that a German pilgrim had been killed that very day in Cremona. The ringing of the bells was spontaneous, and the man, it was said, a certain Gerald from Cologne, had been to Santiago, and had now been passing through on his way to Rome. He had exited one of the gates by the river and appeared to have been robbed and to have died from multiple stab wounds.[24]

Fishermen found the body, which some clerics came to retrieve, and yet they soon found that they could not move it. A messenger reported all this to Bishop Omobono, who ordered that the clerics show due reverence to the body and that the fishermen carry the body, which they were then able to do. Once the religious and communal authorities and the rest of the clergy assembled and formed a procession, they set off through the gate back into the city. Shortly the cross bearer at the head of the procession felt an invisible force diverting him from the planned itinerary, leading him and those following to the church of Saint-Vitale. Inside they found a magnificent marble tomb waiting, as it were, to receive Gerald's sweet-smelling remains. Right away sick people praying at this tomb began to be cured. This church's later rededication to Saints Vitale and Gerald was probably only confirmation of a spontaneous, popular renaming from the time of those miraculous events.

This story of Gerald the pilgrim is not entirely unique, for it belongs to the hagiographical sub-genre of murdered pilgrims. The less known about them the easier it was to invent a substitute identity, which tended to include foreign birth and high social standing. The underlying reason for giving the benefit of the doubt to such mysterious outsiders was that pilgrims were by definition engaging in a penitential act, and so the fact that others took advantage of their vulnerability to the point of even killing them made them into martyrs.[25]

Very different still from Homobono, Raymond, and Gerald was Facio, a gold- and silversmith who went into exile from his native Verona and found refuge at Cremona in the late 1220s.[26] Facio set up shop working at his lucrative trade and earning a good income. He belonged to a confraternity called the Consortium of the Holy Spirit, in which he served in the role of one who distributed alms to the poor. His membership in this organisation, to which nobles, merchants, and others of the elite of Cremona adhered, gives a good indication of relatively high social standing. We do not know whether his family background contributed to this favoured status, but his profession may have more to do with it, for people in his line of work marched near the end of the great city-wide religious processions that included the judges, notaries, and spice merchants, far removed from the tavern keepers, butchers, and porters at the other end. It was an old story: in early Germanic law individuals of various social categories were assigned a wergild – that is, a fixed monetary value – and gold- and silversmiths ranked high on that scale.[27]

The seat of the Consortium of the Holy Spirit was the cathedral, which for four decades or more served Facio as a spiritual home. He made several precious liturgical vessels for that church. A few generations of cathedral canons knew him well; they administered the sacraments to him, preached before him, heard his confessions, and of course at the end laid his body to rest in their church. Even so, the author of his *Life* tells us that Facio visited and prayed in many of the other churches in the city; in addition, he claimed that Facio undertook no fewer than eighteen pilgrimages to Santiago de Compostela and visited Rome the same prodigious number of times. The claims continue. Facio came to be known in his adopted city for his generous charity towards the poor. Besides his personal spirituality of frequent prayer and penitential asceticism, he engaged in an evangelical spirituality, offering hospitality to pilgrims in his home, caring for the sick, visiting prisoners, helping to found a hospital (later named after him), providing dowries to young women that they might marry, and meeting the needs of widows and orphans.

Meanwhile the documentation on Facio does not indicate a consistent record of political leanings. He supported a pro-imperial faction during his early years in Verona, support that led to his expulsion and his eventual relocation in pro-imperial Cremona. Moreover, once settled there in the environment of the cathedral and a consortium or confraternity whose members were mainly drawn from the faction of the *milites*, he seems to have continued to ally himself with the political persuasion of the Ghibellines. However, the *vita* refers to a critical moment, probably in the mid-to-late 1250s, when through a vision of the Virgin he received instruction to form a group of Brothers of the Consortium of the Holy Spirit who, while remaining laymen, in addition to their name adopted some clerical garb and devoted themselves intently to charitable undertakings. As part of this new or renewed commitment to alleviating the sufferings of the poor, we might add Facio's record of fifteen recorded miracles performed while he yet lived, most of them cures of supplicants' illnesses. It remains to mention that the religious conversion dating from the time of his conversion had its political counterpart, for in the final decade of his life Facio joined in fully in the progress and final triumph of Guelf politics.[28]

When Facio died in January 1272, the leading civic and religious leaders of the city met right away and decided together that he should be buried in the cathedral, in that place where, according to the text, he had spent so many nights in prayer. The entire clergy of the city, plus both the knights and the *popoli*, gathered for a grand funeral and saw Facio duly entombed. The burial of someone known to have performed many miracles in his life could not help but create an expectation that he would continue to do so following his death and burial. The cathedral canons formed a commission to look into and make a record of the miracles of their departed friend; they designated one of their own, a priest named John, to serve as secretary with the specific responsibility for writing up the record. The *vita* appears to have been written at about the same time by a different individual but nonetheless a member of the same corporate body. John began his report with an account of the fifteen miracles *in vita* and then continued on with fifty more that he recorded after Facio's death. For two months, from right after the funeral until the end of March, John gathered the testimony of witnesses who were interrogated by the commission. Most of these interrogations took place at the cathedral but members occasionally went instead to the homes of witnesses who were unable to come to them.

These details give us a textbook model of how to organise a successful saint's cult. Facio clearly belonged to the cathedral, not that he was a member of the chapter of canons, or even of course a priest, but that in a proprietary sense he, or more precisely his life story, belonged to the cathedral and its current custodians. It was the latter's responsibility to do all in their power to gather every bit of evidence that could help prove that Facio was a saint, and to do so immediately, before any witnesses left the scene or enthusiasm and memories evaporated.[29]

Seven years after Facio died, chroniclers in Parma, Piacenza, and Reggio Emilia noted in their entries for 1279 that a good man from Bergamo named Alberto who worked as a wine porter in Cremona had died in that city and that shortly after his burial he had begun to perform miracles. Thereafter these chroniclers differed in how much additional information they supplied, while, as we saw, Salimbene left us not just the longest but by far the most opinionated account of all.

To learn more about Alberto we consulted a contemporary account of the scene at his tomb along with twenty-one notarised testimonials to miraculous cures received. We then had to jump to the sixteenth century to read three lives (*vitae*) of Alberto, all of which claimed to be based upon an old historical record kept by the parish priest of Saint-Mattia. That record, not known to be extant, probably dated back to the last two decades of the thirteenth century.

The saint's legend that emerged from these disparate sources did not and could not measure up to the demands of modern biography. More mosaic than oil portrait, its individual components were simply, and often randomly, placed next to one another, rather than fully integrated so as to become inseparable parts of a coherent whole. Hagiographers in general showed little regard for narrative development, chronological sequence, or traits of personality. Their job was to make the holy person worthy of both veneration and emulation. One well-worn trick of the trade was to borrow details from other saints' lives, or even from the Gospels. The latter practice is what explains Homobono's turning water into wine (John 2:1–11), Facio's calming of the winds and waves of a raging storm at sea (Mark 8:26; Luke 8:22–5), and Alberto's walking across the Po on his cloak (Matthew 14:22–7; Mark 6:45–52; John 6:16–21). Thaumaturgical powers of the sort demonstrated by Jesus have been part of many saints' attributes, even down to quite small details. Both the claim that the wine Alberto picked up off the ground tasted better than the wine that had been spilled and the verdict of superior quality at the conclusion of the Homobono miracle of transforming water into wine derive from the miracle of the wedding banquet at Cana. When the servants had followed Jesus' order that they fill the large jars that stood empty nearby with water, he then instructed one of them to draw some off and offer it first to the major domo for his approval. The latter, who was unaware of the miracle, tasted the wine and then turned to the bridegroom and said: 'Hosts generally serve the best wine first, and wait until their guests have drunk freely before serving the poorer sort; but you have kept the best wine until now' (John 2:7–11).

For most of the elements of the Alberto legend, however, even
if several of them have remote precedents, the point instead is to
see how current nearly all of them were in Cremona in 1279 and
immediately thereafter. Alberto's misfortune in having a wife who
disapproved of his charitable offerings and berated him bitterly
was all part of God's plan for trying his patience, the same as God
had for Homobono, right down to the details of the food he had
given away being miraculously replaced. Raymond of Piacenza
was put to that same test, but as Alberto apparently had no children, his story is at least free of any parallel to that appalling scene
in which Raymond begged God to take the life of his sixth child
so that (1) the latter not be separated from the company of his
deceased siblings and (2) Raymond himself would be free to realise
his desire to become a full-time pilgrim. Alberto's wife received no
further notice in the legend so there is no need even to speculate
about a possible connection between her departure from the scene
and his departure for the plain below. There was no need to introduce a turning point into his story either, except for his emigra-
tion, because he was a worker from the time he was a boy until he
died. As with Facio, there was no contradiction between Alberto's
work and his spiritual life, hence the legend contains no apology
for his working, except in the version that insists he was so well
off that he had no need to work, and goes on to claim that, as both
Homobono and Facio, he offered food to the hungry and hospitality to pilgrims in his home.

The consensus among contemporary sources about the career of
a wine porter obviously contradicts the notions that Alberto was
above having to work for a living and that he had a home where
he could receive guests. Even so, there is nothing about his condition that rules out his having been generous in sharing what little
he had with the less fortunate or his occasionally helping care for
the sick. In these matters the legend shows him responding to the
crisis of urban poverty just as, in their respective ways, Homobono,
Raymond, and Facio had done.

The contradiction between pilgrimage – 'a waste of time and
energy', according to Jesus in Raymond's legend – and active assistance to the poor, which marked a major turning point in the life of
Raymond, does not appear in the legends of Facio and of Alberto.
Thus we read of Facio going to both Santiago and Rome eighteen
times, and of Alberto going to Santiago eight times and Rome nine

times. It may be that Facio had sufficient leisure for multiple trips and could pay his way, as his legend suggests, with liturgical paraphernalia that he had made, but the same is not likely in Alberto's case.[30]

The work of these holy men did not detract from their spiritual life but instead provided the occasion for miracles, namely Alberto's picking up the spilled wine and Facio's having one of his chalices survive a fire. The chalice was one that Facio brought as a gift to the shrine of Saint Mary of Finisterra, beyond Santiago at the westernmost point of land in Spain. The chalice happened to be in the sacristy when a fire broke out there. While the fire consumed the entire sacristy the chalice flew up through the crumbling roof and into a window of the church next to it, and landed, unscathed, upon the altar of the Blessed Virgin.

Towards the end of the first week of May in 1279, when Alberto's life came to its end, church bells began to ring spontaneously, sending the memories of persons over forty scurrying back to the day a pilgrim's body with several stab wounds was fished out of the river. Some of these memories of Gerald appear to have kept on working, even being intertwined with more recent material from the funeral of Facio, because the next episode of the Alberto legend showed the grave diggers unable to penetrate the ground with their shovels and the pallbearers directed instead to enter Saint-Mattia to a spot favoured by Alberto when he went there to pray. There they found a tomb awaiting his earthly remains.

Right away, as at the burial sites of all the other new saints of the age, supplicants arrived from near and far, some of whom reported miraculous cures. We saw earlier that a large canopy was set up outside Saint-Mattia to accommodate the crowds. While the list of twenty-one miracles recorded at Alberto's tomb contains no indication of how much time elapsed before the excitement quieted down and the crowds diminished, the commission that gathered testimonies of fifty miraculous cures at the tomb of Facio terminated its work, without saying why, just two months after his death. In the case of one of the other lay saints, however, that of Anthony the Pilgrim of Padua, the notarised reports of miracles shed light on the relationship between the number of miracles and the length of time elapsed since entombment. Anthony's earliest miracles occurred on 2 February 1263, three days after he died. In the two months following, notaries recorded thirty-eight miracles, whereas over the next three years they recorded only eleven more.[31] The period of heightened enthusiasm was thus possibly as brief as a few months, and yet the flow of offerings of cash, objects, cloth, and ex-votos at Saint-Mattia was enough to support the establishment of a monument to Alberto's memory – that is, a hospital. Raymond and Facio each had their hospitals, and Alberto had his.

Alberto's cult spread to Parma and Reggio Emilia, as we learned from Salimbene, where again there were abundant offerings, and in Parma the founding of a hospital. Icons appeared. One of the earliest of these shows Alberto standing, dressed as a pilgrim, receiving a communion wafer brought to his lips by the dove of the Holy Spirit. The two extant versions are the fresco in Saint-Michael in Bergamo from the 1280s and a relief sculpture dated 1357 that was prepared for the Saint-Alberto Hospital in Cremona (see Figure 18).[32] Might both the Bergamo fresco and this Cremona sculpture have been based on a prototype made in Cremona? It would seem likely since the legend originated in Cremona and, we can be reasonably sure, was preserved in a written copy at the church of Saint-Mattia.

The components of Alberto's legend were common currency in late-thirteenth-century Cremona. Stories of the city's popular saints and the annual festivals at which these were repeated often, as well as the continuing recourse to the saints by people in need, kept all these friendly advocates and the tales about them constantly in view and in mind. Their stories were essential parts of the shared culture of all classes of the city's population. In the same way news of miracles at a new burial site got people out into the street and talking with neighbours and strangers, as did scandals or fights or flooding by the Po, or fires, whether spontaneous or the ones planned for public executions such as those burnings of heretics in the years around 1270. Need we worry about whether it is true that Alberto's wife was a complainer? No, it is enough to recall that both Homobono and Raymond also had wives who nagged them. These stories did not remain the preserve of the clerical elite, for they were told over and over from the pulpit; besides, they were retold by jongleurs in the public squares. They were the stuff of popular culture.[33] It is the same with the mythical number of times that saints were said to have gone on pilgrimages. Besides, even the brief 1279 entry in the *Annals of Piacenza* announcing Alberto's death included mention of his persistence in alms-giving and prayer, and his frequent pilgrimages to Rome. So it goes with each piece of this mosaic-like

Figure 18 This sandstone tablet shows Alberto, as in Figure 9, dressed as a pilgrim receiving the viaticum, and specifically identified (although the inscription at the top is barely legible) as *S[anctus] Albertus*. The tablet is one of a pair (each 41 × 23.5 cm) found in the Museo Civico Ala Ponzone of Cremona. The inscription on the other one bears the date 1357.

legend. We find each piece, each element, no matter how much it may seem to stretch credibility, to be a standard part of the pervading cultural expectations of a saint, and therefore perfectly plausible within the context of the immediate aftermath of Alberto's death. The question we need to look at is just who put the legend together and, more broadly, who orchestrated Alberto's cult.

Canonisations do not occur spontaneously. Some would-be saints expend great effort on preparing the way for their own canonisations, but although we expect generals and political figures to spend fortunes and years polishing their respective images for posterity, campaigning for one's own sainthood is really rather unseemly. Much of what is relevant in these matters is or can be very personal and thus well out of public view, and therefore the role of a confidant such as a parish priest or, especially, a confessor, can be crucial in determining whether the memory of a very holy, but also very humble, person simply slips into oblivion or gets widely enough talked or written about to come to the attention of an entire community. In one way or another somebody has to gather up information about the deceased holy person in order that it not be lost and then do something to pass it along to others. Practically always this meant that the information would get written down because even in a society made up mainly of illiterates, literate clerics had the responsibility (and power) to preserve the communal memory in written form.

In totally illiterate communities oral tradition had of necessity to serve this function. In the 1240s in a rural backwater north of Lyons a Dominican inquisitor came across the cult of a saint named Guinefort, who was, strange to tell, a greyhound. Poor Guinefort, the inquisitor found out, had been killed by his master, the local lord, who mistakenly assumed that once when he and his lady were briefly absent from their chateau this aristocratic pet had killed their infant son, when in fact Guinefort had saved the child's life from the attack of a large serpent. The repentant master buried his faithful pet with all the honours due a martyr – a martyr to babysitting – and the local people, mothers especially, took their sick children to Guinefort's grave to be cured. The good friar, needless to say, did all he could to extirpate this outlandishly irregular cult, and probably left the scene satisfied with the results of his effort, and yet six hundred years later folklorists found that the cult had lasted into the middle of the nineteenth century.[34] In settings that were the very antitheses of rural backwaters, namely the northern Italian

communes of the thirteenth century, not only did matters of importance need to be put in writing but the writing itself was best put
into the hands of persons who enjoyed public faith, i.e. notaries.[35]
Someone must have called upon notaries to take down the record
of Alberto's miracles, but still a significant difference between the
Alberto story and those of his immediate predecessors on the local
scene is the absence of any explicit naming of those responsible for
assembling his legend and launching his cult.

The case of Homobono relied principally upon three individuals: Homobono's confessor at Saint-Egidio, Bishop Sicard, and
Pope Innocent. The others who accompanied Sicard to Rome were
undoubtedly committed to the cause but we do not know their
names or what precise contributions they made. The main advocates for Raymond of Piacenza included his son, who in spite of
his father's prayers survived into adulthood and became a priest;
the author of his *vita*, Master Rufino; the latter's fellow canons of
the church of the Twelve Apostles; the bishop; and the communal
officials of Piacenza. Gerald the murdered pilgrim belonged to no
community associated with Cremona, but Bishop Omobono, upon
being told of the discovery of his body, took the entire matter in
hand. By applying what he knew of the tradition that a person who
is killed while on a pilgrimage is to be considered a martyr, and then
by calling in all of the city's clergy to participate in the funeral, the
bishop effectively and on the spot made Gerald a member of the
community of Cremona and thus the cause of Gerald's sanctity a
matter for the entire city population.

The cause of making Facio a saint we have already characterised
as a how-to or textbook case. The members of the cathedral chapter
were methodical in setting up a special commission to investigate
the claims that Facio secured miraculous cures for supplicants; they
chose one of their own to write the *vita* of Facio; and in a sense
they attempted to anticipate all the questions that could eventually
be raised in a canonisation process, and then set about getting precise, well-documented answers. The opening lines of the *vita* make
clear, in addition, that they were not going to yield to anyone or any
counter-argument in establishing their claim.

> Here begins the life of the most holy Facio whose body rests in the
> principal church of Cremona, which is named the Church of Saint-
> Mary. As for it being all right to call him a saint, you should know
> that the Church is twofold: there is the Church Militant, which is

made up of us, and the Church Triumphant, made up of the saints. Even if he is not canonised in the Church Militant, that is, down here, he is canonised up above in the Church Triumphant.[36]

The case of Alberto stands out as an exception in this regard. There is no indication of participation or assistance on the part of any high authority. We can assume the active engagement of the parish priest of Saint-Mattia, and there were those other secular clerics and some friars, along with a few notaries, who showed up to lend a hand in dealing with the crowds of people who came in search of miracles at the burial site of Alberto. It was also in that parish church, as mentioned more than once before, that the original text of his legend was said to be kept. Not one of these observations, however, points to a person or persons responsible for organising his cult. We do not even know who took responsibility for getting him buried. Who then could have been interested in him and/or had an interest in perpetuating his memory?

We come back to the wine porters. Salimbene is very explicit in assigning to them full responsibility for extending the cult from Cremona to both Parma and Reggio Emilia, and then for fostering its development in both places. Not least of their accomplishments in those cities was their successful recruiting of many secular clerics and especially of the bishops to support the cult. Among the explanations Salimbene pointed out for the devotion to Alberto in Cremona, besides the desires of the sick and the curious, was the greed of the secular clerics, as well as their envy of the new orders of friars.[37] If Salimbene was right, and if indeed the technique used for spreading the cult was to put up images of Alberto, then it is permissible to speculate that the wine porters of Bergamo had similarly gone to Cremona and brought back a prototype of that image of Alberto dressed as a pilgrim and receiving the Eucharist from the dove. After all, the relief sculpture in Cremona was made for the Hospital of Saint-Alberto, which had been paid for by funds collected by the wine porters.

One can only speculate that the wine porters were behind the launching of this cult, and that various other parties had their own reasons for supporting it. As far as we know the porters were not yet officially organised into a guild, and yet already by this time, in guilds that did exist and in the confraternities and other types of *societates* that had started to proliferate in the communes, one provision of the by-laws that they commonly shared was that all members – i.e. all people in that category or organisation – had as we learned earlier an obligation to attend the funeral of any one of their number. The deathbed miracle of the dove bringing the sacred host to Alberto came about, according to Benaglio's version of the legend, because the priest who was summoned as Alberto lay dying was slow to arrive. The episode suggests that the person or persons attending him were able to make do without any clerical intervention. Perhaps, too, the wine porters gathered many or even all of the elements that went into the legend but, given their illiteracy, would have had to seek out a scribe to set these down. Speculation about the origins of the cult aside, the wine porters were indisputably the ones who kept it going.

With one major exception, the elements of the Alberto cult were thus recognisably specific to the brief period centring on 1279. They would not have made sense much earlier in the thirteenth century, at least not earlier than the much-revised version of Homobono's *vita*, and probably not earlier than the death of Facio and the founding of his cult. But now to that one exception, which would not have made sense at any time in the thirteenth century – namely Alberto's supposed membership in the Third Order of Saint Dominic.[38]

Notice of this affiliation first appears in the available sources in negative form – that is, as a denial – in Benaglio's version of the legend, and then in positive terms in Ludovico Cavitelli's *Annals of Cremona* of 1588. What Cavitelli says is that Alberto took on the habit of a tertiary of the Dominican Order, and he then recites the list of the many forms of Alberto's devotion. What he leaves out is any mention of Alberto's vocation. And although he says Alberto gave alms to the poor, he says nothing of any sort of active assistance to the poor such as caring for the sick or burying the dead. Cavitelli's Alberto is more cleric than layman.[39]

The Dominicans and Franciscans both had third orders; the first and second were respectively for men and women who took vows and thus, not unlike monks and nuns, devoted their lives wholly to religion, while the third was for laypeople. Dominic and Francis strove to establish and make prosper their companies of religious men. When they and their successors failed to discourage the development of corresponding female branches, they at least denied women the right to participate in their day-to-day active engagement in urban life, imposing upon them instead a strictly cloistered life based upon the centuries-old monastic model. Such were the second orders. The origins of the third orders, which afforded pious men and women an opportunity to retain their lay status while associating themselves closely with one or another of the new orders of friars, in a real sense go back to the third quarter of the twelfth century, to a few decades even before Dominic and Francis were born. This was when, as indicated earlier, mention of urban poverty and poor people, *pauperes*, began to appear in documents, while at the same time there is evidence of laypeople trying to square the lives they were living with their growing awareness of the social responsiveness demanded of them by the Gospels. These people, ranging in social terms from very poor servants and labourers to well-off merchants and some nobles as well, stayed in town, kept their lay status, practised devotions on a regular basis, and devoted some of their resources and/or energies to charitable assistance for the poor. Some of them formed associations that helped feed, clothe, and shelter poor people, and some also left money or property to those same causes in their wills. These decades mark as well the appearance of the hospital and the confraternity, and an organisation that dispensed social welfare and whose name in many communes celebrated the virtue of mercy: *misericordia*. People found various ways to maintain their lay status: some married couples continued to live together as before; some lived together in chastity; some joined resources to enter with others into communal living – a lay variant on the monastic life; and most continued to make their livings as before.

Prior to the establishment of the friars, the lack of formal organisation among these laypeople meant also a lack of documentation upon which a historian might attempt to reconstruct their past. Starting, though, with Francis's teachings about the penitential life, the friars encouraged laypeople to participate more fully in religious worship as well as to maintain their charitable commitments. Here and there some of them formed groups that called themselves Brothers and Sisters of Penance and that did leave some documentation of their existence.[40] As some of the daring and spontaneity of the early, heroic days of the new mendicant orders wore off, and these took on more and more the look of carefully structured, conservative organisations – Max Weber's phrase for this process was 'the routinization of charisma', the point at which priests took over from the prophets[41] – the orders sought to rein in these amorphous groups of lay fellow-travellers. The Franciscans were ahead of the Dominicans in this by preparing a rule for the lay Brothers and

Sisters of Saint Francis in 1285. The Dominicans sought to catch up by producing a similar rule the following year, but were out-manoeuvred by a former minister-general of the Franciscan Order who became the first Franciscan pope, Nicholas IV, in 1288. To the great annoyance of the Order of Preachers, he inserted into the bull giving official approval to the Order of Friars Minor tertiary rule in 1289 a provision placing all lay penitents under Franciscan control. Meanwhile Dominican tertiaries had to wait until 1405 for final papal approval of their rule.

To state the obvious: Alberto could not have joined the Dominican Third Order. It is not impossible, though, that he belonged to some sort of loose organisation of laypeople, or perhaps to the Penitential Brothers of Saint Dominic, whom we can think of as forerunners of the Third Order, but even this is highly unlikely. To return yet again to Salimbene, this time to his story about the relic of Alberto – the supposed little toe of his right foot that turned out to be a clove of garlic – it is significant that he introduced the story by telling of some secular clerics who taunted the Friars Minor and the Preachers vociferously, saying: 'You think that nobody can work miracles but your own saints, but this will show that you are evidently deceived.' His clear intent was to pin some of the blame for instituting this cult on the secular clergy, but if Alberto had had any connection whatever with the Dominicans, Salimbene could not have set up his account of this ludicrous incident in such a way. As a result, we can rest assured that for persons living in the final decades of the thirteenth century, the question of whether Alberto was a member of the Dominican Third Order simply did not come up. However, this very question did become a matter of considerable importance in the seventeenth and eighteenth centuries, when it stirred up lively controversy.

In the meantime, to one and all Alberto had been a layman who was a legitimate – not an unofficial or a second-class – saint, the kind whose cult was recognised by episcopal authority, for whom altars were erected, and to whom believers could and did pray.

9

Sainthood by the papacy

Whether the planting of Alberto's cult is properly credited mainly or even exclusively to wine porters and some members of the clergy in a few cities, or as in the case of both Cremona and Bergamo the bishops played key roles as well, it took root and flourished for centuries. Moreover, for their part the people of Villa d'Ogna founded a confraternity as well as a hospice and a chapel, all in his name. Scattered pieces of documentary evidence give assurance of the cult's continuity through time but otherwise reveal little in the way of development or change.

In 1588, however, Ludovico Cavitelli introduced in his version of the Alberto legend the claim that Alberto had belonged to the Third Order of Saint Dominic. Iconography lends support to the view that what Cavitelli reported about Alberto's Dominican connection was a recent addition to the legend, because no known portrait of Alberto dressed in a Dominican habit dates from before his time. On the contrary, as late as 1530 Giulio Campi painted an altarpiece for the church of Saints-Mattia-and-Alberto that depicts the Virgin and Child with three saints: Matthew, Anthony of Padua, and Alberto. While the great Franciscan preacher Anthony appears just as one would expect, in a Franciscan habit, Alberto is dressed in the garb of a pilgrim, with no sign whatever of a Dominican or any other kind of habit. Had Alberto had any official connection with the Order of Preachers, the point would have escaped neither the persons who commissioned the work nor the painter, a citizen of Cremona who was executing this commission in his native city.[1] The earliest extant image of Alberto in Dominican garb, an oil painting by an unknown artist, dates from the second half of the seventeenth century (see Figure 19). Thus instead of Alberto's having gone to knock at the Dominicans' door back in the thirteenth

Figure 19 This anonymous portrait of Alberto, unmistakably a saint because of the halo over his head and unmistakably a Dominican tertiary because of the habit he wears, is a highly polemical campaign poster on behalf of Alberto's canonisation. Painted in Lombardy in the late seventeenth century, it is in the church of Saint-Matteo-and-the-Sacred-Heart, Villa d'Ogna.

century, it seems far more probable that it was the Dominicans who came knocking at his some three centuries later. Such posthumous appointments were not unheard of at that time. King Louis IX, who had died just nine years before Alberto, was listed as a Dominican saint in about 1480, and as a Franciscan one as well in 1547. Since he was well known to be a friend, admirer, and patron of both orders, and they in turn participated energetically in the campaign on behalf of his canonisation, their later claims had the benefit of verisimilitude. The historical truth mattered little given that he had become a saint for all eternity back in 1297. No one was going to have to prove that the king of France belonged to any religious order. Not so for the wine porter of Cremona.[2]

Meanwhile, the same early modern centuries brought important changes to the canonisation process.[3] Back when the papacy began attempting to take control of canonisation at the close of the late twelfth century, the protocols for initiating cases were not tightly structured, but after just a few decades of experience the popes became skittish about allowing the number of saints – all, but especially lay saints – rise too high, too fast. Thereafter while they still moved expeditiously on cases that they favoured, they also began to be far more selective about which cases to pursue and in general to keep down the number of canonisations. In fact the figures for cases undertaken and of canonisations proclaimed in Rome in the thirteenth century declined by over one-half in the following century.[4]

At the same time, though, the demands placed upon the saints and their cults experienced no such decline. Indeed they were kept busy by one natural catastrophe or institutional crisis after another, to cite only: the advent of a 'little ice age' and the Great Famine of 1315–22; the arrival from Central Asia of a lethal pandemic of plague starting in 1347; widespread warfare; outbreaks of civil strife; and the spectacle both bewildering and degrading of rival claimants to the papacy.[5]

Politics, which are present in every canonisation proposal, even if in different degrees and not always in plain sight, occasionally had roles so conspicuous as to outshine most other factors in some cases. One such was that of the Dominican reformer Girolamo Savonarola, whose many followers regarded him as a saint but who even so went to his death at the stake as a heretic in Florence in 1498. By his diatribes against the rule of Lorenzo de' Medici right to the latter's death in 1496 and against that of his successor Piero, Savonarola earned the undying hatred of the Medici family and their allies. Any thought on the part of his devotees of getting him canonised had thus to remain dormant during the reigns of the three Medici popes of the sixteenth century. As it happened, the closest the advocates for Savonarola's sainthood came to success was during the reign of a Florentine pope, Clement VIII (1592–1605), precisely because his family were rivals of the Medici. Such a highly politicised case could do little to enhance the sacred aura of either the process or its stated goal, and political influence was only one problem among several that called into question the validity and viability of saints' cults.[6]

The criticisms launched by Erasmus and other Christian humanists of the fifteenth and early sixteenth centuries left no aspect of this complex web of devotional practices free of ridicule, whether pilgrimages, shrines, relics, images, intercessory prayers, miraculous cures, or the demands for payment for the services rendered.[7] These same criticisms intensified as they shifted from satire, in the spirit of encouraging reform, into weapons, in the frontal attack launched by Protestants. The sharp decline in the number of canonisations by the papacy in the sixteenth century, in particular the lengthy period 1523–88, in which there were none at all, gives some indication of the sensitivity of the popes on this matter and of the intramural debates between reformers and hard-line traditionalists then going on within the Roman curia. The eventual responses came in actions spread over a period of eighty years, from the 1560s to the 1640s.[8]

First of all, the Council of Trent reasserted in 1563 the validity of the cult of saints and even elevated its importance by asserting that the faithful could seek grace from God only through the mediation of the saints. Furthermore the council reaffirmed the goodness and utility of images and, as we saw earlier, gave specific instructions on how to depict saints properly.[9] Then, to get to the implementation of the conciliar decrees, a completely separate department or agency of the papal government for handling all matters pertaining to canonisation, the Congregation of Rites, came into being in 1588; its procedures called for the intervention in each case of the promoter of the faith (*promotor fidei*), popularly known as the 'devil's advocate' (*advocatus diaboli*), to assure that every argument in favour of canonisation be subjected to critical examination.[10]

It was Pope Urban VIII who in 1625 introduced and defined the two-tiered system of *beati* and *sancti*; no one could henceforth be considered for sainthood unless first made a *beatus*. Promotion to the higher rank required just one further miracle. Pope Urban also forbade absolutely the cult of any blessed or saint not approved by the papacy.[11] This latter provision was hardly innovative, since it merely restated what was canon law already in the thirteenth century, law that popes at the time were unable to, or at least did not, enforce but that remained an ideal in the view of many people, including Salimbene. What changed in 1625, however, was that this time the law was backed up with severe sanctions, which were to be meted out by the Inquisition.[12] Suddenly the cult of Saint Alberto, one in a class of hundreds if not thousands, appeared to face a serious threat of extinction.

Yet there was hope, for Pope Urban inserted an exemption to this law for all 'ancient cults', defined as having existed already for a century or more. Alberto's cult met this 100-year rule with 245 years to spare. But then any rejoicing was short-lived. Four years after the one-century exception, the Congregation of Rites ruled that even for a cult that began before 1525 there would have to be a full beatification process, should its devotees wish to qualify it for the celebrating of mass and reciting of the office in honour of the holy person in question. The specific criteria for such a process as spelled out in several different rulings were: publish a life of the subject; demonstrate that the cult existed 'from time immemorial'; demonstrate that the holy person exemplified 'heroic virtue'; and offer proof of one postmortem miracle. If all these criteria were met, one could expect the following positive outcome: the subject would be qualified as a *beatus* and as worthy of a cult, whether in the entire world or, in many cases, only in a specified diocese or region or religious order.[13]

Finally, to avoid a rush to judgement fuelled by uncritical enthusiasm for a live or recently deceased potential candidate, a waiting period of fifty years following the subject's death was to lapse before an official case could be initiated. Urban VIII had all these new principles and procedures published together as the new dispensation for naming saints in 1642.[14]

As the new order of regulations was coming into operation between the 1580s and the 1640s, the Inquisition went to work on its new assignment. This included, for example, snuffing out unwelcome popular enthusiasm before a potentially new cult could take hold. A glimpse at this policy of pre-emptive strikes is offered by a papal legate's candid observations on five budding cults he encountered in Germany and Switzerland in 1625. He reassured his superiors in Rome that he should not have difficulty in quashing the attempts to venerate three of the five candidates because they had died relatively recently, their fame had not spread very far, and he knew of no images of them with halos that had yet been put in circulation. In the other two cases, though, he predicted that repressive intervention would backfire. One of these concerned the cult of a Third-Order Franciscan woman who died with the stigmata in 1420 in the diocese of Constance; it had a vast popular following as well as the backing of princes and prelates throughout the German empire. The other cult honoured a Swiss hermit known to be a mystic and prophet as well as to have saved the people of his region on more than one occasion. Images and biographies of this holy hero circulated widely. In both cases, the legate advised, the likelihood of grave disorders rendered any attempts to restrain these cults too risky to undertake. If this report from the field to headquarters is any indication, the role of inquisitors in canonisation matters was considerable, even though its full extent is not likely ever to be known.[15]

The religious orders also had to get to work bringing their claims and practices into line with the new regulations. The same was true of cities and of all institutions that had patron saints who had not been canonised by the Roman Church. While the chief patrons of the religious orders, who in most cases were their famous founders – the likes of Benedict, Francis, Dominic, or Ignatius – had their papers in order, the religious orders had in addition long lists of saints whom they venerated, not least the friars with their third orders and their many locally venerated spiritual heroes. Not only did each order want to get its own cults legitimised but each felt itself in competition, as always, with the other orders. For the fate of Alberto's cult, the sponsorship of the Dominican Order was perhaps going to turn out to be fortuitous.[16]

The new regulations of 1642 in fact threatened the legitimacy of many hundreds of saints' cults. Those based on nothing more than local folklore, even if their protagonists were human beings and not greyhounds, had little chance of surviving the rigorous new tests of authenticity. The more extensive the documentation, as well as the more precise and official in nature, the better equipped the petitioner for a saint's cause would be. The petitioner could not of course be a lone devotee of the prospective saint. Here at least, although unspoken, was a survival of pre- and non-papal canonisation, namely the need that there be a recognisable community devoted to the cause, be it a particular church congregation, a trade or professional organisation, an entire city, or some other geo-political unit. Wealth and power, plus the influence these provided, also helped. It is not surprising that the lion's share of canonisations in the sixteenth and seventeenth centuries went to the Spanish kings, who for much of that time controlled all of Iberia, much of Italy, much of Central Europe, the Catholic lowlands, and vast portions of the 'New World' with its sparkling treasures of gold and silver.

Kingdoms and cities had other things to think about in addition to saints. It was, though, the religious orders, even if with a myriad of preoccupations, that were by far the communities most heavily and intensely, indeed emotionally, invested in the veneration of saints. Among the orders, it was the Franciscans and Dominicans that within a generation of their beginnings in the early 1200s, having so captured the religious imagination of Latin Christian culture, came to dominate the hagiographical scene then and in the centuries immediately following. They had their detractors, especially among the secular clergy, and their competitors among the other religious orders such as the Carmelites or, from the mid-sixteenth century on, the Jesuits. The keenest of these competitions, though, was typically that between the two leading orders of friars themselves, the Franciscans and Dominicans. In the rush to put their hagiographical rosters in order after 1642, these orders had both the most to gain and the most to lose. Besides their share of saints duly canonised by the papacy, each order had dozens more, many of them laymen and laywomen whom they as communities, perhaps together with the faithful of some city or diocese, venerated. These many saints were vital to their self-image, if not their very existence.

The first American-born saint was a Dominican tertiary named Rose of Lima. After her death in 1617 and completion of the mandatory fifty-year waiting period, the order was well prepared to advance her cause. Already in 1668 she was beatified, and three years later she was made a saint. Between then and 1700 the Preachers gained six more blesseds, three of whom had lived in the thirteenth century. In the first two decades of the eighteenth century they got a Dominican pope, Pius V (1566–74), canonised, and two members of the order who lived in the thirteenth century beatified. In the reign of Benedict XIII (1724–30), himself a Dominican, one of the ten saints he canonised was a Dominican, as was one of those he beatified. His successor, Clement XII (1730–40), named two blesseds, one a fourteenth-century Dominican pope, Benedict XI, and the other a sixteenth-century Dominican sister.[17] In general the new saints of this period beginning in the reign of Benedict XIII represented a notable change from both the heroic model of the Jesuit martyr-missionaries and the Counter-Reformation mystical model, exemplified mostly by women whose experiences included levitation, prophecies, visions, and the like. A more humble spirituality marked by simplicity, populism, and healing, besides being exercised close to home, became the new paradigm.[18]

The revised regulations had become so Rome-centred that it may come as something of a surprise to observe that a major new force in hagiography came out of the Spanish Netherlands in the middle decades of the seventeenth century. In 1643, one year after Urban VIII had the complete set of new regulations governing canonisation published, a team of Jesuits working in Antwerp published the first two volumes of one of the most ambitious scholarly projects ever undertaken, the *Acta sanctorum*.[19] The project's first director was Jean Bolland (1596–1665) and its purpose was to locate, transcribe, and publish the *vitae* of all Christian saints; however, far from making it a catch-all of fantastical tales, the editors sought to subject whatever material they collected to rigorous historical criticism. This approach placed them in the vanguard of an intellectual movement that had its counterparts elsewhere in Europe. At the Abbey of Saint-Germain in Paris, for example, there was a group of Benedictine scholars known as the Maurists (from the Congregation of Saint-Maur, of which their abbey was the principal house), who travelled throughout France to read and transcribe medieval manuscripts.[20] Out of these *voyages littéraires* as they called them came the dictionary of medieval Latin produced by Charles Du Cange; the classic study of the forms of medieval documents by Jean Mabillon; and the vast collections of texts on the religious life by Luc d'Achery, of royal charters by Etienne Baluze, and of liturgical texts by Edmond Martène – all these published between 1655 and 1738. They remain today indispensable tools for practitioners of the medievalist's trade.

The Italian counterpart was not a team but an individual, Ludovico Antonio Muratori (1672–1750). Born outside Modena and educated by the Jesuits in that city, at age twenty-two he became a priest and a Doctor of the Ambrosiana Library in Milan, where he started to publish previously unedited manuscripts. A few years later the Estense duke summoned him back to Modena to be the archivist and librarian of the ducal library, a post he held until his death fifty years later. He remained always a conscientious, evangelically inclined priest, while also exchanging letters – his collection numbers in the many thousands – with erudite correspondents all over Europe. Besides encouraging the growth of an Italian literature, seeking to rid the religion of his time of superstition and various cultic and devotional excesses, and laying the documentary groundwork for a comprehensive history of Italy in his twelve-volume *Annali d'Italia* (1744–49), his most lasting achievement was the *Rerum italicarum scriptores, 500–1500* (*Writers on Italian Matters*), published in twenty-eight folio volumes starting in 1723.[21]

The Jesuit project on saints, while unique in its scope, was thus part of a European-wide intellectual trend. Given that it has been in operation for nearly four centuries, there is unforeseen irony in the approval granted Bolland by his superiors to carry it out 'in his leisure time'. Still today, just as through the intervening generations, all of the project's collaborators have been known as 'Bollandists'. One of Bolland's earliest decisions was to organise the work by the dates on which the saints were commemorated, and so those first two volumes dated 1643, folio volumes with a combined total of 2,500 pages, contained the lives of saints honoured in January. Only after issuing the three February volumes in 1658 did the Bollandists undertake research outside their home territory, essentially Flanders. For two-and-a-half years, two of their number travelled through Germany, Austria, Italy (with stays totalling over a year in Rome), and France.[22] Many scholars volunteered to assist them, and patrons gave them the means to hire copyists. They returned home with over 1,400 *vitae*, leaving behind a network of helpers prepared to send them additional material. March, in three volumes, followed in 1668, and April, also in three volumes, in 1675. By 1680 the amount of material they were including had so expanded that the second volume for May covered just the fifth day of that month through the eleventh. Among the entries for 7 May was one titled *De S. Alberto Agricola*.[23]

The entry on Alberto, which covered one full folio page, relied principally upon the lives published by Pellegrini in 1553 and Mozzi in 1614, the latter of which in turn incorporated much of the work of Benaglio. The Jesuit scholars had also seen a book on Saint Homobono published by a Cremonese scholar named Tromboni in 1618, which mistakenly placed Alberto in Cremona a full century too early and made of him a sort of apprentice to Cremona's patron. As these Jesuits apparently had no access to any of the contemporary chronicles or urban annals, which all agreed on the date of Alberto's death, and as the lives of Alberto written in Bergamo gave no time-specific references, they probably accepted Tromboni's mistaken chronology because his book works Alberto's sojourn in Cremona into the particularly well-documented chronological scheme for Homobono.[24]

But what would have caught the eyes of Dominican readers of that page, and perhaps also the eyes of their detractors, was the line that the Jesuit scholars included quoting Pellegrini, who wrote of Alberto: 'he belonged to no religious order of friars'. Just as startling in a way was the total absence of any mention of the Order of Preachers. Nonetheless, the seventeenth- and eighteenth-century Preachers of Cremona were set on rescuing their saints from the oblivion that inaction on the new canonisation protocols promised.

The leading protagonists in the cause of Alberto included some of the key figures who expanded and sustained the corps of Dominican saints in the first half of the eighteenth century: a pope, a bishop, and an inquisitor. The pope who conferred the honour of sainthood on Alberto was Benedict XIV (1740–56), a Bolognese cleric of great intellectual distinction named Prospero Lambertini.[25] From his studies in law and theology in Rome he moved directly to the papal court where over a period of three decades he served under four popes. Shortly after he arrived there a senior curia official who was also from Bologna took him on as an assistant in the Congregation of Rites. He became an expert in matters pertaining to canonisation from serving in the role of promoter of the faith for two decades. Custodian of the papal library was one more of the many posts he held, one that gave him much in common with his friend Muratori. Another formative experience came with his assignment to take charge of a diocesan synod called by Benedict XIII in 1724. The pope, in his capacity as the bishop of Rome, apparently astonished the clergy of his diocese by summoning them to a gathering in order to put forward an extensive programme of reform, something no pope in living memory had done. Besides publishing a book on diocesan synods, Lambertini convened such a synod in his own diocese when he was appointed to the bishopric of Ancona, and again when he became archbishop of Bologna.

Once back in Bologna, Lambertini was in every sense at home. He enjoyed the companionship of writers, mathematicians, astronomers, medical doctors, publishers, and book sellers. He was famously supportive of some very accomplished women scholars. He participated in the meetings of academies. His intellectual openness and wit drew praise and admiration from Voltaire. It was during his Bologna years that he produced a truly *magnum opus*, four folio volumes on *The Beatification of Servants of God and the Canonisation of Blesseds (De servorum Dei beatificatione et beatorum canonizatione).*[26] It covers an extraordinary range of topics. The laws and procedures are of course all included but there is much more, for Lambertini found the critical historical approaches of the Bollandists, the Maurists, and Muratori compatible with his own thinking. Like these other learned devotees of rationality, Lambertini did not hide his lack of enthusiasm for mystics. He believed that there is nothing inherently laudable in mystical behaviour, or in immoderate asceticism for that matter, because what counts is the spiritual end, not the means. He had a very limited view of the significance of miracles, and when miracles were being discussed, he gave a considerable role to medical doctors, not by asking them to pronounce on their authenticity but to testify whether the phenomenon under discussion could or could not be explained by current scientific knowledge.[27] And as for defining the main task of those participating in a canonisation inquiry, he stressed that it was not so much a matter of searching out the truth as of detecting the false, a remark in which one can perhaps discern the voice of the former devil's advocate.

The bishop of Cremona in the 1740s was Alessandro Litta, born in Milan in 1671; following his studies in both civil and ecclesiastical law at Pavia he became much involved in the political life of his native city, serving as emissary on missions to Austria, Lorraine, Paris, Naples, and Rome. He remained in Rome from 1714 to 1718, at which time he was named to the see of Cremona, where he remained until his retirement in 1749. It is highly likely that from those years in Rome he would have known Prospero Lambertini. Like the latter, he was inspired by Benedict XIII's holding of a diocesan synod, for he organised one in Cremona in 1727. It was very thoroughly prepared with an agenda based upon carefully constructed surveys of the problems and needs of every parish in the diocese. As with his colleagues his major concerns were to improve the preparation, training, discipline, and preaching of the clergy. He wrote tracts on these subjects. He devoted resources and effort to reforming the diocesan seminary, often teaching there himself and also sitting in on exams.[28]

Like Lambertini, Litta was a friend of Muratori, whose admiration he reciprocated. They shared their reservations about popular devotions, believing that these needed to be carefully regulated, especially those relating to Marian cults. Litta for example approved of laypeople reciting litanies before images painted on the walls of houses in their neighbourhoods, but drew the line at such add-ons popular at the time as nocturnal luminaria or concerts.[29] As for his peers among the well-educated elite, he hosted meetings of local literary and scientific academies in his palace or, the season and weather permitting, in his garden, and he particularly enjoyed the company of learned doctors of medicine. Finally, Litta strove to promote the cult of the saints, especially those connected with the various religious orders in his adopted city. Just as it surely did not harm the cause of Homobono in 1199 that Bishop Sicard of Cremona and Pope Innocent III had a great deal in common, so can it also be said that the similarities of culture, training, experience, and views on holiness held by their respective successors, Litta and Lambertini in the 1740s, boded well for the cause of Alberto.

On the part of the Dominican Order in Cremona at the same time there was another erudite man, Ermengildus Todeschini, a native of Mantua and a master of sacred theology assigned by his order to keep watch over the faith of the people. One reference to him in *Cremona literata* published in 1741 called him *Inquisitor vigilantissimus*.[30]

The bishop and the Order of Preachers of Cremona decided to open their campaign on behalf of their diocese's Dominican saints during the pontificate of the Dominican Benedict XIII. As their first candidate they selected a female tertiary named Stefana Quinzani (1457–1529). A native of the province of Brescia, she was brought as a small child to Soncino in the northern part of the province of Cremona. As her father found live-in employment at the Dominican convent in that town, Stefana practically grew up as a member of the order. One of the friars there took over her 'spiritual formation', which resulted already when she was seven years old in a vision in which Jesus appeared before her to say that he wished to have her as his spouse. Their mystical marriage followed in due course, a wedding at which the bride's family effectively included the friars themselves. Extraordinary events took place throughout her long life, such as when she entered the Third Order and received her habit, mystically of course, directly from Saint Dominic. On one Good Friday when Stefana was in her early thirties, she suffered the agonies of Jesus on the cross, stigmata and all. This scene recurred on most subsequent Fridays, often with well-born spectators in attendance, many of whom signed notarised documents describing in detail what they had seen. While rich and poor alike continually sought her out for spiritual comfort and advice, she readily accepted the hospitality of the former, especially the Gonzaga and Este families of Mantua and Ferrara. The Este were among the principal patrons of a convent of Dominican sisters that Stefana established at Crema late in life.[31]

Whilst the drive to get Stefana's cult recognised began during the reign of Benedict XIII, it was after the departure of Lambertini from Rome for Ancona. The case then wound its way through the curia over the decade-long pontificate of Benedict's successor, Clement XII. It had cleared all the requisite hurdles short of the final papal approval when Clement died in 1740. Thus did this matter land on the desk of Prospero Lambertini, who took the name Benedict XIV in honour of the last of the popes he had served, the one who had promoted more saints and blesseds than any of his predecessors and who had also promoted him to both the episcopacy and the cardinalate. One could expect that the case of Stefana Quinzani would have raised all the objections to the excesses of mystical experiences that so troubled the new pope and his like-minded friends. But he chose to see this case as one of heroic virtue – on the basis of Stefana's consistently penitential manner of life – graced by numerous signs of divine approval of her genuine sanctity. In December 1740 Benedict signed and promulgated the beatification of Stefana, while also approving that her feast day be inserted into the liturgical calendars of the Dominican Order and of the dioceses of Cremona and Brescia.[32]

No known text informs us about a gathering of the power brokers of Cremona who thereupon decided that it was now Alberto's turn. All we know is that within months of the Quinzani beatification Friar Todeschini published a book – in Bologna and anonymously – about Alberto. Labelled a 'historical dissertation' on Saint Alberto of Bergamo, confessor and tertiary of the Order of Preachers, it is an octavo volume with a text in Italian that runs barely over fifty pages. It dispenses with Alberto's 'life' or legend in just five pages. In the first sentence on page 6 the author lets us know what this book is really about. Since, he says, many writers of lives of Saint Alberto place his death in 1190, 'by which time the Holy Father Dominic had surely not established any order whatever', he, the author, is going to show this to be a false opinion and go on to demonstrate in addition that Saint Alberto did indeed belong to the Third Order of Saint Dominic.[33]

The obstacle to getting Alberto's venerable cult reaffirmed was thus that single page published by the Bollandists in 1680, with its damning assertions that Alberto was a contemporary of Homobono – which would have made him at least one generation older than Saint Dominic – and that he belonged to no religious order whatever. Perhaps some individual Dominicans might have wanted to go forward with an attempt to get Alberto canonised without refuting the Jesuits' authoritative scholarship, but the Dominican Order, given the premium its leaders always placed on learning, would surely not have supported such an effort. For them, the obstacle had absolutely to be removed.

As to how they should go about it, they had before them the example of the approach taken by the Carmelites in an earlier dispute with the Bollandists, an approach that they wished, also absolutely, to avoid. The origins of the Carmelite order date from the late twelfth century when in the wake of the Crusades a group of hermits settled on Mount Carmel, which was traditionally regarded as the home of the prophet Elijah. As the order grew, a foundation myth took form that involved tracing the beginnings of the order back to disciples of Elijah among the earliest Christians. In the course of their articles on some of the Carmelite saints of the twelfth century, the Bollandists quite effectively dismantled the Carmelites' collective autobiography. The latters' reaction was predictably fierce. They attacked the Antwerp scholars by accusing them of bad faith and even of heresy. That they took offence and fought back is not surprising, and perhaps the same goes for their decision to attack the messengers rather than the message. However, what is notable about this story is that for two decades they found very influential allies, chief among them Pope Innocent XII (1691–1700), thus exposing and exploiting deep-seated hostility in the upper reaches of the Roman hierarchy to the Bollandists' new historical methods.[34]

Clearly the Carmelite approach was not for the Dominicans, and not just because the Bollandists had done nothing as devastating to them as, say, arguing that Saint Dominic had never existed. The Dominicans were nothing if not intellectuals and well trained in the art of disputation. The Bollandists were obviously capable scholars and in this case they had read the printed books of Pellegrini, Mozzi, and Tromboni. In effect, Todeschini clearly had to oppose the Jesuits' assertions by fighting fire with fire, in this case using the same critical historical approach that the Jesuits themselves had used.

For Todeschini the first half of his task was relatively easy; he needed simply to bring the Bollandists' work up to date. The one incontestably established date in Alberto's life – namely 1279, the year of his death – was, as we have seen, attested to by the *Annals* of Parma, Reggio Emilia, and Piacenza, as well as by Salimbene. Although the latter two annals and Salimbene's *Chronicle* did not come into print until the nineteenth century, Muratori in fact edited and published the *Annals of Parma* in 1726, well after the disputed Bollandist publication of 1680. Score one point for Todeschini, with an indispensable assist from Muratori.[35]

Establishing Alberto's membership in the Preachers' Third Order was rather more daunting. The same *Annals of Parma*, though, as Todeschini pointed out, call the hospital founded there by the wine carriers as the Hospital of *Frater* – i.e. Friar or Brother – Alberto. This same title applied to Alberto appears as well in three versions of the statutes of the commune of Cremona in the fourteenth century. The job of explaining away the silence concerning Alberto on the part of Dominican writers before the sixteenth century tested Todeschini's ingenuity. He makes a sensible observation by noting that Dominican writers were well informed about those brothers or sisters who lived in convents, whereas they had little information on those who lived *extra ordinem* – that is, in their own houses, usually with spouses – and belonged to secular parishes. He is perhaps less convincing in arguing that some famous people of the thirteenth and fourteenth centuries who were regarded as Dominican tertiaries are also not mentioned as such by Dominican authors of those same centuries; 'not even Simon de Montfort', he bemoans – the great crusader against heretics in southern France – or again not even (here Todeschini was being clever if not actually funny) Hugolino Lambertini, one of the most noble and wealthy men of thirteenth-century Bologna, obviously an ancestor of the current pope.

In truth, Todeschini had access to a great deal of information that had not been available to the Belgian scholars. Concerning the age of the cult, for example, Todeschini was able to point out that the communal statutes of Cremona of 1356 set the date for the annual celebration of Saint Alberto's feast day. He also knew that 'the wine porters' guild of Cremona chose him as their patron in 1493 and that they had undertaken to care for his tomb in Saint-Mattia, to decorate it decently with images, to keep the oil lamp always burning there, and to participate in the solemn rite of his saint's day'. The corresponding guild in Bergamo also chose Alberto for its patron, although, as he wrote: 'no memory of when that happened has survived'. He then reported on what Carlo Borromeo had noted during his visit to Villa d'Ogna in 1575, both in the village and by the bridge over the Serio.

Finally, Todeschini provided some entirely new information about the cult of Alberto, namely that it had spread to Spain, especially Catalonia. In fact the woollen cloth workers in Catalonia, he reported, had chosen Alberto to be the patron of their guild, adding astutely that Cavitelli had said back in 1588 that Alberto was at times a wool carder. The cloth workers' guild at Vich celebrated the feast of Saint Alberto at that city's Dominican convent, which had a painting of their patron dressed in the habit of the Third Order. He also added that in the choir of the Preachers' convent of Saint-Catherine in Barcelona there was a statue of Alberto showing him holding a cloth maker's card, i.e. a comb. A recent survey of several Dominican books in libraries in Barcelona – books listing saints of the order or dealing specifically with the Third Order's saints and spiritual practices – yielded no mention of Alberto in the sixteenth century, or most of the seventeenth, until 1674, whereas his name is routinely present in such works published thereafter. Many of these tell the essentials of Alberto's legend, always including of course his frequent pilgrimages to Spain, e.g.: 'seven times he came from Italy to Santiago in Galicia'.[36] It is a testimony to the thoroughness of Todeschini's research that very little evidence subsequently introduced into the proceedings was not already present in his short treatise of 1741.

In the following year there came into print the statutes of the wine porters' guild of Cremona, sporting an image on the cover showing a robed, haloed, and kneeling holy man receiving a communion wafer from a dove; this figure is identified just as we would expect as 'S. Alberto, Protector of the University of Brentatori' (see Figure 20).[37] The earliest document included in the canonisation dossier on Alberto in the papers of the Congregation of Rites in the Vatican Archives dates, like this edition of the guild's statutes, from 1742.[38] It is a notarised report, written in Italian, of action taken

STATUTI

DELL' UNIVERSITA'

D E'

BRENTADORI

DELLA CITTA' DI CREMONA

Riconofciuti da' Nobili Signori Prefidenti al Governo
della Città foddetta, ed approvati dall'Eccellen-
tiffimo Senato di Milano

S T A M P A T I

Efsendo Confole Giacomo Antonio Moruzzi.
Giufeppe Vigani Mafsaro de' Vecchj.
Girolamo Trojano   )
Bartolomeo Moruzzi) Mafsari Nuovi.
Giovanni Boino   )

In Cremona 1742. Nella Stamperìa del Ricchini.

Figure 20 This printed version of the *Statutes of the University of Wine Porters of the City of Cremona*, with its prominent display of the iconic symbol of Alberto's sanctity, appeared in 1742 just when the canonisation campaign on his behalf was gearing up.

on 'an exceptional matter' during the annual meeting of the wine porters' guild of Cremona on 7 May. That was a Monday, but the sixty-nine wine porters in attendance had the day off, of course, for the Feast of Saint Alberto, so they could attend as a group the mass in his honour at Saint-Mattia and also hold their annual meeting to elect officers and deal with other, mostly routine, matters.

The exceptional matter brought up on this particular day came from the guild's lawyer, who informed the members that 'certain persons, devoted to and concerned for the greater glory of Saint Alberto, sanctified by *il Popolo*, intend to promote the cause of this saint's immemorial cult, virtue, and miracles and to assure [the continuity of] his mass and special office'. In view of this development and of the fact that Alberto was the protector of this guild, the lawyer maintained that the wine porters had a duty to join with the others in this cause so that it succeed and bring honour to their city, 'of which this saint is a citizen'. His specific advice was that they deputise and give power of attorney to an agent (*procurator*) together with the other parties so that, both in Cremona and in other cities, the person chosen might do all that is called for in organising and shepherding their common cause. In addition, he advised that they allot an amount of money, in keeping with the guild's financial capabilities, to support the work of the agent for as long as needed.

The members were all in favour of the bishop's pursuing the canonisation of Alberto and accordingly acted on both of the lawyer's recommendations. First, in order to avoid having to call a special meeting, they there and then authorised the officers to consult with the other parties and agree upon the selection of an agent. As for the funds needed, they decided that since the guild's ordinary finances would not suffice they would petition the bishop for permission to solicit contributions, from guild members of course, but also from the general public.

Did the lawyer reveal the source of his information? Did he name the other interested parties, or even some of them? The account of the wine porters' meeting is silent on these points, but there are six documents following it in the dossier that tell us who those other parties were and suggest something, although not all, of what had been going on behind the scenes.[39] One month to the day after the wine porters' meeting, the parish priest of Villa d'Ogna went down to the little hospice and chapel of Saint-Alberto by the Serio to meet with the Franciscans in residence there. Also present was a hermit from the nearby village of Piario. In addition there were three visitors from the diocese of Cremona: Friar Todeschini himself, the parish priest from Saint-Mattia, and a notary they had brought along from Soncino. Their purpose was to procure written approval of a protocol by which the Franciscans of Saint-Alberto were being asked to name Todeschini their agent for advancing the cause of Alberto's canonisation. The resulting protocol was a highly formal Latin document bearing the signatures of the hermit and the two parish priests as witnesses. The visitors from Cremona and the witnesses remained in place while all the others withdrew, and then the secular magistrates of Villa d'Ogna, Ogna, both Upper and Lower Vultra Senis, and Piario came in for the signing of a similar protocol on behalf of the people of those village communities. Two days later the three Cremonese visitors were down in the city of Bergamo at the Dominican convent of Saint-Bartholomew in Borgo Sant'Antonino. There the entire company of local Preachers attested in writing to their support of the same cause and to the choice of Todeschini as their representative in pursuing it.

Back in Cremona, Todeschini held three more such gatherings. On 11 December 1742 he met with his confrères, the Dominicans of Cremona, in the chapter house of their convent. A second meeting took place in the inquisitor's residence, located in the same convent; that was on 29 January, when it was the turn of the wine porters' guild, represented by the five officers who had been deputised by the full membership the previous May. And finally there came on 19 February 1743 the leading civic authorities of the city of Cremona. The document signed by this last group has an exceptional paragraph in Italian at the end that includes a passing yet notable observation about Alberto's having 'spent the greater part of his life in this city'.

The six documents choosing the agreed-upon agent, two from Villa d'Ogna, one from Bergamo, and three from Cremona, pretend in a way to be spontaneously initiating this entire campaign. By not referring to any previous steps taken or even to the 'certain persons' who might have been thinking about undertaking some such steps, each of these groups could appear to be suggesting by default that its own members came up with the idea. This notion of spontaneity calls to mind Lambertini's candid explanation in his work on sainthood that when some collective entity such as a city or a family wishes to sponsor a candidate for sainthood, since not all the city's inhabitants or all the family members would be able to go to Rome, they would need to have a representative make their case for them.[40] But what these documents from 1742–43 demonstrate is just the opposite, namely that this operation was coming not from the bottom up but from the top down. Todeschini was certainly not doing this entirely on his own but he was the front man, the one who could be seen coordinating the six 'spontaneous' groups, attending and directing each of the gatherings, always with a notary at the ready by his side. Those gatherings clearly demanded careful advance preparation, especially the three held at some distance from Cremona.

In the spring of 1743 Todeschini had to drop out, having been promoted to the post of head inquisitor for the archdiocese of Milan. However, he took the time to follow through on his obligation to the six parties to place before the bishop of Cremona their request that the latter open a cause for the canonisation of Alberto. Then, because Todeschini had prudently included a provision in the six documents that gave him authority, should the necessity arise, to name a substitute for himself, he proceeded to put forward a fellow Dominican, Francesco Domenico Zanenga.

Bishop Litta's acceptance of these requests was surely never doubted by anyone. Over the next few months he appointed three clerics to the investigative commission while in the meantime Zanenga prepared his case. Then in May of 1744 the commission examined twelve witnesses.[41] From the written record of their testimonies, it appears that Zanenga sent each witness beforehand a copy of a life of Alberto written by a Cremonese writer named Giuseppe Bresciani in 1630, plus a copy of Todeschini's anonymous historical treatise of 1741.[42] The witnesses represented the various categories of priests and of religious orders then present in the diocese of Cremona. No layperson testified. The questions dealt mainly with the life, virtues, miracles, and cult of Alberto. Zanenga sought to get the witnesses to go beyond their bookish or abstract knowledge of these matters to speak of their personal experiences of them, such as how they first learned of Alberto or what recollections they had of seeing images of him. Their replies, in Italian, constitute the only fleeting moments of spontaneity introduced into this massive dossier of relentlessly formal and repetitious legal language.

A Franciscan named Francesco Antonio testified that when Alberto carried wine for a poor person he wanted no compensation for his effort. In recounting the criticisms directed at Alberto by his wife, he added: 'I read these things in the life by Signor Bresciani and in the dissertation printed in Bologna.' He mentioned having seen the oil lamp maintained by the wine porters in Saint-Mattia and he described paintings he had seen there showing the miracles of the spilled wine and of the crossing of the Po.

Friar Antonio said that because of the miracles surrounding and following Alberto's death, 'all Cremona' believed him to be a saint; the same was true in other cities, especially Parma, and also in far-away places like Spain, where he made several trips to Santiago. Not only had this good opinion of him continued, it had continued to grow: both in Villa d'Ogna, 'where our reformed Franciscan brothers built a convent in 1608', and in Naples, where a new church had been built in honour of Alberto to house two of the saint's teeth that Bishop Litta had had extracted and sent southwards. The friar's source for this unique story of teeth sent to Naples was a certain Don Ignazio Bertolotti, who, he claimed, lived in a house near Saint-Mattia once inhabited by Alberto.[43]

The provost of the cathedral of Cremona, Carlo Bongiovanni, who gave his age as 'about sixty or sixty-one', began his testimony with this disclaimer: 'I have not been instructed by anyone apart from Father Zanenga, who asked me to testify ... because he wanted to question me on certain articles that he showed me last autumn when he gave me a biography of Saint Alberto and a dissertation.' An interesting variant on this disclaimer appears in the testimony of Giulio Cesare Lazari, an eighty-year-old brother of the Order of Saint Augustine of Cremona: 'Not only have I not been instructed by anyone but I was taken by surprise by Father Zanenga, and the more I tried to excuse myself because of the many things I have to do the more he exhorted me and insisted until I gave in and agreed to come to give testimony.' Another personal touch by Lazari is this folksy anecdote: 'For years I'd heard of Blessed Alberto. In fact each year at Epiphany we fathers have a tradition whereby each of us chooses by lot a saintly protector for the year, and three or four years ago I got Alberto, but to this day I still say an Our Father and a Hail Mary to him every day.' He was careful to say how he knew what he had to say: 'I read in books that he was born in ... I have not seen any of his miracles but I read ... of the spilled wine and it was found to be of the finest quality.' That he knew that Alberto was the protector of the 'brentadori or wine porters' and that their devotion to him still continued was, he testified 'common knowledge'.

'I learned about him from my parents when I was a boy', said Giuseppe Antonio Madoni, a canon of Saint-Agata of Cremona, but later cited both the book by Bresciani and the dissertation. Similarly, Giovanni Battista Rapari, theologian of the cathedral, cited his sources for the story of the spilled wine in this way: 'I have heard it said, and moreover I have read ...'. The sub-prior of Saint-Dominic, Friar Giuseppe Maria Mazzani, then seventy years old, recalled his experience of over thirty years earlier:

> It was in 1708 that I came back from Rome and saw a painting in the entry to our refectory, and though there was an inscription saying it was of Blessed Alberto, Dominican Tertiary, the image is still there but the inscription says 'Blessed Martino Porrey'. In the parish chamber of Saint-Vito, there is an older painting with an inscription naming Blessed Alberto. But I first learned of him from the refectory painting and from hearing, as one still does today, that he is the protector of the University of Brentadori.[44]

Copies of all of the books mentioned in the course of the proceedings were introduced as material evidence, moves that engendered several documents certifying their authenticity.

The commission got to examine evidence of a quite different sort when a cloth banner, no longer extant, that belonged to the Congregation of the Brentatori of Bergamo was brought into the hall and unfurled before them. Two experts on painting from Bergamo, Giuseppe Platti and Geronomo Ragnoli, described as 'persons who work with paintings every day, especially old ones', were present to testify on the meaning, use, and age of this artefact. The image painted on the cloth was perhaps the standard icon for Alberto with its incongruous mix of the upright figure receiving his deathbed communion, and yet the experts made no mention of details that would prove the point. On the other hand, one of them did mention a brenta in the image without specifying where it was placed, such as on the ground near the figure of Alberto, or on his back. The fact remains that no known image of Alberto depicts him as a brentatore. One of the two experts did testify that he had no difficulty in saying the banner was 150 years old. 'I cannot say who painted it, but it is old and ... I know it is carried every year by the wine porters' guild in the Corpus Domini procession.'[45]

In just under two years, from May 1744 to March 1746, the entire procedure at Cremona was over. Bishop Litta's chancery produced a summary of the proceedings, and so did the three members of the commission, both to be sent to the Congregation of Rites in Rome. In addition to reporting on the *processo* at Cremona, both made reference to a 'little *processo*' at the Franciscan hospice of Saint-Alberto, perhaps referring to the meeting organised there by Todeschini for getting approval of his serving as *procurator*, but remained silent, as do all the other sources, about anything of the sort taking place in the city of Bergamo. The commission declared that the cult of Alberto satisfied the requirements set forth in the reforms of Urban VIII and thus favoured Alberto's beatification, although without pronouncing on the disputed question of his membership in the Third Order of Preachers. This matter they left to the judgement of the Congregation of Rites.[46]

At this point the documents went off to Rome where everything had to start all over, except that this time the *processo* was to be the real thing. The formal request to the pope that the process be allowed to commence was made in a speech during a solemn ceremony. The person officially designated as *orator* for the occasion was Thomas Ripoll, the master-general of the Order of Preachers. This was no casual choice. The presence in this key role of Friar Ripoll, whose very family name is that of a city in Catalonia, helps explain the Catalonian connection. Clearly some Dominican(s) had brought knowledge and experience of the cult of Saint Alberto from Lombardy to Catalonia, about as the name of Saint Martin of Porres, a Third-Order Dominican from Peru, had been relayed in the opposite direction to become known at Saint-Mattia in Cremona. Such cultural transfers are not difficult to imagine given the Spanish presence in Lombardy, and Rome as well, in the sixteenth and seventeenth centuries. Along with the Spanish publications by and concerning the Dominicans that refer to the cult of Alberto and are now located in the Library of Catalonia or in that of the University of Barcelona, there is a copy of a work about the Dominicans' convent in Cremona published there in 1767; the bookplate in it names a friar who resided at his order's convent in Barcelona, named for Saint Catherine of Siena, O. P. Tertiary.[47] Although Catalonia had no *métier* that matched that of the wine porters, it did have a flourishing woollen cloth industry, so Cavitelli's calling Alberto a cloth maker turned out to be useful.

The Dominican master-general's appeal addressed to the pope came with a supporting document signed by a number of important individuals, starting with James III, the Stuart pretender to the throne of England, Scotland, and Ireland, then in residence in Rome (and living on a handsome papal annuity for life).[48] Also signing on for the cause were the archbishop of Milan; Bishop Litta of Cremona; Bishop Redetti of Bergamo; the magistrates of these last two cities; the head of the Reformed Franciscans of Brescia (and thus the superior of the community at the hospice in Villa d'Ogna); and, at a more modest social level, the entire community of Villa d'Ogna. The pope acceded to their request and so the case began.

The documentation available to the authorities in Rome consisted of all the material that had been forwarded from Cremona, with at least one notable difference. This was a Latin translation of Todeschini's anonymous 1741 treatise in Italian about Alberto; it appeared in Milan in 1746 and now took the place of the Italian original in the dossier. The translator's preface identifies Todeschini as the author of the original version. As for the translator, one could hardly imagine a more devoted standard bearer for the Dominican Order. He was Tommaso Agostino Ricchini (1695–1779), the editor of an anti-Cathar treatise by the thirteenth-century Dominican theologian who had founded the order's convent at Crema. Ricchini had delivered the funeral oration for the Dominican pope, Benedict XIII, in Rome in 1730, and also published a hagiographic treatise on a Dominican cardinal in 1742. His stated purpose in translating Todeschini's tract was 'to vindicate Saint Alberto of the Order of Preachers'.[49]

The requisite meetings of the commissions of the Congregation of Rites appointed to handle this particular case took place in 1747 and early 1748. In his final summary and report (*Positio super dubio*) the promoter of the faith did not avoid that nagging doubt concerning whether Alberto had been a Dominican tertiary. Indeed he pointed out that the Dominican sponsors of the case made no claims about Alberto belonging to their Third Order for the first two centuries following his death. However, what carried the day was the abundant written and iconographic testimony on this matter that existed from the sixteenth century on. The main question of whether the Alberto cult could continue to be celebrated was put before Pope Benedict XIV one final time at the beginning of May. He specified in his positive response that the cult could be observed in the dioceses of Cremona and Bergamo as well as in the Dominican Order, a result that is exactly parallel to the one worked out for Beata Stefana Quinzani. The papal broadside dated 9 May 1748 announced 'The

Canonisation of Blessed Alberto of Bergamo, of the Third Order of Preachers', followed four months later by specific permission for the celebration of masses in honour of Blessed Alberto.[50]

The Alberto canonised in 1748 was very different from the Alberto first venerated as a saint in 1279. Already during the final phase of Alberto's life powerful elements in the clergy were seeking to curb the enthusiasm for lay sainthood, which they saw, just a few decades after it began, as already getting out of hand. Salimbene gave voice to these views in his story of how the people of Cremona, Parma, and Reggio Emilia had been made fools of through the Alberto cult, and then linked it with similar instances in other cities. One of these that aggravated him especially was the case of Padua, a city that had its own great Franciscan saint, Anthony, but whose people and communal government seemed enthralled by the miracles flowing from the tomb of the hippy wanderer Anthony the Pilgrim, who died in 1267. 'Truly the Lord came not only in His own person', Salimbene lectured his readers, 'but in the Blessed Francis, the Blessed Anthony [of Padua], Saint Dominic, and their sons; and sinners ought to believe in them in order to merit salvation'. This kind of thinking was what led also to the measures taken against lay penitents by the heads of both the Dominican and Franciscan Orders, especially the one who became the first Franciscan pope in 1285.[51]

The development of the Alberto legend in the three centuries after his death documents the clericalisation of the once poor layman who made his living as an unskilled labourer. By the seventeenth century at the latest he was no longer any of those things, but a figure clothed in clerical garb as a Dominican tertiary who, if he worked upon occasion, did so only to display his humility and to gain something that he could dispense as charity to the poor.

The earlier canonisation of Alberto was the work of the wine porters of Cremona with support on the part of at least some of that city's secular clergy. This later canonisation, however, was almost entirely the work of the Dominican Order. The Preachers engaged various other parties in the cause, all of them perfectly willing participants to be sure, but none of whom could match the friars' corporate interest, intellectual and political energy, and contacts for building a case, lobbying for it in the right places, and carrying through in every phase of the process. The next most capable participant in this affair was Bishop Litta, who could surely have counted upon getting a favourable hearing from Benedict XIV, and yet for all his imposing role in Cremona, he could not have commanded the same level of resources and support for such a campaign outside his diocese, especially in Rome, as a major religious order could.

In looking back over all that was made of the Third-Order problem, one might wonder whether it really mattered. It certainly was not a formal criterion for sainthood, nor in the end was it really crucial for gaining sainthood for Alberto. What it was crucial for was stirring up and maintaining the interest of the Order of Preachers. No role as tertiary for Alberto would have meant no interest whatever on the part of the Dominican Order in anything having to do with this man. Perhaps the most disappointing result that the order was risking would have been to have Alberto sainted but at the same time declared officially as not having been a tertiary, which is the way things appeared to be heading when the case moved on from Cremona to Rome. Having invested so much in the cause of this truly minor figure up to that point, once the matter was in the hands of the papal curia the Dominicans had to pull every string available in order to get the desired outcome – and it worked.

The people of Villa d'Ogna and their pastor, and the Reformed Franciscans who ran the hospice, surely lacked the resources to mount such a campaign. Their whole stake in the matter relied solely upon the coincidence of their living in the place where Alberto was born and grew up. He lived most of his adult life elsewhere and they had no knowledge of that life except for the invented life we call the legend. Bergamo, as we saw, was not a very active partner in this enterprise. Even if the lack of evidence about the continuity of the cult in Bergamo were due only to lost documentation or deficient research, the fact remains that no one from Bergamo testified in 1744 to the maintenance of an altar dedicated to Alberto in any of that city's churches.

Someone introduced the banner of the Bergamo wine porters into the proceedings, but no other indication of their participation in the cult, let alone those proceedings, remains. That silence only underscores the value of the information concerning the maintenance of the Alberto cult by the wine porters of Cremona. It is plainly evident that their corporate identity was inextricably linked to his cult, and plainer still that no one from among them was called upon to give testimony before the commission in Cremona. Nonetheless, it is also clear that they were the only ones mentioned as having to pay, or help pay, for the costs of the process, and yet it is highly unlikely that the sixty-nine brentatori present at their annual meeting on 7 May 1742 would have been able to meet the costs of a lengthy and complex judicial procedure called for by a case such as this.[52]

As for the final, make-or-break phase in Rome, with the exception of Friar Ripoll and any of his Dominican confrères present, there was no one personally involved there who had any close connection with either the cult or the believers in it. The list of those authorities supporting the petition to the pope is mainly a list of prestigious titles, not of persons in any way involved in or committed to a cause. Few people associated with the papal court, except for the pope himself and those of his staff he brought along from his native Bologna, would even have known, in case it could have mattered, what a brentatore was or did.

What the wine porters and other laypeople, along with a few clerics, accomplished at Cremona in canonising Alberto in the thirteenth century was to build a cult that perhaps gave some people comfort and hope, but for sure at least gave the wine porters their group identity. Yet what took place in Cremona and Rome in the eighteenth century was an altogether different matter. A more meticulously choreographed process would be hard to imagine. During the initial phase of the inquiry in Cremona, Friar Zanenga's interrogation of witnesses was farcical. His first question, 'Did anyone tell you beforehand how you should testify?', always drew a negative response. Then he asked for specific information about the subject's piety, virtues, etc. Once the witness replied, he asked the witness where he had learned what he had just stated, and the response invariably named the books supplied by Zanenga himself as the source. Then in Rome the matter was re-examined and judged by people with no direct knowledge of either the protagonist or his context. In short, what the learned Dominicans and canon lawyers and prelates accomplished in eighteenth-century Rome by canonising a fictional holy man of the sort they could admire was instead a lengthy, pretentious, costly, and, as it was to turn out although they could not have foreseen it, unnecessary charade.

Epilogue: Dignity and memory

Corporate memory is the stuff of much if not most historical thought and writing. We were all brought up, for better and worse, on our respective national histories, vestiges of nineteenth-century nationalist sentiment. But we all have multiple allegiances and these, too, come with histories, whether of religious bodies, ethnic groups, professional organisations, or still other types of corporate entities. For corporate memory to flourish, the corporate body needs to be alive. The end of Yugoslavia meant the end of teaching Yugoslavian national history to the school children of Slovenia, Croatia, Bosnia and Herzegovina, Serbia, Montenegro, and Kosovo. Dissolution of the guilds in the final decades of the eighteenth century did not of course necessarily put an end to the myriad kinds of work previously organised into corporations, for bakers and book sellers and lawyers there continued to be. For the wine porters, though, the dissolution of the guilds did effectively mean the end of their *métier*. In a few communities some wine porters acting as free agents carried on their obsolete ways of working into the nineteenth century, in Parma even into the early twentieth. But whatever concerns these last of their kind had, investigation into the history of their *métier* was not remotely among them.

Romantic artists, folklorists, and local historians stepped into this void in the nineteenth century to take up the lapsed memory of the wine porters. There is a large mural painted by Ferdinando Manzini, a set designer in late-nineteenth-century Modena, who sought to depict his city's main square as he imagined it to have looked in the Middle Ages. The view is from the south side of the square looking across towards the long southern side of the cathedral; there in the foreground are two wine porters, seen from behind, seated at their station waiting to be summoned by clients.[1]

Another nineteenth-century painting, this one from 1855 by a Bergamasque artist, Giovanni Battista Epis, shows the interior of a wine merchant's cellar. The scene includes huge vats to one side and to the other the merchant making a sale with a client who holds a money bag. There is a servant woman holding a pitcher who seems to be waiting her turn, and in the background a wine porter seen from behind, a view that gives prominence to the brenta on his back as he walks up the stairs to the ground level outside. Everything about this painting suggests a sleepy, provincial setting where old-fashioned ways still prevail.[2]

Writers, too, on occasion made nostalgic references to wine porters, as for example Massimo D'Azeglio in his memoirs, which came out in 1867. At a certain point he tells some stories of people he considered true heroes, and these came from all different social classes. One of the best in his view was a poor, typically illiterate peasant from the Valley of Lanzo, which place, he says in passing, had by long-standing tradition the mission of providing Turin with servants and wine porters.[3] Edmondo De Amicis wrote in a similar vein in his *Military Life* (*Vita militare*) of 1880, where he spoke of the harsh lives of the good people of the mountains to the west of Turin. He listed the valleys and their numerous towns, recalling how their sons came down each winter to be wine porters or wood cutters, or to go still further afield to earn their living at the hardest jobs, with just one supreme ambition, namely to succeed at placing stone upon stone in their mountains to be able to die there under a roof, saying: 'I'll die in my valley and in my house!'[4]

In the final decades of the nineteenth century, the rapid pace of industrialisation stimulated erudite gentlemen to try to preserve or recapture the collective memory of ways of life that were disappearing. Some of these devoted their energies mainly to folklore, while others did archival research in local history. These were of course not mutually exclusive enterprises, for the publications on guilds that then emerged usually combined a sense of pride with a certain nostalgia for the hard-working people who were for centuries well-known figures on the local scene but were now gone. 'Quarrelsome men, these wine porters', as one Modenese notable put it, 'raw-edged and loud but also courageous ... blasphemers in the excitement of horseplay and in their sudden outbursts of anger, yet they had a religious side all their own as well'. Bortolo Belotti (1877–1944), a native of the Val Brembana, distinguished lawyer, jurist, politician, and, on the side, author of a multi-volume history of Bergamo, found nothing funny about the wit of Folengo, that 'slanderer and fraud' who could jest that 'porters come only from Bergamasque stock', while showing no appreciation for 'the dedication to work and love of family of our highlanders', nor for the sacrifices they made by going far from home to be able to support their children. Belotti felt equally indignant about the frequent expressions of disdain for what he called 'our dialect', which he pronounced capable of standing up to 'the trivial verses of Folengo'.[5]

A rapid bibliographical review shows that archival studies of local wine porters' guilds in northern Italian cities appeared all within a period of just a few decades: Bologna (1872), Mantua (1884), Venice (1894), Vicenza (1895), Ferrara (1896), Parma (1896), Trent (1899), Padua (1902), and Pavia (1915).[6] One fundamental characteristic of all these studies about an obsolete trade in many different cities is the gentle, perhaps mildly patronising but generally sympathetic view they present of the workers. The author of the study on Ferrara probably spoke for all of them in expressing the view that the cause of writing such studies was noble. Indeed, 'for one who doesn't engage and take delight in historical studies the attempt may seem bold if not strange to disinter from the dust of archives documents and traditions that recall the modest existences of obscure and forgotten workers ... and to reconstruct the history of institutions already faded away ... but it is useful and our duty'.[7] In a somewhat later work about Parma (1952), much the same attitude towards workers of the past is applied to the last of the wine porters in that city, who ceased activity only in 1910: 'The elderly still remember seeing wine porters bent forward as they plodded along at a regular, ponderous pace under the weight of the brenta ... memorable, too, was their aim when they poured out the liquid; they did it on the side [over one shoulder] without spilling a drop.'[8] As obsolete as the trade itself was the disdainful and insulting attitude towards its practitioners that so permeated the aristocratic culture of the Old Regime. It was henceforth as if the governing yet unspoken rule were to speak no ill of the dead.

In spite of the frequent use of the term *brentatore* in those several studies, it found no place in the *New Universal Dictionary of the Italian Language* edited by P. Petrocchi and published in Milan in 1900.[9] *Brenta* was in there of course because the object it named was still in use. Yet it was in use only in the countryside, especially for the grape harvest. Gone were the tall, curved containers whose widely flared tops loomed over the heads of generations of wine porters. It would be a rare find indeed if someone were to discover one in the future, but we can rest content with such depictions of them as those by Andrea of Bologna or Annibale Carracci.[10] Only the smaller, straight-sided model is now found, properly, in museum collections of rural implements; those used in cities have disappeared. The brenta itself both preceded and outlasted the specialised urban trade of the brentatori.

One particularly notable representation of a brenta has been, while not forgotten, at least lost sight of in the long history of the famous Austro-German family named Brentano. Their origins go back to Lombardy, more specifically the area around Lake Como, where names such as Rogerius de Brenta and Johannes de Brenta first appeared in twelfth-century documents. They were merchants and landowners, and in the following centuries their clearly successful clan branched out into neighbouring parts of Lombardy, while one branch extended their trade beyond the Alps and eventually settled in Austria. By the fifteenth century the names Brentani and Brentoni appear and the family, like most of Como's old clans, adopted a coat of arms. The standard heraldic practice was for the initial image on a family's crest to occupy a smaller and smaller portion of the overall design as succeeding generations' marriage alliances with other important families called for divisions and sub-divisions of the design in order to accommodate the symbols of newly acquired relatives. Eventually the Brentano crest was typically crowded such that virtually lost in the crowd of different families' symbols was a small square that showed an unpretentious barrel-like container with shoulder straps. Yet in the library of the Civic Museum of Como one can find the original coat of arms; it is in the second oldest book of heraldry in Lombardy, dated 1480, and it consists of an utterly simple, unadorned brenta. Above it is written the family name *de brentanis* (see Figure 21).[11]

There is a more recent romantic variant on recalling the wine porters that might be mentioned in passing. Founded in 1970 and appropriate for its time, it verges, up to a point, on the acting-out or re-enactment sort of history. The Company of the *Métier* of the Brentatori has its base in Bazzano, a town set amidst vineyards in the hills west of Bologna.[12] The only qualification needed for

Figure 21 This is the oldest known, and almost certainly the first, coat of arms of the Brentano family, painted at Como in 1480.

membership appears to be an interest in and appreciation of wine. The members call themselves *brentatori* and they dress up for their meetings in elaborate costumes based on those they claim were used by the wine porters of Bologna in the sixteenth century on ceremonial occasions. They conduct their meetings at a castle in Bazzano, or in the villas or castles of vintners where they hold splendid dinners and taste not a few wines. There are local branches within the larger organisation and these are called *trebbi*, which we noted earlier was the Bolognese term for the several taxi-stand-like places in Bologna where the wine porters used to wait their turn to be hired. From northern Italy they have spread into German Switzerland, where the term for brentatore is *Brententraeger*. Overall this company's view of brentatori is to the real thing about as the Alberto legend was to the historical Alberto.

As long as the wine porters' *métier* lasted, Saint Alberto played a major role in their well-being. They were mainly immigrants or sons thereof who did hard work for little pay; painful and humiliating as their urban existence was, it was better than having nothing to eat back in their Alpine villages. Poverty is such a universal presence in human history, and the poor are so obviously less well off materially than the rich, that it is easy to think of these matters entirely in economic terms – easy but insufficient. In societies where the poor have virtually no chance to improve their standard of living and the rich have little inclination to help them do so, the notions of poverty and of the poor take on a variety of meanings. The term *poverty* itself, even though an abstract noun, refers to a state or condition whose meaning is best defined for us in relative terms such as 'having less wealth than', 'having a lower income than', and so on. In fact in Europe during approximately the seventh-through-tenth centuries, when the economy was barely at subsistence level and made very little use of money, the principal meaning of *poverty* was lack of power. Then as always power and wealth were linked, but it is clear, for example, that when individuals of high social rank became monks or nuns (virtually the only class of people who did so), the standard rhetoric for describing what they had done was of course biblical, and so they said that they were abandoning their wealth in order to become poor. In fact though, they mostly brought at least some of their wealth to their new communities and so it was their power that they were abandoning in order to become poor. They lived in relative comfort in their monasteries, often waited upon by servants, but they were 'poor'. Widows of high-ranking nobles together with their children were 'poor' because they were deprived of protection. With the great increases in wealth and mobility from the eleventh century on, people no matter how well off who went on pilgrimages were 'poor' because they were away from the relative warmth and familiarity and security of home. People who were sick were 'poor' in relation to the healthy. People in towns who were disenfranchised were 'poor' in relation to those who could vote.[13] And thus, to come back to the condition of the wine porters, even if there was little that could to be done or at least little that anyone cared to do for them about their low pay, crucial for understanding the meaning of their poverty was their lack of identity and lack of dignity. These were the needs filled by Alberto. Unlike the Swiss migrants who tried to circumvent the monopolies of the porters' and wine porters' guilds in Milan, and were denounced for causing 'evil disorders' and called *brugnoni*, those who could and did belong to a guild thereby had their own socially acknowledged leader to honour and to call upon for help.[14] Those with Alberto as their patron had a banner bearing his image that identified them when they marched on his special day and when they joined the city's other guilds and societies in observing the major religious festivals. All of this added up to a measure, a small but not negligible measure, of self-esteem.

In recompense it is only fair to consider the role of wine porters in the cult of Alberto, for the relationship was reciprocal. Indeed the wine porters were crucial for sustaining the afterlife, meaning of course the cult, of Alberto. One need only review the major institutional players in the papal canonisation and note that they all survived into the nineteenth century and beyond, all except the guilds of wine porters, which vanished with the end of the Old Regime. The point is that so, too, at about the same time as the demise of the guilds did the cult of Alberto fade away in each city where it had flourished. Neither the papacy nor the dioceses of Cremona and Bergamo, and not even the Dominican Order, which had mounted such a vigorous campaign to get the canonisation, did anything to keep the cult going. The dissolution of the wine porters' guilds was what led to the collapse of the Alberto cult, a fact that clinches the argument that it was the porters in the first place and all along who had a clear and good reason to initiate the cult and then keep it going. Without their interest and support, the cult could not and did not continue. No more wine porters' guilds meant no more cult of Saint Alberto.[15]

This phenomenon of collective forgetting played out differently, and in differing tempos, in different places. Parma and Piacenza are both cities where people were well acquainted with the cult of Alberto of Villa d'Ogna from the start, and the wine porters of Parma after all were the pioneers in spreading it from Cremona. In whatever fashion the wine porters were organised at first and may or may not have venerated Alberto, once they were granted the rights to have a guild – that was in 1553 in Parma and in 1627 in Piacenza – the Carmelites had already become established and clearly relished having guilds select their Alberto of Trapani as their patrons. It is thus not difficult to see how at those later dates the wine porters could have chosen this other Alberto. Besides, in Parma the order got an immensely impressive painting by Antonio Bresciani in 1762, showing the saint restoring a dead child to life with his signature brand of miraculous water.[16]

In both Bologna and Ferrara, where there was no initial attachment to the person or cult of Alberto of Villa d'Ogna, the Carmelites had arrived in the late thirteenth century, and the guilds, once officially recognised in the early fifteenth century, received hospitality from the Carmelites and chose to venerate Alberto of Trapani. However, we find that in 1752 the wine porters of Bologna named 'Blessed Alberto of Villa d'Ogna, a Dominican Friar' their patron.[17] This denomination clearly echoes the language of the 1748 canonisation of Alberto by the Bolognese pope. It indicates that the papal canonisation, which undeniably played down Alberto's *métier*, at least did not suppress all mention of it, and so someone presumably told the brentatori of Bologna after May 1748 that there was a new saint who had once been a wine porter. The setting for this half-century-long cult of Alberto of Villa d'Ogna in Bologna was the Oratorio of Saint-Alberto in the Via de' Pignatari, where the wine porters had had their base all along.[18] The same thing happened in the 1750s in Modena, although we do not know the identity of the Modenese wine porters' patron prior to that time.

At Reggio Emilia, the church of Saint-George, where the wine porters maintained an altar in honour of Saint Alberto, ceased to be a parish church and passed into the hands of the Jesuits in 1610. Forty years later they began construction on the same site of a much larger church. If there was an altar to Saint Alberto in the new church it would have gone out of use when the Jesuits were suppressed and the church secularised at the end of the eighteenth century.[19] That no one from there testified at the canonisation proceedings in the 1740s could signify, but does not prove, that the cult had been suspended before that date. In any case, the cult flourished in Reggio for a minimum of a bit over three centuries.

Some specialists in the history of Parma came across both Alberto of Villa d'Ogna and the wine porters incidentally from the 1970s on, for example in writing about the local wine trade or about their city's fire fighters or about its conservatory of music. How they encountered our saint and his line of work in studying either of the first two topics, wine or fire fighting, is self-evident. As for the less obvious connection with the conservatory, though, it happens that in the nineteenth century the conservatory came to be housed in the building that had once been the Carmelite convent, yet in this case the historians in question failed to understand the confusion of the two Albertos. However, as they were all well versed in the work of their famous compatriot, Salimbene, they relied upon his chronicle for their information on the workers and the saint. Furthermore, as they lacked the genteel nostalgia of the folklorists of a century earlier, these historians depicted the wine porters as greedy, dull, and earthy peasants (*terragni*), and Alberto in particular as a heavy drinker whose spurious cult never gained the official approval of the Roman Church. Little did they know that that cult had flourished in their city several centuries earlier, that it had gained papal approval in the eighteenth century, or that for most of those centuries Salimbene's book had very few readers.[20]

Still other modern readers of Salimbene have also been led to think that by his witty exposé he brought the cult of Alberto to a deservedly abrupt, early end. One of these is a very eminent historian who, it turns out, is a Dominican friar. In the course of a lengthy and complex historical study of religion in the age of the communes, his error of relying solely upon Salimbene is surely a minor transgression, but it also indicates in passing a lapse of memory even on the part of the Dominicans, who as we well know went to great lengths in the eighteenth century to get their supposed confrère Alberto canonised. These memory losses on the part of a few local historians and of one Dominican historian thus include any memory of the papal canonisation itself.[21]

In 1799 the French forces then occupying Cremona closed the church of Saints-Mattia-and-Alberto and in 1805 agents of the Cisalpine Republic ordered it demolished. Alberto's relics found refuge in the cathedral, where they were placed in the main altar of the crypt. As for the Giulio Campi painting of the Virgin and Child with saints that included Alberto, it officially entered the collection of the Brera Gallery in Milan in 1811.[22] Although Alberto's feast day remained in the ecclesiastical calendar of the diocese of Cremona, there is little indication of his cult being actively continued even in the cathedral at or after that time.

The side effects of the prolonged Napoleonic campaign for control of the Iberian Peninsula, 1808–14, included massive ecclesiastical property losses and clerical fatalities. If the Dominicans or the woollen cloth workers were able to keep the Alberto cult going in Catalonia thereafter, then it was possibly the anti-clerical agitation of the 1830s or, finally, the Spanish Civil War of a century later that put an end to it. No traces of the cult or the guild have emerged in either the municipal or diocesan archives of Vich. Neither are there any painted or sculptured representations of Alberto in the episcopal museum there. Photographs remain to document the destruction of the Dominicans' church in Vich, and while the one in Gerona still stands, even if somewhat restored, there are no written records extant to complement it. Last of all, nothing remains of the order's Convent of Saint-Catherine in Barcelona, except that the market that now stands on the site bears her name.[23]

In Bergamo the late-thirteenth-century fresco in the church of Saint-Michael-by-the-White-Well bearing the image of Alberto had been forgotten when it was covered over with other frescos in the fifteenth century. However, when the original fresco was rediscovered in the early 1940s, anyone could see that the inscription over the figure said 'S. Albertus', but the local experts were left wondering: Yes, but which Saint Alberto? The art historian who then published the fresco, even though he considered as candidates both the Carmelite Alberto and our wine porter, opted for the famous Dominican theologian Albert the Great.[24]

A few decades later there came to light in the Civic Museum of Cremona two matching sandstone tablets, each measuring 41 × 23.5 cm. Each has high-relief carving on one side, one with an image that was mentioned earlier (see Figure 18) and an inscription over it, and the other with writing only. Both sculpted surfaces are so worn as to make deciphering very difficult. The first published analysis of either tablet appeared in 1976 and dealt only with the one bearing an image. The entire centre and right half of the image is taken up by a standing person wearing a full-length dress or cloak and whose right hand reaches out to grasp either a post or a very thick walking stick. In the upper-left corner a flying creature approaches, its beak coming close to the person's right ear. Without being able to make out what was written over the image, the author of that 1976 study surmised that it represents an Annunciation. This was not a bad guess, but although the surface of the image is indeed badly worn, anyone knowledgeable about the cult and iconography of Alberto would have recognised the standard icon of him dressed as a pilgrim and about to receive the viaticum from the beak of the dove. Just as happened at Bergamo in the 1940s, at Cremona three decades later the erudite establishment appeared to have forgotten this iconographic composition, which for centuries graced several works on display in their city. Within a few years of the 1976 article, though, another scholar suggested that the inscription above the image says: 'S Albertus', and from there the search to identify the correct Saint Alberto moved quickly. Along the way crucial help came from Todeschini's anonymous book of 1741; this contains a transcription of the inscription on the other tablet, which reads: 'Frater Ambrose, minister of the Hospital of Saint-Albert, had this work made in 1357.'[25]

It turns out that not all memory of Alberto had vanished from his adopted city, although it was holding on, and still holds on, by the thinnest of threads. When the calendar of saints for the diocese of Cremona underwent reorganisation in 1962, with amendments added in 1986, each saint still found in the calendar had to be assigned to one of three categories of liturgical celebration or else be eliminated. The highest and most important category was *solemnitas* (solemnity, must be celebrated annually with great pomp); next was *memoria*, or *memoria obligatoria* (commemoration, must be celebrated annually); and last came *memoria facultativa* (optional commemoration, annual celebration at the discretion of the pastor). The results of the reform were as follows: Homobono was henceforth to be honoured with solemnity; Stefana Quinzani with obligatory commemoration; Facio and Alberto with optional commemoration; and Gerald of Cologne, the pilgrim, with expulsion.[26] *Sic transit gloria altarium.*

In Bergamo no altar to Saint Alberto has ever been identified, no matter how likely that there was one somewhere in the city. Up in the Serio Valley, though, where the cult has had its longest run, a terrible misfortune brought an end to the cult at the hospice and chapel of Saint-Alberto by the river's edge. A landslide completely demolished the site in 1823 and it was not rebuilt.[27]

In these various ways, the oil lamps that for centuries were kept lighted in honour of Saint Alberto eventually went dark, snuffed out in an instant at the chapel by the edge of the Serio, but elsewhere allowed to sputter and die out at their own pace. Only in Villa d'Ogna and a few other communities of the upper valley of the Serio does the cult survive, bolstered by the classification 'optional commemoration' granted by the post-Vatican II reforms.[28] To be sure, here as elsewhere the cult had become confused with that of the Carmelite Alberto from at least as far back as the time of Carlo Borromeo's visit in the late sixteenth century. He noted that a standard feature of the feast-day festivities held there was the distribution of 'water of Saint Alberto', believed good for reducing fevers and in general for keeping illnesses away. This part of the celebration has continued to the present, with the water having been blessed by a priest using the reliquary made in the shape of Alberto's forearm and hand for making the sign of the cross.[29]

However, as we learned from the painting in the 'Chapel of the Brentadori' located in the Carmelites' convent in Ferrara, an image showing a male saint wearing a black tunic with some form of white cape over his shoulders and reviving sick or even deceased persons by pouring water on them indicates unmistakably Saint Alberto of Trapani. We noted such use of water with prophylactic as well as life-restoring properties also in the altarpiece of the Carmelite church in Parma, where the wine porters worshipped. In both cases the saint was correctly identified. However, following upon a rather simple confusion between two saints with the same name there then comes a more complicated confusion when the distinguishing features of one saint's legend get transferred to the other's, as appears to have happened at Ferrara, Parma, and even Villa d'Ogna. But the confusion goes further still, facilitated by similarities between the Dominican and Carmelite habits, which combine white and black. To be sure, they are different; those of the Dominicans consist of a white habit with a black cape or scapula over it, while those of the Carmelites are just the opposite. The

Figure 22 The relics of Alberto arrive at Villa d'Ogna on 26 August 1903. These had travelled by train from Cremona to Bergamo on 28 May and then, after being duly venerated for three months in the cathedral there, made the final leg of the journey home by wagon train.

effect of this difference of color is though mitigated by the action taking place in the scenes, by the gestures of each of these saints pouring water upon human bodies. The result is a number of depictions of Saint Alberto of Villa d'Ogna, dressed in a white robe with a black cape, stretching his arms out in front of him to pour water from a large pitcher on figures in a pit below. In contrast to the ill and deceased to whom Alberto of Trapani ministers, those looking up towards Alberto of Villa d'Ogna are souls in purgatory, albeit represented as naked human bodies, whom he appears to be rescuing. Three of these images remain in the churches of three very small villages in the Serio Valley not far from Villa d'Ogna, while in the western part of Bergamasque territory, closer to the Adda, there is a fourth, an altarpiece, dated 1643 in Caprino Bergamasco; it is the work of Giovanni Battista Discepoli, a Ticinese painter who lived in Lugano.[30]

The cult survived up in the mountains not in spite of the demise of the wine porters' profession but simply because up there the cult never had any connection with wine porters.[31] Alberto's status as indispensable immigrant had expired. As he was no longer indispensable elsewhere, the time had come for him to return home (see Figure 22). The exclusive connection with Villa d'Ogna had always been simply that Alberto was born there. Thus Villa d'Ogna was the obvious place where what was left of him, since it was no longer of interest to anyone else, came back home in 1903 – home being what Robert Frost once defined as 'the place where, when you have to go there, they have to take you in'.[32] The memory of Alberto preserved at Villa d'Ogna is not that of an emigrant who made his living by carrying wine on his back in a city down in the plain, but of the imagined person depicted in the colourful processional banners that retell his legend each year as they pass by.

Appendix

Sources and studies pertaining to brentatori

There being no general study of the *métier* of the brentatori, the following bibliography of primary sources and secondary works that concern this subject and were consulted for this book is arranged by cities.

Bergamo

Civica Biblioteca A. Mai, Archivio Storico Comunale, Antico Regime, Serie 61: Sindacati delle arti, 1683–1794, pp. 1461–76. Azioni del Consiglio comunale di Bergamo, Vol. XLVI, fo. 272v. *Ordini, Leggi, e Statuti de' Spett. Sig. Giudici Alle Vettovaglie di Bergamo* (Bergamo, 1607): 'De Brentatori', pp. 20–1. Statuta Civitatis Pergami, Collatio XIII.31, in *Historiae Patriae Monumenta*, 22 vols in 23 (Turin, 1836–1955), Vol. XVI, Part II (1876), col. 2009. C. Storti Storchi (ed.), *Lo Statuto di Bergamo del 1331* (Milan, 1986), p. 147. G. Forgiarini (ed.), *Lo Statuto di Bergamo del 1353* (Milan, 1996), p. 174. R. Taschini, 'Popolazioni e classi sociali a Bergamo tra XV e XVI secolo', tesi di laurea (Università di Padova, 1970–71). *Storia economica e sociale di Bergamo*, Vols II.1–III.4 (Bergamo, 1993–95).

Bologna

Archivio di Stato (where I was ably assisted by Dr Rossella Rinaldi), Cod. min. 32: Statuti della Società dei Brentatori; a second copy of these statutes, but lacking the initial image (Vatican Library, Patetta 933), was brought to my attention by Dr Massimo Zaggia (University of Bergamo). Archivio di Stato, Assuntaria d'Arti,

Notizie, Brentadori. G. Fasoli and P. Sella (eds), *Statuti di Bologna, 1288*, 2 vols, Studi e testi, 73, 89 (Vatican City, 1937, 1939). G. Fasoli, 'Catalogo descrittivo degli Statuti bolognesi conservati nell'Archivio di Stato di Bologna', *L'Archiginnasio: Bulletino della Biblioteca comunale di Bologna*, 26 (1931), 34–57. G. Fasoli, 'Le compagnie delle arti a Bologna fino al principio del secolo XV', *L'Archiginnasio: Bulletino della Biblioteca comunale di Bologna*, 30 (1935), 237–80 and 31 (1936), 56–80. G. Guidicini, *Cose notabili della città di Bologna*, 6 vols (Bologna, 1872), Vol. IV, pp. 188–91. A. I. Pini, 'Alle origini delle corporazioni medievali: Il caso di Bologna', in his *Città, comuni e corporazioni nel medioevo italiano* (Bologna, 1986), pp. 219–58; and 'Coltura della vite e consumo del vino a Bologna dal X al XV secolo', in his *Vite e vino nel medioevo* (Bologna, 1989), pp. 51–145.

Brescia

Archivio di Stato, Archivio Storico Civico, 1056: 'Statuta paratici gerulatorum', fos 122–30. L. Tedoldi, 'Servizio pubblico e cittadinanza: Il caso degli zerlotti bresciani dal seicento al settecento', in M. Meriggi and A. Pastore (eds), *Le regole dei mestieri e delle professioni, sec. XV–XIX* (Milan, 2000), pp. 75–89.

Como

Archivio di Stato (where I was ably assisted by Dr Cesare Sibilia), Libri degli estimi, 168 (for 1439). [G. Manganelli (ed.)], *Statuti di Como del 1335 volumen magnum*, 3 vols (Como, 1957), Vol. I, pp. 86, 121; Vol. II, pp. 307–8. F. Cani and G. Monizza, *Como e la sua storia* (Como, 1993).

Cremona

Archivio Storico della Camera di Commercio, Corp. A.11: Arte e paratico dei Brentatori, Statuti e Matricola. U. Gualazzini (ed.), *Statuta et ordinamenta comunis cremonae, 1339* (Milan, 1952). *Statuta civitatis Cremonae* (Cremona, 1578). P. Merula (ed.), *Santuario di Cremona* (Cremona, 1627). *Statuti dell'Università de' Brentadori della Città di Cremona* (Cremona, 1742). C. Almansi, *L'università dei mercanti e le corporazioni d'arte a Cremona dal medioevo all'età moderna,* exhibit catalogue (Cremona, 1982), pp. 64–6. A. Cavalcabò, 'Gli antichi mercati del vino a Cremona', *Cremona,* 12 (1940), 295–9. G. Miglioli, *Le corporazioni Cremonesi d'arti e mestieri nella legislazione statutaria del Medio Evo* (Padua, 1904), pp. 137–43.

Ferrara

Archivio di Stato di Modena, Statuti, Capitoli, e Grazie, 1: Statuta civitatis ferrarie, lib. 2, cap. 32–4. Biblioteca Comunale Ariostea, Statuti delle corporazioni, 30: Statuti dell'arte de Brentadori della Città di Ferrara (1610), fos 2r and 35; Consignatis capellae Artis Brentatorum in Sancto Paulo carmelitorum (1602), fo. 14r; and Collegium seu scolla brentatorum et mastellatorum (1402), fos 2v–13r. R. Greci, 'Le associazioni di mestiere, il commercio e la navigazione nel Ferrarese dal XII al XIV secolo', in A. Vasina (ed.), *Storia di Ferrara,* 7 vols in 8 (Ferrara, 1987–2004),Vol. V (1987), pp. 275–322. P. Sitta, 'Le università delle arti a Ferrara dal secolo XII al secolo XVIII', *Atti della Deputazione ferrarese di storia patria,* 8 (1896), 7–244. *Chiese e monasteri di Ferrara: Devozione, storia, arte di una città della fede* (Ferrara, 2000), pp. 75–82.

Imola

A. I. Pini, 'Produzione e trasporto del vino a Imola e nel suo contado in età medievale', in his *Vite e vino nel medioevo* (Bologna, 1989), pp. 147–69.

Lodi

Archivio Storico Comunale, Atti notarili, Fondo Borgognoni Maurizio, 30 March 1600 and 17 February 1602; Fondo Maldotti Gaetano, 12 February 1759: Provisioni del Paratico dei Brentadori.

Mantua

Archivio di Stato, Archivio Gonzaga, Libri dei decreti, Vol. V, p. 277v; Vol. XLIII, p. 22; Vol. XLIV, pp. 122v–5; Schede Davari, buste 13, 306. A. Portioli, *Le Corporazioni artiere e l'Archivio della Camera di Commercio di Mantova* (Mantua, 1884).

Milan

Archivio Storico Civico, materie, 362, s.v. *Facchini*; Gride, 1, fasc. 13. *Mediolensium Statuta*, cap. 493 (Bergamo, 1594), fo. 211v. C. Comoletti, *I mestee de Milan* (Milan, 1983), p. 33. C. Santoro, *Collegi professionali e corporazioni d'arti e mestieri della vecchia Milano* (Milan, 1955). P. Mainoni, *Economia e politica nella Lombardia medievale: Da Bergamo a Milano fra 13. e 15. secolo* (Cavallermaggiore, 1994), Chapter 4. A. Tremolada, *Mestieri milanesi d'altri tempi* (Milan, 1995), p. 89.

Modena

Archivio di Stato, Arti e mestieri, 6.2; Inventario della Cantina ducale (1527); Mappe e disegni, n. 21 (1525). Archivio Storico del Comune, Atti della Comunità, Filza V, KKK, 1727: Statuto dell'Arte dei Brentatori; Grida sugli Incendi (1710); Repertorio degli Atti del Consiglio (1576). *Monumenti di storia Patria delle provincie Modenesi, ser. statuti*, 23 vols, Vol. XII.1 (Parma, 1864), lib. 2, cap. 22: Statuta civitatis Mutine (1327): De portatoribus vini. R. Bergonzini, *Arte dei brentatori a Modena* (Modena, 1983). G. Lucchi, *'Camera segreta': Codici, statuari, registri ed atti costitutivi della Comunità e delle arti* (Modena, 1963), pp. 12–13, 74. R. Rölker, 'Per uno studio delle corporazioni modenesi tra XIII e XV secolo', *Atti e memorie della deputazione di storia patria per le antiche provincie modenesi*, ser. 11, 9 (1987), 47–58.

Padua

M. Roberti, *Le corporazioni padovane d'arte e mestieri* (Venice, 1902), pp. 126–7, 136, 147–54, 213.

Parma

Archivio di Stato: Gridario, Vol. XXVII, n. 50; Vol. XXX, n. 34; Vol. XXXI, n. 127; Vol. LV, n. 72; Vol. LVI, n. 38; Vol. LXIII, n. 79; Vol. LXIV, n. 84. Raccolta Mappe e Disegni, Vol. II, n. 85 (oldest plan of Parma, 1460). Archivio del Comune di Parma, Sez. I, ser. 22, Arti, Buste 1850, fos 86–110; 1858, fos 66–101v; 1861, fos 1–22v. I. Affò, *Storia della città di Parma*, 4 vols (Parma, 1795), Vol. IV, pp. 32–5. G. Micheli, 'Le corporazioni parmensi d'arti e mestieri', *Archivio Storico per le provincie parmensi*, ser. 4, 5 (1896), 1–137, esp. pp. 48–53, 62–63. A. Scotti, 'I Brentatori', *Aurea Parma: Rivista di lettere arte e storia* 36 (1952), 100–2.

Pavia

Biblioteca Civica Bonetta di Pavia, MS A III 11, A III 4 X. Archivio Storico Civico di Milano, Materie 362, s.v. *Facchini*, fos 1–7v: Paratico dei Brentatori di Pavia. G. Baracca *et al.*, *Pavia: Ambiente, storia, cultura* (Novara, 1988). F. Fagnani, 'Gli statuti medioevali di Pavia', *Archivio Storico Lombardo*, ser. 9, 4 (1964–65), 90–130. G. Magnani, 'Lo statuto dei brentatori di Pavia del 1553', *Bollettino storico pavese*, 2:1 (1939), 1–31. R. Soriga, 'Sulle corporazioni artigiane di Pavia nella età comunale', *Bollettino della Società pavese di storia patria*, 15 (1915), 76–93.

Piacenza

Archivio di Stato, Collegio dei mercanti e dei paratici, busta 2: Brentori (1621–1803); busta 5, Statuti. E. Nasalli Rocca (ed.), *Statuti di corporazioni artigiane piacentine, sec. XV–XVIII* (Milan, 1966). P. Casignoli and P. Racine (eds), *Corpus statutorum mercatorum Placentiae (s. XIV–XVIII)* (Milan, 1967).

Reggio Emilia

Archivio di Stato, *Liber focorum* (1315). Archivio del Comune di Reggio, Provigioni del Consiglio Generale del Popolo, anno 1318; Società d'Arti, 4 (printed pamphlet): *Statuti et ordini dell'arte delli brentatori di Reggio* (Reggio Emilia, 1670) (contains the rule of 1503, printed in 1697 but sewn into a pamphlet dated 1670); Statuti, Statuta communis Reggii (1411). A. Balletti, *Storia di Reggio nell'Emilia* (Reggio Emilia, 1925). G. L. Basani, 'Appunti sulle arti reggiane nell'età di mezzo', *Nuova Rivista Storica*, 48 (1964), 359–68. M. Mussini and G. Varini, *Il Battistero di Reggio Emilia: Storia e restauro* (Reggio Emilia, 1999). U. Nobili, *Le chiese della città*

(Reggio Emilia, 1986). M. Pirondini, *Reggio Emilia, Guida Storico-Artistica* (Reggio Emilia, 1982). P. Scurani, *Storia della chiesa di San Giorgio (e della presenza dei Gesuiti) in Reggio Emilia* (Reggio Emilia, 1896). A. Spaggiari, 'Artigianato e mestieri nella storia reggiana', in *Reggio Emilia: Una terra, la sua storia* (Reggio Emilia, *c.* 1985), pp. 130–3.

Trent

Archivio di Stato, 3872: Capitoli di li portatori di vino, fos 8–9. G. Alberti, 'L'antica corporazione dei portatori di vino a Trento', *Tridentum*, 2 (1899), 49–90, 149–65. G. B. Zanella, *S. Maria di Trento, Cenni storici* (Trento, 1870).

Treviso

Archivio Storico Comunale, 792: Fraglie delle arti, 1319–95; 793: Vacchette e registri portatori, 1508–1626; 794: Fraglie delle arti, 1520–1718; 798: Registri portatori, 1644–86; 800: Registri portatori, 1705–96. Biblioteca Comunale, MSS 542, fos 52–3; and 606, fos 78–87. B. Betto (ed.), *Gli Statuti del comune di Treviso (sec. XIII–XIV)*, 2 vols (Rome, 1984–86), Vol. I, p. 326. A. Marchesan, *Treviso medievale*, 2 vols (Treviso, 1923), Vol. I, pp. 265–83. L. Pesce, *Vita Socio-Culturale in Diocesi di Treviso nel primo quattrocento* (Venezia, 1983). G. M. Varanini, *Comune cittadino e documentazione scritta: Il caso trevignano* (Treviso, 1993).

Turin

Archivio Storico Comunale, Carte sciolte, nn. 1096, 1101, 1111. Statuta civitatis taurinensis, 51, in *Historiae Patriae Monumenta*, 22 vols in 23 (Turin, 1836–1955), Vol. II: *Leges municipales* (1838), col. 642. D. Balani, 'Il commercio dei prodotti agricoli nella Torino moderna', in R. Comba and S. A. Benedetto (eds), *Torino, le sue montagne, le sue campagne: Rapporti, metamorfosi, tradizioni produttive, identità (1350–1840)* (Turin, 2002), pp. 289–318; D. Balani, 'Il commercio del vino nella Torino sei-settecentesca', in R. Comba (ed.), *Vigne e vini nel Piemonte moderno*, 2 vols (Cuneo, 1992), pp. 439–59. R. Greci, 'Il commercio del vino negli statuti comunali di area piemontese', in Comba, *Vigne e vini*, pp. 245–80.

L. Picco, *Tra filari e botti: Per una storia economica del vino nel Piemonte dal XVI al XVIII secolo* (Turin, 1989).

Venice

Biblioteca del Museo Correr, Mariegola 104. Archivio di Stato, Arti 718: Arte dei Travasadori, Portatori e Venditori di Vino, 1789–1806. D. Beltrami, *Storia della popolazione di Venezia dalla fine del secolo XVI alla caduta della Repubblica* (Padua, 1954). G. Bonfiglio Dosio, 'Le Arti cittadine', in G. Cracco and G. Ortalli (eds), *Storia di Venezia*, Vol. II (Rome, 1995), pp. 577–625. E. Concina, *Venezia nell'età moderna: Struttura e funzione*, 2nd edn (Venice, 1994). V. Gottardo, *Ora è tempo di bere: Una breve storia del vino a Venezia* (Venice, 1991). S. Gramigna and A. Perissa, *Scuole di arti mestieri e devozione a Venezia* (Venice, 1981). C. A. Levi, *Sopra alcune antiche scuole di arti e mestieri scomparse o ancora esistente a Venezia: Notizie storiche* (Venice, 1894). A. Manno, *I Mestieri di Venezia: Storia, arte e devozione delle corporazioni dal XIII al XVIII secolo* (Cittadella [Padua], 1995). G. Marangoni, *Le associazioni di mestiere nella Repubblica Veneta (vittuaria-farmacia-medicina)* (Venice, 1974). R. T. Rapp, *Industry and Economic Decline in Seventeenth-Century Venice* (Cambridge, MA, 1976). G. Vio, *Le Scuole piccolo nella Venezia dei dogi: Note d'archivio per la storia delle confraternite veneziane* (Costabissara, 2004). G. Zompini, *Le arti che vanno per via nella città di Venezia* (Venice, 1785).

Verona

Archivio di Stato (where I initially received assistance from Professor Gian Maria Varanini), Casa dei Mercanti, Registro 1: Liber statutorum Misteriorum et Artium civitatis et burgorum Verone, fos 25v–27v; Registro 94: Statuta et ordinamenta … super arte portitorum portantium vinum; Registro 95: Statuti dell'arte dei Portatori di vino; Compagnie d'arte o fraglie, Registro 1: Arte dei Portatori di vino. G. Maroso and G. M. Varanini (eds), *Vite e vino nel medioevo, da fonti veronesi e venete: Schede e materiali per una mostra* (Verona, 1984), pp. 50–5. F. Scarcella, *Feste, santi, chiese e gonfaloni delle Arti Veronesi*, Quaderni di Vita Veronesi, 1 (Verona, 1948). A. Tagliaferro, *L'economia veronese secondo gli estimi dal 1409 al 1635* (Milan, 1966).

Vicenza

Archivio di Stato, Estimo 985: Statuta et ordinamento super datio civitatis Vincentie, 1576, fos 20–3. F. Brunello, 'Fraglie e società artigiane a Vicenza dal XIII al XVIII sec.', in *Vicenza illustrata* (Vicenza, 1976), pp. 86–116. F. Pozza, 'Le corporazioni d'arti e mestieri a Vicenza', *Nuovo Archivio Veneto*, 10 (1895), 247–311. *Jus municipale Vicentinum* (Venice, 1567), pp. 147–9, 160; or (Vicenza, 1628), pp. 237–8, 258.

Notes

As the notes that follow will make clear, I am the beneficiary – and for that deeply appreciative – of the expertise and labours of a great many scholars, only a small minority of whom I have ever met. They cleared pathways that gave me access to several subject matters and historical eras that, until fairly recently, I never imagined I would one day explore. What bibliographical notes fail to convey, though, are the many kindnesses and helpful suggestions extended by friends, colleagues, and strangers, thereby facilitating my task of (1) disentangling the myth of a virtually unknown individual and the history of a forgotten *métier*, and then (2) re-entangling them in a way that I find reasonably coherent.

In addition to the persons whom I thank in the notes for specific references, my imperfect recollections of gratitude bring to mind Carrie Beneš (New College of Florida), who did a preliminary investigation for me of the canonisation proceedings concerning Alberto in the Vatican Archive; Lisa Bitel (University of Southern California) and the anonymous readers for Manchester University Press, who read an early draft of this work with challenging criticism; Orazio Bravi and Sandro Buzzetti (the Civic Library of Bergamo), who with their unmatched knowledge of all matters pertaining to Bergamo supplied me with countless answers, and questions, too; Roisin Cossar (University of Manitoba), Mary Doyno (California State University, Sacramento), the late Shona Kelly Wray (University of Missouri at Kansas City), Areli Marina (Indiana University), Dr Maria Teresa Brolis and Don Giovanni Brembilla (independent scholars), and Andrea Zanca (Archive of the Diocese of Bergamo), who all made available to me the results of some of their research that was pertinent to mine; Lucio Del Bianco, for a photo; Chris Duncan, for generously sharing his talent in the art of topography; Nino Gandini, for supplying me with documentation both written and photographic; Sandra Piccinini, for assistance in Reggio Emilia; Nicolas Pluchot (University of Lyons 2), who tracked down evidence of the cult of Alberto that the Dominicans spread to Catalonia, and whom I was able to reach with the assistance of his

doctoral adviser, Professor Nicole Bériou; Don Luigi Zanoletti, who gra-
ciously received me on more than one occasion at the parish archive of Villa
d'Ogna; and Tullio Zini, architect and friend, both for a most instructive
tour of Modena and, with the able assistance of Antonella Ferraguti, for
securing an important document for me in a timely fashion.

Nearly all of the material I consulted for this book I found in archives
and libraries in over twenty northern Italian cities and in the Vatican. The
level of professionalism I encountered in the numerous archivists and librar-
ians I met, or in a few cases corresponded with, was without exception of
the highest order. I have acknowledged in the notes the help I received
from some of them in specific instances. In addition, I am grateful for the
opportunities I had to receive helpful criticism when lecturing or giving
seminars on this topic at the American Academy in Rome; the Athenaeum
of Science, Letters, and Arts of Bergamo; the Civic Library of Bergamo;
Harvard University; the Mid-America Medieval Association meeting at
the University of Missouri at Kansas City; Mount Holyoke College; Saint
Louis University; the University of Southern California; and the University
of Venice.

My ties with Italy have been just one of the felicitous benefits of my
decades-long companionship with Lella Gandini. With regard to this book
project in particular, we are beholden to Reinhold Mueller and Laura
Lepscky, Claudio Rosati and Annalia Gallardini, and Claudio Zanier and
Veronica Prestini for lively conversations and correspondence – not limited to wine porters – as well as warm hospitality. Lastly, by invoking the
name of Bob Brentano in the dedication of this book, I wish to do more
than express the esteem and affection that Lella and I both felt for him.
Since this part of the book is supposed to be bibliographical, I should at
least point out that he wrote three of the most engaging books any historian has ever written about the religious culture of Italy. Several years ago,
Bob gathered a group of colleagues for a day in Berkeley to celebrate the
presence there of Antonio Rigon from Padua. His request to each of us
was to tell what we 'currently had in mind about the century after Francis'.
We all played our parts and had an energising day, yet Bob's question has
lingered in my mind ever since. This book is in a sense a longer version of
the answer I gave that day.

Prologue: The setting, the main characters, and two questions

1 E. Panofsky, *Gothic Architecture and Scholasticism* (Latrobe, PA, 1951).
2 J. B. Schneyer, 'Alberts des Grossen Augsburger Predigtzyklus über den hl. Augustinus', *Recherches de théologie ancienne et médiévale*, 36 (1969), 100–47.

3   *Ibid.*, p. 146.
4   See below, Chapter 4.

1 The legend of Saint Alberto

1   Food miracles, based upon the example of Jesus, were common episodes in saints' legends. That the particular food mentioned here was polenta, however, is clearly an anachronism, since well over two centuries were to elapse before maize arrived from the Americas.
2   H. Delehaye, *The Legends of the Saints*, trans. D. Attwater (New York, 1962), pp. 3–9.
3   Marcantonio Benaglio, 'De antiquitatibus et gestis divorum Bergomensium', Bergamo, Civica Biblioteca, MMB 258, fos 80–2.
4   The social distinctions among the different versions of the legend are well set out in an unpublished paper by A. Zonca, 'La vita di S. Alberto da Villa d'Ogna, agricoltore', which the author kindly made available to me.
5   Bartolomeo Pellegrini, *Opus divinum de sacra ac fertili Bergomensi vinea* (Brescia, 1553), fo. 22. A Cremonese scholar, Antonio Campi, reports in his *Cremona fedelissima città e nobilissima colonia de' Romani* (Cremona, 1585), p. 26, that he read about Alberto in Pellegrini's book but also consulted the legend, which the rector of Saint-Mattia showed him.
6   Lodovico Cavitelli, *Annales Cremonensis* (Cremona, 1588), fos 98–9.
7   To be sure, illustrated manuscripts served the same purpose, but these were seen by only a tiny elite of readers, whereas fresco was a comparatively popular art. C. Hahn, *Portrayed on the Heart: Narrative Effect in Pictorial Lives of the Saints from the Tenth through the Thirteenth Century* (Berkeley, 2001).
8   See below, Chapter 9.
9   The banners are kept at the Sanctuary of Blessed Alberto in Villa d'Ogna. Photographs of the banners are in the collection of the Centro Studi del Museo Adriano Bernareggi in Bergamo.

2 The life of Alberto

1   Even so, 7 May soon came to be regarded as the date of Alberto's death and has remained so ever since. L. Ginami, *Il Beato Alberto di Villa d'Ogna: Esempio di santità laica nell'Italia dei Comuni* (Milan, 2000), pp. 56–7, 158–9.
2   For more on the social and political history of Cremona in the thirteenth century, see below, Chapter 8.
3   These works are discussed in the following chapter.

3 The afterlife of Alberto

1 *Annales Placentini Gibellini*, Monumenta Germaniae Historica, Scriptores, 18 (Hanover, 1863), pp. 571–2.

2 The description of the scene at Saint-Mattia and the account of these miracles are found in a *Liber miraculorum*, written probably in 1279 or shortly thereafter, but which is extant only in a copy dated 1474: Villa d'Ogna, Archivio parrocchiale, 'Regola de li devotie honesti zoveni de la tera de Vila', fos 6–14v; detailed analysis in L. Ginami, *Il Beato Alberto di Villa d'Ogna: Esempio di santità laica nell'Italia dei Comuni* (Milan, 2000), pp. 63–94, 158–70. In the third quarter of the nineteenth century, A. Tiraboschi transcribed three of the miracle accounts, nos 1, 2, and 4, and then commented: 'One could report another twenty such miracles that date from right after the death of Blessed Alberto, but the above examples can suffice for giving an idea of the manner and style of that era.' See his collected transcripts of manuscripts in Bergamo, Civica Biblioteca, MMB 583, Vol. VII, Part XIV, piece 18/2, pp. 11–15; cited by M. T. Brolis, 'Confraternite bergamasche bassomedievali: Nuove fonti e prospettive di ricerca', *Rivista di Storia della Chiesa in Italia*, 49 (1995), 337–54, esp. pp. 345–6.

3 Albertus Milliolus, *Liber de temporibus et aetatibus et cronica imperatorum*, Monumenta Germaniae Historica, Scriptores, 31 (Hanover, 1903), p. 553.

4 *Annales Parmenses Maiores*, Monumenta Germaniae Historica, Scriptores, 18 (Hanover, 1863), p. 687.

5 Salimbene de Adam, *Cronica fratris Salimbene de Adam ordinis minorum*, Monumenta Germaniae Historica, Scriptores, 32 (Hanover, 1913), pp. 501–3; Salimbene de Adam, *The Chronicle of Salimbene de Adam*, trans. J. L. Baird (Binghamton, NY, 1986), pp. 512–14.

6 D. Calvi, *Delle chiese della Diocesi di Bergamo (1661–1671)*, ed. G. Bonetti and M. Rabaglio (Milan, 2008), p. 9.

7 M. Boskovits (ed.), *I Pittori bergamaschi*, Vol. I: *Le origini* (Bergamo, 1992), pp. 76–7, 156.

8 L. K. Little, *Liberty, Charity, Fraternity: Lay Religious Confraternities at Bergamo in the Age of the Commune* (Northampton, MA, 1988), pp. 61, 123–37.

9 E. Bellantoni, 'Gli affreschi della Sala di Giustizia nella Rocca di Angera', *Arte cristiana*, 75 (1987), 283–94.

10 G. Locatelli, 'I più antichi documenti intorno alla chiesa ed all'ospedale di S. Alberto da Villa d'Ogna', *Bollettino della Civica Biblioteca di Bergamo*, 11:1 (1917), 24–8. Ginami, *Il Beato Alberto*, pp. 95–6. A. Grion, *Alberto di Villa d'Ogna: Laico santo del Medioevo* (Clusone, 1979), pp. 199–203.

11 L. K. Little, 'Una confraternita di giovani in un paese bergamasco, 1474', in C. Fonseca (ed.), *Società, Istituzioni, Spiritualità: Studi in onore di Cinzio Violante* (Spoleto, 1984), pp. 489–502. Ginami, *Il Beato Alberto*, pp. 107–22, 152–6. *Gli atti della visita apostolica di S. Carlo Borromeo a Bergamo (1575)*, ed. A. G. Roncalli (Florence, 1939), Vol. II, Part I, pp. 328–37.

12 E. Moretti, *Breve storia della vita e del culto del B. Alberto da Villa d'Ogna, scritta sopra documenti autentici* (Bergamo, 1897), p. 43.

13 C. Bertinelli and M. Mantovani, 'Potere politico e vita religiosa nei secoli XIII e XIV', in A. Caprioli, A. Rimoldi, and L. Vaccaro (eds), *Diocesi di Cremona* (Brescia, 1998), pp. 114–16.

14 Marcantonio Benaglio, 'De antiquitatibus', Bergamo, Civica Biblioteca, MMB 258, fo. 81v: 'in quo transitu non de vita ad mortem, sed potius … de morte ad vitam eternam'.

15 For the cult at Pavia, Piacenza, Parma, Bologna, and Ferrara, see the following chapter, and for its presence in Catalonia, Chapter 9.

4 The brenta and the brentatori

1 *Lessico etimologico italiano* (Wiesbaden, 2000), s.v. *brenta*; cf. M. Cortelazzo and C. Marcato (eds), *Dizionario etimologico dei dialetti Italiani* (Turin, 1998), s.v. *brenta*. Where German is spoken in the Alps, Switzerland especially, the term for brenta is *die Brente, -n* (see *Das grosse Wörterbuch des deutschen Sprache* (Mannheim, 1993), Vol. II, p. 588), and similarly where French is spoken, in Switzerland and Savoy, the term is *la brante* or *la brande* (see *Dictionnaire culturel en langue française* (Paris, 2005), Vol. I, p. 1078). For other variants such as *bränta* (German) and *brentes* (French) in use in Switzerland, see P. Scheuermeier, *Il lavoro dei contadini: Cultura materiale e artigianato rurale in Italia e nella Svizzera italiana e retoromanza*, trans. I. Gaudenzi and K. D. Egger, 2 vols (Milan, 1980), Vol. II, pp. 104–6.

2 Scheuermeier, *Il lavoro dei contadini*, Vol. I, pp. 153–6, 158; and Vol. II, pp. 99–110.

3 K. Jaberg and J. Jud, *Sprach- und Sachatlas Italiens und der Südschweitz*, 8 vols (Zofingen, 1928–40); for use of the brenta for carrying milk or water, see Vol. VI, map 1203.

4 Both *brentarius* and *brentifer* appear in documents as variant Latin spellings for *brentator*.

5 For the principal sources and studies concerning wine porters, see the Appendix.

6 Jaberg and Jud, *Sprach- und Sachatlas*, Vol. VII, Part I, maps 1319, 1322, 1325. On the cultural differences between the eastern and western parts of the Venetian Terraferma, see G. M. Varanini, 'Le strade del

vino: Note sul commercio vinicolo nel tardo Medioevo', in G. Archetti (ed.), *La civiltà del vino: Fonti, temi e produzione vitivinicole dal Medioevo al Novecento* (Brescia, 2003), pp. 635–63, esp. p. 649.

7 G. Bonfiglio Dosio, 'Le arti cittadine', in G. Cracco and G. Ortalli (eds), *Storia di Venezia*, Vol. II (Rome, 1995), p. 586.

8 Mantua: A. Marescalchi and G. Dalmasso, *Storia delle vite e del vino in Italia*, 3 vols (Milano, 1931–37), Vol. III, pp. 105, 112. Ferrara: Biblioteca Comunale Ariostea, Collegium seu scolla brentatorum et mastellatorum (1402), fos 2v–13r. Cremona: *Statuta civitatis Cremonae* (Cremona, 1578), p. 184: 'Rubrica quod portatores vini portent solios et brentas copertas'.

9 Some other local variants include *brentadùr* (Bergamo), *brentadòo* (Como), *el brentador* (Milan), *brintlador* (Modena), *brentadùr* (Pavia), *brentori* (Piacenza), *brintadòur* (Reggio Emilia), and *brindor* (Turin).

10 The theory was put forth by Antonio I. Pini; see 'Alimentazione, trasporti, fiscalità: I "containers" medievali', in *Vite e vino nel medioevo* (Bologna, 1989), pp. 183–4. For a map of Celtic settlements in Italy, see Ian Barnes (ed.), *The Historical Atlas of the Celtic World* (Edison, NJ, 2009), pp. 64–5. Brief mention should be made of what appears to be a Tuscan anomaly. A former Irish diplomat who is a scholar of the history of Montepulciano, Mr Gearoid O'Broin, kindly provided me with copies of notes he made on the account books of the 1560s and 1570s concerning properties of the Nobili lords. The Nobili were one among several important families to settle at Montepulciano following the submission of Siena to the Florentine State in 1559. The documents in question, from the Conti e Ragioni de SS Nobili in the Archivio Diocesano de Montepulciano, all mention amounts paid for so many brentas of wine and most specify that the payments were made to a brentatore, referred to always as 'frate Brentatore'. Dr Claudio Rosati, former director of the Museums Section of the Region of Tuscany, kindly carried out on my behalf an informal survey of views about these texts on the part of three leading scholars of Tuscan dialectology, who confirmed that such usage in Tuscany was in their view unique and suggested that it be explained as an importation from north of the Apennines.

11 P. Jones, *The Italian City-State, from Commune to Signoria* (Oxford, 1997), pp. 152–332. R. S. Lopez, *The Commercial Revolution of the Middle Ages* (Englewood Cliffs, 1971). L. K. Little, *Religious Poverty and the Profit Economy in the Middle Ages* (London, 1978), pp. ix–x, 3–34. For climate, see the lectures of B. Campbell, 'The Great Transition: Climate, Disease and Society in the 13th and 14th Centuries', www.econsoc.hist.cam.ac.uk/podcasts.html, consulted 18 July 2013.

12 F. Menant, *L'Italia dei comuni (1100–1350)* (Rome, 2011). Jones, *The Italian City-State*, pp. 333–650. E. Coleman, 'Cities and Communes', in J. Davis (ed.), *Italy in the Central Middle Ages, 1000–1300* (New York, 2004), pp. 27–57. D. Waley, *The Italian City-Republics*, 3rd edn (London, 1988). A. I. Pini, *Città, comuni e corporazioni nel medioevo italiano* (Bologna, 1986). J. K. Hyde, *Society and Politics in Medieval Italy* (London, 1973).

13 Statuta Civitatis Pergami, Collatio XIII.31, in *Historiae Patriae Monumenta*, 22 vols in 23 (Turin, 1836–1955), Vol. XVI, Part II (1876), col. 2009. P. Mainoni, 'Le arti e l'economia urbana: Mestieri, mercanti e manifatture a Cremona dal XIII al XV secolo', in G. Chittolini (ed.), *Storia di Cremona: Il Quattrocento. Cremona nel Ducato di Milano (1395–1535)* (Cremona, 2008), pp. 116–47 (pp. 116–19). Pini, *Città, comuni e corporazioni*, pp. 228–43. For Modena see G. L. Basani, *L'uomo e il pane: Consumi e carenze alimentari della popolazione Modenese nel cinque e seicento* (Milan, 1970); and *Sul mercato di Modena tra cinque e seicento: Prezzi e salari* (Milan, 1974).

14 F. Parcianello (ed.), *Statuti di Rovereto del 1425, con le aggiunte dal 1434 al 1538* (Venice, 1991).

15 Bonfiglio Dosio, 'Le arti cittadine', p. 610.

16 D. Zardin (ed.), *Corpi, 'fraternità', mestieri nella storia della società europea* (Rome, 1998), pp. 9–39.

17 B. Pullan, *Rich and Poor in Renaissance Venice: The Social Institutions of a Catholic State, to 1620* (Cambridge, MA, 1971); L. K. Little, *Liberty, Charity, Fraternity: Lay Religious Confraternities at Bergamo in the Age of the Commune* (Bergamo, 1988), pp. 107–21.

18 C. Black, 'Introduction: The Confraternity Context (including a bibliography)', in C. Black and P. Gravestock (eds), *Early Modern Confraternities in Europe and the Americas, International and Interdisciplinary Perspectives* (Burlington, VT, 2006), pp. 1–34.

19 R. Greci, *Corporazioni e mondo del lavoro nell'Italia padana medievale* (Bologna, 1988). A. I. Pini, 'Le arti in processione: Professioni, prestigio e potere nelle città-stato dell'Italia medievale', in *Città, comuni e corporazioni*, pp. 266–72.

20 L. Frati (ed.), *Statuti di Bologna (1245–67)*, 3 vols (Bologna, 1869), Vol. II, p. 254; G. Fasoli and P. Sella (eds), *Statuti di Bologna, 1288*, 2 vols, Studi e testi, 73, 89 (Vatican City, 1937, 1939), Vol. II, p. 220.

21 L. Rockinger, *Briefsteller und Formelbücher des elften bis vierzehnten Jahrhunderts*, 2 vols (New York, 1961 [1863]), Vol. I, pp. 121–7.

22 O. Niccoli, *La vita religiosa nell'Italia moderna, secoli XV–XVIII* (Rome, 2008), pp. 26–8. Lodi, Archivio Storico Comunale, Atti notarili, Fondo Maldotti Gaetano, 12 February 1759, fo. 3.

23 Bologna, Archivio di Stato, Cod. min. 32, fo. 1r.

24 C. Eisler, *The Genius of Jacopo Bellini: The Complete Paintings and Drawings* (London, 1989), Plate 22, p. 111. This is drawing no. 14 in the sketchbook in the British Museum (BM). Eisler identifies the figure, following an index made not by the artist and perhaps as late as the beginning of the following century, as a 'coal bearer', but the curved shape of the vessel is that of a brenta. He identifies in the same way a quite similar figure in the Louvre volume, no. 70 (*ibid.*, Plate 18, p. 95), which in this instance, however, is more convincing, given the mainly straight edges of the container. One might note that BM no. 52 (*ibid.*, Plate 24, p. 113), called *Two Men Carrying Vintage*, shows two men carrying a mastello.

25 G. C. Zanella and V. Zanella, '"Città sopra monte excellentissime situada": Evoluzione urbana di Bergamo in età veneziana', in *Storia economica e sociale di Bergamo*, Vol. III.1 (Bergamo, 1995), pp. 66–91; M. Sanudo, *Itinerario di Marin Sanuto per la terraferma veneziana nell'anno MCCCCLXXXIII* (Padua, 1847), pp. 77–8. Giovanni da Lezze, *Descrizione di Bergamo e suo territorio, 1596*, ed. V. Marchetti and L. Pagani (Bergamo, 1988), pp. 137–8.

26 A. Marina, *The Italian Piazza Transformed: Parma in the Communal Age* (University Park, PA, 2012).

27 For the 1614 trial, I am indebted to Dr Sandro Buzzetti who referred me to this text: Civ. Bib., Misericordia, 839, fos 1–10v. For the ties with confraternities, I am grateful to Professor Roisin Cossar for several references, which can now be found in her book, *The Transformation of the Laity in Bergamo, 1265–c. 1400* (Leiden, 2006), pp. 106–8. In later research Professor Cossar has found mention of a *portator vini* in Treviso who inherited some property. Still concerning confraternities, see also M. T. Brolis, G. Brembilla, and M. Corato (eds), *La matricola femminile della Misericordia di Bergamo (1265–1339)* (Rome, 2001), p. 103. For Bologna my debt is to the late Professor Shona Kelly Wray, both for the reference to the *ministralis* (Bologna, Archivio di Stato, Memoriali, 119, busta 9) and for the reference to the will (Bologna, Archivio di Stato, Memoriali, 203, fo. 122); see also her book, *Communities and Crisis: Bologna during the Black Death* (Leiden, 2009), pp. 187–91, 206. At the Archivio di Stato of Bologna I was greatly assisted by Dr Rossella Rinaldi.

28 Bologna, Archivio di Stato, Assunteria d'Arti, Notizie, Brentadori; Statuti del 1614, fo. 13v, Chapter 50.

29 C. H. Lawrence, *The Friars: The Impact of the Early Mendicant Movement on Western Society* (New York, 1994). On the Indic imports, see L. White, Jr, 'Medieval Borrowings from Further Asia', *Medieval and Renaissance Studies*, 5 (1971), 17–18.

30 B. Walters, V. Corrigan, and P. T. Ricketts, *The Feast of Corpus Christi* (University Park, PA, 2006), pp. 3–54; M. Rubin, *Corpus Christi: The Eucharist in Late Medieval Culture* (Cambridge, 1991), pp. 164–76.

31 Rubin, *Corpus Christi*, pp. 243–71; Pini, 'Le arti in processione', pp. 272–8. Bergamo: Archivio Storico Comunale, Proclami, XXV, 10: *Proclama per la processione del Corpus Domini*. M. Rabaglio, 'Festa del popolo, festa dello stato: Politica e società nella processione del *Corpus Domini* tra XVII e XIX secolo', *Archivio Storico Bergamasco*, n.s. 3 (1995), 42–61. Como: Archivio di Stato, Fondo notarile, cart. 473: Atti del Notaio Paolo Della Torre.

32 Cremona: *Statuti dell'Università de' Brentadori della Città di Cremona* (Cremona, 1742), p. 6. Piacenza: Archivio di Stato, Collegio della mercanzia e paratici, busta 5, Brentori matricola, fo. 25.

33 Piacenza: Archivio di Stato, Collegio della mercanzia e paratici, busta 5, Brentori matricola, fo. 22.

34 I. Vizzini *et al.* (eds), *Bibliotheca sanctorum*, 12 vols (Rome, 1961–71), Vol. I, pp. 676–81.

35 G. Magnani, 'Lo statuto dei brentatori di Pavia del 1553', *Bollettino storico pavese*, 2:1 (1939), 1–31 (p. 26). G. Mismetti, *Vita popolare illustrate di S. Alberto da Villa d'Ogna* (Crema, 1917), p. 82.

36 Ferrara: Biblioteca Comunale Ariostea, Statuti delle corporazioni, 30: Statuti dell'arte de Brentadori della Città di Ferrara (1610), fos 2r and 35; Consignatis capellae Artis Brentatorum in Sancto Paulo carmelitorum (1602), fo. 14r. The painter of the altarpiece was Francesco Pellegrini.

37 Parma: Archivio di Stato, Antichi ospizi di Parma, busta 12, items 8, 50; busta 13, item 65.

38 M. T. Brolis, 'All'origine dei primi ospedali in Bergamo: L'iniziativa dei laici nel XII secolo', *Rendiconto dell'Istituto Lombardo*, 127 (1993), 53–77; 'Comunità ospedaliere dell'Italia centro-settentrionale (sec. XII–XV): Modelli, episodi e protagonisti', in Zardin, *Corpi, 'fraternità', mestieri*, pp. 73–83. J. Henderson, *The Renaissance Hospital: Healing the Body and Soul* (New Haven, 1996).

39 Cremona: Archivio di Stato, Ospedale S. Maria della Pietà, Sez. I, Scat. 13: Documenti relativi all'Ospedale di S. Alberto.

40 C. B. Almansi, 'La soppressione delle corporazioni d'arti e mestieri nella provincia cremonese dello Stato di Milano', *Archivio Storico Lombardo*, ser. 9, 8 (1969), 3–31. The guild at Venice maintained records until 1806, when it listed sixty-three members and still had dues coming in and expenditures for wax; Venice: Archivio di Stato, Archivio delle arti, busta 718, Arte dei travasadori, portadori, e venditori di vino, 1789–1806, fos 101–3.

41 T. Unwin, *Wine and the Vine: An Historical Geography of Viticulture and the Wine Trade* (London, 1991), pp. 254–6.

5 Topography and migration

1 A tourist folder published by the Province of Cremona features a conservation area along the Adda River that includes, near the town of Pizzighettone, a section of stagnant pools and swamp called 'Dead Adda' (Adda Morta).

2 F. Cenerini, 'La via Emilia e la Romanizzazione', in M. Montanari, M. Ridolfi, and R. Zangheri (eds), *Storia dell'Emilia-Romagna*, 2 vols (Rome, 2004), Vol. I: *Dalle origini al Seicento*, pp. 32–44.

3 A. Namias (ed.), *Storia di Modena e dei paesi circostanti*, 2 vols (Bologna, 1969 [1894]), Vol. I, pp. 59–61.

4 G. Sassatelli, 'I primi insediamenti umani e gli etruschi', in Montanari, Ridolfi, and Zangheri, *Storia dell'Emilia-Romagna*, Vol. I, 18–31. F. Soldi, *La capitale del Po* (Cremona, 2007), pp. 57–65; the course change of the main channel of the Po at Ficarolo in the years around 1152 caused the river to go from passing along the southern edge of Ferrara to bypassing the city 5 km to its north.

5 P. Jones, *The Italian City-State: From Commune to Signoria* (Oxford, 1997), pp. 152–332.

6 *Ibid.*, pp. 152–5; A. I. Pini, *Città medievali e demografia storica: Bologna, Romagna, Italia (secc. XIII–XV)* (Bologna, 1996).

7 F. Panero, 'L'inurbamento delle popolazioni rurali e la politica territoriale e demografica dei comuni piemontesi nei secoli XII e XIII', in R. Comba and I. Naso (eds), *Demografia e società nell'Italia medievale* (Cuneo, 1994), pp. 401–40.

8 P. Grillo, 'Il richiamo della metropoli: Immigrazione e crescita demografica a Milano nel XIII secolo', in Comba and Naso, *Demografia e società nell'Italia*, pp. 441–54. F. Braudel, *The Mediterranean and the Mediterranean World in the Age of Philip II*, trans. S. Reynolds, 2 vols (New York, 1972 [1949]), Vol. I, pp. 72–3.

9 M. M. Postan (ed.), *The Cambridge Economic History of Europe*, Vol. I: *The Agrarian Life of the Middle Ages*, rev. edn (Cambridge, 1966), pp. 147, 370, 443.

10 For example Lodi: *Statuta vetera Laudae*, §xci: 'Quod immunes sint rustici qui aliunde venerint in locum novum', in *Codice diplomatico laudense*, 3 vols (Lodi Nuova, 1879–85), Vol. II, p. 568.

11 M. Ginatempo and L. Sandri, *L'Italia delle città: Il popolamento urbano tra Medioevo e Rinascimento (secoli XIII–XVI)* (Florence, 1990). M. W. Flinn, *The European Demographic System, 1500–1800* (Baltimore, 1981), p. 22: 'virtually all towns in early modern Europe … were net consumers of population; that is to say, deaths normally exceeded births, so that towns could maintain their populations and grow only by constant replenishment from rural areas'.

12 A. I. Pini, *Campagne Bolognesi: Le radici agrarie di una metropolis medievale* (Florence, 1993), pp. 5–7.

13 *Ibid.*, p. 20.

14 Braudel, *The Mediterranean*, Vol. I, pp. 25–102. The title of the first chapter is noteworthy: 'The Peninsulas: Mountains, Plateaux, and Plains'. For the ice cream, see Vol. I, pp. 27–9. On Braudel's career and accomplishments, see 'The Age of Braudel', Chapter 3 of P. Burke, *The French Historical Revolution: The 'Annales' School, 1929–89* (Stanford, 1990), pp. 32–64.

15 Flinn, *The European Demographic System*, pp. 72–5. Braudel, *The Mediterranean*, Vol. I, pp. 41–5. On chestnuts, see G. Cherubini, 'La "civiltà" del Castagno in Italia alla fine del Medioevo', *Archeologia medievale*, 8 (1981), 247–80.

16 C. M. Belfanti, 'Dalla stagnatione alla crescita: La populazione di Bergamo dal Cinquecento a Napoleone', in *Storia economica e sociale di Bergamo*, Vol. III.1 (Bergamo, 1995), pp. 172–219.

17 B. Pullan, 'Town Poor, Country Poor: The Province of Bergamo from the Sixteenth to the Eighteenth Century', in E. E. Kittell and T. F. Madden (eds), *Medieval and Renaissance Venice* (Urbana, IL, 1999), pp. 213–36; C. Carlsmith, *A Renaissance Education: Schooling in Bergamo and the Venetian Republic, 1500–1650* (Toronto, 2010), p. 75.

18 F. Menant, 'Nouveaux monastères et jeunes communes: Les Vallombrosains du S. Sepolchro d'Astino et le groupe dirigeant bergamasque (1107–1161)', in F. G. B. Trolese (ed.), *Il monachesimo italiano nell'età comunale* (Cesena, 1998), pp. 269–316; L. K. Little, *Liberty, Charity, Fraternity: Lay Religious Confraternities at Bergamo in the Age of the Commune* (Bergamo, 1988), pp. 34, 44, 57, 66, 89, 101–6.

19 G. Pettinari, *Dalle montagne alla pianura: Storie di transumanza e di Bergamini* (Lodi, 2001), p. 11.

20 Braudel, *The Mediterranean*, Vol. I, pp. 85–91.

21 For a cautionary statement on the extensive research of recent decades that calls for a more nuanced reading of Braudel's views, see P. Viazzo, 'La mobilità nelle frontiere alpine', in P. Corti and M. Sanfilippo (eds), *Migrazioni*, Storia d'Italia: Annali, 24 (Turin, 2009), pp. 91–105. Cf. the incisive historiographical observations in the preface and introduction of R. C. Mueller, *Immigrazione e cittadinanza nella Venezia medievale* (Rome, 2010); see also R. Rao (ed.), *Bergamo e la montagna nel Medioevo: Il territorio orobico fra città e poteri locali*, conference proceedings, *Bergomum*, 104–5 (2009–10), pp. 5–215.

22 W. H. McNeill, *The Pursuit of Truth: A Historian's Memoir* (Lexington, KY, 2005), pp. 56–7.

23 C. M. Belfanti, *Mestieri e forestieri: Immigrazione ed economia urbana a Mantova tra sei e settecento* (Milano, 1994), pp. 87–8.

24 R. Greci, 'Immigrazioni artigiane a Bologna tra due e trecento', in Comba and Naso, *Demografia e società nell'Italia*, pp. 375–99.

25 R. Comba, *Contadini, signori e mercanti nel Piemonte medievale* (Rome, 1988), pp. 87–92. D. Balani, 'Il commercio del vino nella Torino sei-settecentesca', in R. Comba (ed.), *Vigne e vini nel Piemonte moderno*, 2 vols (Cuneo, 1992), pp. 439–59 (pp. 444–7).

26 Belfanti, *Mestieri e forestieri*, pp. 67–76, 88–9, 111–12.

27 F. Menant, 'Bergamo comunale: Storia, economia e società', in *Storia economica e sociale di Bergamo*, Vol. II.2 (Bergamo, 1993), pp. 15–181.

28 F. Menant, 'Aux origines de la société crémasque: L'immigration bergamasque et crémonaise', in *Crema, 1185: Una contrastata autonomia politica e territoriale* (Crema, 1988), pp. 109–36.

29 F. Menant, 'Il lungo Duecento (1183–1311): Il Comune fra maturità istituzionale e lotte di parte', in G. Andenna (ed.), *Storia di Cremona: Dall'Alto Medioevo all'Età Comunale* (Cremona, 2004), pp. 362–3. The pattern on the south or Apennine side of the Po Valley differed, for some of the flocks that summered at higher elevations went up and over the mountains so as to come down on the south – that is, the sunnier and warmer Tuscan side – for the winter. See A. Silvestri, *Fanano Sacra: Cielo e terra d'Appennino* (Nonantola, 2005), p. 69.

30 Statuta Civitatis Pergami, an. 1248, Collatio XIII.1: 'De mercatore posse ire ad Cremonam cum mercato', in *Historiae Patriae Monumenta*, 22 vols in 23 (Turin, 1836–1955), Vol. XVI, Part II, col. 1999. For the 1308 contract, see A. Mazzi, *Corografia Bergomense* (Bergamo, 1880), pp. 145–6.

31 E. Plebani Faga, 'Vecchi mestieri', *Atti dell'Ateneo di scienze, lettere ed arti di Bergamo*, 62 (1998–99), 378.

32 G. Bonfiglio Dosio, 'L'immigrazione a Brescia fra trecento a quattrocento', in R. Comba, G. Piccinni, and G. Pinto (eds), *Strutture famigliari, epidemie, migrazione nell'Italia medievale* (Naples, 1984), pp. 355–71.

33 Grillo, 'Il richiamo', pp. 449–50.

34 P. Soglian, *Terra d'Urgnano: Documenti e immagini per la storia* (Urgnano, 1980), pp. 219–32.

35 P. M. Piergiovanni, 'La Compagnia dei Caravana: I facchini bergamaschi del porto di Genova', in *Storia economica e sociale di Bergamo*, Vol. III.2 (Bergamo, 1995), pp. 194–217. A. Mazzi, 'I bergamaschi in Genova e la sua Riviera nel secolo XIII', *Bergomum*, 3 (1909), 19–34.

36 A. Zannini, 'L'*altra* Bergamo in laguna: La communità bergamasca a Venezia', in *Storia economica e sociale di Bergamo*, Vol. II, pp. 174–93. G. Gullino, 'L'exploit dei bergamaschi in Laguna: Colonia numerosa ma estranea al potere', in *Storia economica e sociale di Bergamo*, Vol. III.4 (Bergamo, 1995), pp. 166–93. S. R. Ell, 'Citizenship and Immigration in Venice, 1305–1500', Ph.D. dissertation (University of Chicago, 1976).

37 G. Priuli, *Diari, 1494–1512*, ed. A. Segre, 4 vols (Città del Castello, 1912–41), Vol. IV, p. 47. S. Battaglia and G. Bàrberi Squarotti, *Grande dizionario della lingua italiana*, 21 vols (Turin, 1961–2002), Vol. V, s.v. *facchino*.

38 Giovanni da Lezze, *Descrizione di Bergamo e suo territorio, 1596*, ed. V. Marchetti and L. Pagani (Bergamo, 1988), pp. 148, 190.

39 See the following chapter for several expressions of this view.

40 G. Albini, 'La populazione di Bergamo e del suo territorio nei secoli XIV e XV', in *Storia economica e sociale di Bergamo*, Vol. II.2, pp. 222–3.

41 Braudel, *The Mediterranean*, Vol. I, pp. 334–8.

6 Porters of the imagination

1 Teofilo Folengo, *Baldo*, trans. A. E. Mullaney, 2 vols, I Tatti Renaissance Library, 25 (Cambridge, MA, 2007), Vol. I, pp. 232–7; Teofilo Folengo, *Baldus*, ed. and trans. M. Chiesa, 2 vols (Turin, 1997), Vol. I, pp. 350–3.

2 *Dizionario Biografico degli Italiani* (*Diz. Biog. Ital.*), 75 vols to date (Rome, 1960), Vol. XLVIII, pp. 546–2. The first edition of *Baldus* bore the title *Liber macaronices* and carried the pseudonym Merlin Cocai. In a sense Folengo never stopped working on *Baldus*, for he issued a second, much expanded edition accompanied by fifty-three woodcuts in 1521. A third followed in 1530 and a fourth, posthumously, in 1552.

3 Folengo, *Baldo*, trans. Mullaney, Vol. I, pp. 404–7; *Baldus*, trans. Chiesa, Vol. I, pp. 526–9.

4 *Diz. Biog. Ital.*, Vol. VIII, pp. 740–6. Ruzzante [A. Beolco], *Teatro*, ed. L. Zorzi (Turin, 1967); R. Ferguson, *The Theater of Beolco: Text, Context and Performance* (Ravenna, 2000), pp. 7–8, 42, 150–7; A. Beolco, *La moschetta*, trans. A. Franceschetti and K. R. Bartlett (Ottowa, 1993).

5 *Diz. Biog. Ital.*, Vol. LII, pp. 449–53. Tomaso Garzoni, *La piazza universale di tutte le professioni del mondo, e nobili et ignobili*, ed. G. B. Bronzini, 2 vols (Florence, 1996).

6 Garzoni, *La piazza universale*, Vol. II, Chapter 114, pp. 973–8.

7 In New Orleans in the years following Hurricane Katrina, the plight of migrant labourers from Latin America, mainly Mexico, Honduras, and Guatemala, was widely reported in the press. Particularly vulnerable because of their illegal status, they got paid in cash and for that were known popularly as 'walking ATMs'. Armed robbers, sometimes alone but often in groups, lay in wait for them to take their wages. Sometimes the people who hired them simply refused to pay them and dismissed any protests by threatening to call the police (*New York Times*, 16 February 2009). Ed Blakely, head of the New Orleans Office of Recovery Management, referred to these Latino workers as being, even though undocumented, 'vital to the success of rebuilding New Orleans' (*PBS Online Newshour*, 28 August 2007). Thus they were immigrants and, in the view of at least one highly placed government official, they were indispensable. They were also easy prey for robbers.

8 See the illuminating discussion of this apparent ambivalence of Garzoni by M. Santoro, '"Professioni": Origini e trasformazioni di un termine e di un'idea', in D. Zardin (ed.), *Corpi, 'fraternità', mestieri nella storia della società europea* (Rome, 1998), pp. 117–58.

9 C. Vecellio, *De gli Habiti Antichi e Moderni di Diversi Parti di Mondo* (Venice, 1590).

10 *Diz. Biog. Ital.*, Vol. XX, pp. 623–6. D. Posner, *Annibale Carracci* (New York, 1971); A. W. A. Boschloo, *Annibale Carracci in Bologna: Visibile Reality in Art after the Council of Trent*, 2 vols (The Hague, 1974); E. Fiori (ed.), *Talento e impazienza: Annibale Carracci nella Pinacoteca nazionale di Bologna* (Milan, 2006); C. Robertson, *The Invention of Annibale Carracci* (Milan, 2008).

11 Juan Huarte de San Juan, *Examen de ingenios para las ciencias* (Baeza, 1575); *Essame de gl'ingegni hvomini* (Venice, 1586); *The Examination of Men's Wits* (London, 1959 [1594]). On the English translation, see this work kindly brought to my attention by Professor Stefano Villani of the Universities of Pisa and Maryland: S. Tomika, *A Bibliographical Catalogue of Italian Books Printed in England, 1558–1603* (Farnham, 2009), pp. 358–9. Cf. G. Rosaccio, *Il microcosmo del Dottore in Filosofia e Medicina Gioseppe Rosaccio cosmografo nel quale si tratta brevemente dell'anima vegetale, sensibile et rationale dell'Huomo* … (Bologna, 1688). The work of the art historian Sheila McTighe is essential for understanding the role of diet in both paintings and literature of this period: 'Foods and the Body in Italian Genre Paintings, about 1580: Campi, Passerotti, Carracci', *The Art Bulletin*, 86 (2004), 301–23.

12 Translation adapted from Huarte, *The Examination of Men's Wits*, p. 310.

13 Giovanni Battista Segni, *Trattato sopra la carestia e fame, sue cause, accidenti, provisioni, reggimenti; varie moltiplicazioni e sorti di pane* (Bologna, 1602).

14 *Diz. Biog. Ital.*, Vol. XXXI, pp. 214–19. Giulio Cesare Croce, *Le sottilissime astuzie di Bertoldo: Le piacevoli e ridicolose semplicità di Bertoldino* (Turin, 1978). M. Rouche, *Les Communautés rurales de la campagne bolonaise et l'image du paysan dans l'oeuvre de Giulio Cesare Croce (1550–1609)* (Lille, 1984).

15 Most of the major works on Carracci have little to say about these drawings, e.g. Posner, *Annibale Carracci*, pp. 17–19; Boschloo, *Annibale Carracci*, pp. 33–5; and Robertson, *Invention*, p. 36, who finds the *Arti* compositions 'remarkable, not only for their sympathy, but also for their gentle humour: figures balance impossible loads of their wares', and gives as examples the baker's delivery man and the brentatore. To check on 'humour' and the 'impossibility' of the former, search online for 'bread delivery Cairo' to see images of Egyptian delivery boys who now carry as much bread in Cairo as their counterparts in Bologna did years ago, *but do so on bicycles, in chaotic automobile traffic*. As for the latter, enough evidence has been amassed above in Chapter 4 to assure us that Carracci was not exaggerating the size of the brenta. Again the work of Sheila McTighe is essential, in this case for understanding the purpose, style, and fate of Carracci's drawings: 'Perfect Deformity, Ideal Beauty, and the *Imaginaire* of Work: the Reception of Annibale Carracci's *Arti di Bologna* in 1646', *Oxford Art Journal*, 16 (1993), 75–91.

16 K. F. Beall, *Kaufrufe und Strassenhändler: Eine Bibliographie* (Hamburg, 1975); D. Miller, *Street Criers and Itinerant Tradesmen in European Prints* (Stanford, 1970).

17 McTighe, 'Perfect Deformity', p.85. Not only was Carracci related to a tailor and to butchers, but, as McTighe points out (p. 84), two of his sisters married wine porters.

18 *Ibid.*, p. 87. The wine porter depicted on the cover of the present volume is one of these works by Mitelli based upon drawings by Carracci.

19 *Diz. Biog. Ital.*, Vol. LXV, pp. 460–7; J. B. Lynch, 'Lomazzo and the Accademia della Valle di Bregno', *The Art Bulletin*, 48 (1966), 210–11; C. Apa (ed.), *Rabisch: Il grottesco nell'arte del Cinquecento. L'Accademia della Val di Blenio, Lomazzo e l'ambiente milanese* (Milan, 1998).

20 Giorgio Vasari (1511–74) published the first edition of his lives of Florentine artists in 1550 and a second edition in 1568.

21 Giovan Paolo Lomazzo e i Facchini della Val di Blenio, *Rabisch*, ed., trans., and intro. D. Isella (Turin, 1993).

22 *Diz. Biog. Ital.*, Vol. III, pp. 776–7; Apa, *Rabisch: Il grottesco,* pp. 57–69, 186–92, 199–202.

23 *Diz. Biog. Ital.*, Vol. XX, pp. 260–9. F. Buzzi and D. Zardin (eds), *Carlo Borromeo e l'opera della 'grande riforma': Cultura, religione e arte del governo nella Milano del pieno cinquecento* (Milan, 1997).

24 N. P. Tanner (ed.), *Decrees of the Ecumenical Councils,* 2 vols (London, 1990), Vol. II, pp. 774–6.

25 Gabriele Paleotti, *Discorso intorno alle immagini sacre e profane,* ed. S. Della Torre (Città del Vaticano, 2002), Chapters 37–41, pp. 214–31.

26 Paleotti, *Discorso,* p. 214.

27 G. Bora, 'Milano nell'età di Lomazzo e San Carlo: Riaffermazione e difficoltà di sopravvivenza di una cultura', in Apa, *Rabisch: Il grottesco,* pp. 37–56.

28 D. Isella, 'Per una lettura dei Rabisch', in Apa, *Rabisch: Il grottesco,* pp. 111–19.

29 S. Favalier, 'L'immagine dei Bergamaschi nella letteratura veneziana minore del secondo Cinquecento', in *Storia economica e sociale di Bergamo,* Vol. III.1 (Bergamo, 1995), pp. 305–26. F. Novati, 'Milano prima e dopo la peste del 1630 secondo nuove testimonianze', *Archivio Storico Lombardo,* 18 (1912), 5–54. My thanks to Dr Massimo Zaggia for elucidating this literary fabrication called 'Bergamasco'.

30 Piacenza: Archivio di Stato, Statuti del Paratico delli Brentori di Piacenza, Chapters 26, 29, fo. 25. Reggio Emilia: *Statuti et ordine dell'arte delli brentatori di Reggio* (Reggio Emilia, 1670), pp. 7, 12–14. Parma: Archivio del Comune di Parma, *Libro degli statuti delle arti di Parma,* Brentatori, Chapters 3, 5, 11, fo. 86r–v.

31 A. Cavalcabò, 'Gli antichi mercati del vino a Cremona', *Cremona,* 12 (1940), 295–9. A similar mix of unfavourable reputation and apparently direct experience figured in a dispute between a community of Florentine nuns and a group of porters (from Norcia, elevation 604 m, in Umbria) who were their immediate neighbours. In the nuns' formal complaint brought in 1564, they claimed that they needed more space since they could not even use that part of their own property contiguous with that of their neighbours because of the latters' foul behaviour. As the offer they made to take over the porters' space and give them a property of similar value in exchange was rejected, they went to court and won their case. The image the nuns presented of the porters' behaviour clearly did not harm their cause. My gratitude goes to Professor Carol Bresnahan for bringing this case and the reference to my attention. Florence: Archivio di Stato, Pratica segreta 7, no. 23: Dispute between the nuns of San Giovanni de' Cavalieri and the porters of Norcia.

32 Modena: Archivio di Stato, Arti e mestieri, Brentatori, busta 22.

33 Venice: Archivio di Stato, Signori di Notte al Crim., reg. 6, fo. 50v; reg. 9, fo. 16.

34 In Italy the illegitimate ones are called 'abusive' (*abusivi*); in New York they are known as 'gypsy cabs'.

35 Milan: Archivio Storico Civico, Gride, 1, fasc. 13. F. Cherubini, *Vocabulario Milanese-Italiano* (Milan, 1839), p. 158.

36 Modena: Archivio di Stato, Mappe e disegni, cart. 1, n. 21, anno 1525; Inventario della Cantina ducale, anno 1527.

37 Salimbene de Adam, *Cronica fratris Salimbene de Adam ordinis minorum*, Monumenta Germaniae Historica, Scriptores, 32 (Hanover, 1913), p. 501; *The Chronicle of Salimbene de Adam*, trans. J. L. Baird (Binghamton, NY, 1986), p. 512. Robert Brentano noted how Salimbene in his frequent travels made a point of trying the local wines: *Two Churches: England and Italy in the Thirteenth Century* (Princeton, 1966), p. 333. Going beyond the easy association of a wine porter and wine drinking, the seventeenth-century French editor of one of the *cries de Paris* accused even a fictitious water carrier of wishing his burden were wine so he could drink it; the caption under the image of this water carrier in a 1676 print says: 'You can tell from his looks that he'd like to change his water into wine and that he'd then drink so much of it he'd swallow his earnings' (Beall, *Kaufrufe*, pp. 224–5).

38 M. Mutio, *Sacra Historia di Bergamo*, 2nd edn (Bergamo, 1621), p. 217.

7 Making saints

1 H. Delehaye, *Essai sur le culte des saints dans l'antiquité* (Brussels, 1927), pp. 24–59; P. Brown, *The Cult of Saints: Its Rise and Function in Latin Christianity* (Chicago, 1981); S. Boesch Gajano, *La santità* (Rome, 1999); A. Vauchez, *Sainthood in the Later Middle Ages*, trans. J. Birrell (Cambridge, 1997); D. Weinstein and R. Bell, *Saints and Society: The Two Worlds of Western Christendom, 1000–1700* (Chicago, 1982).

2 J. Dalarun, in P. Levillain (ed.), *Dizionario storico del Papato*, 2 vols (Milan, 1996), Vol. I, p. 148.

3 Athanasius, *The Life of Antony*, trans. R. C. Gregg (New York, 1980), Chapter 46, pp. 65–7; Cyprian of Carthage, *De mortalitate*, ed. M. L. Hannan (Washington, DC, 1933), pp. 27–39.

4 E. E. Malone, *The Monk and the Martyr: The Monk as the Successor of the Martyr* (Washington, DC, 1950); J. Anson, 'The Female Transvestite in Early Monasticism: The Origins and Development of a Motif', *Viator*, 5 (1974), 1–32.

5 Athanasius, *The Life of Antony*; Sulpicius Severus, *The Life of Saint Martin*, trans. B. Peebles (New York, 1949); Gregory the Great, *The Life of Saint Benedict*, trans. T. G. Kardong (Collegeville, MN, 2009).

6 Gregory of Tours, *The History of the Franks*, trans. L. Thorpe (Harmondsworth, 1974), pp. 584–6.

7 For a thorough account with brilliant analysis of a classic instance of such a struggle in the twentieth century, namely the case of Padre Pio, see S. Luzzatto, *Padre Pio: Miracoli e politica nell'Italia del Novecento* (Turin, 2007).

8 E. W. Kemp, *Canonization and Authority* (London, 1948), p. 58.

9 Vauchez, *Sainthood*, pp. 187–215; cf. A. Murray, *Reason and Society in the Middle Ages* (Oxford, 1978), pp. 337–441.

10 G. Duby, *The Three Orders: Feudal Society Imagined*, trans. A. Goldhammer (Chicago, 1980).

11 J. Le Goff and J.-C. Schmitt (eds), *Dictionnaire raisonné de l'Occident médiéval* (Paris, 1999), s.v. *Moines et religieux*.

12 J. M. Wallace-Hadrill, *The Long-Haired Kings* (London, 1962), pp. 245–8; J. L. Nelson, *The Frankish World, 750–900* (London, 1996), pp. 99–131.

13 H. Fichtenau, *Living in the Tenth Century: Mentalities and Social Orders*, trans. P. Geary (Chicago, 1991). L. K. Little, 'Romanesque Christianity in Germanic Europe', *The Journal of Interdisciplinary History*, 23 (1993), 453–74, esp. pp. 456–62; and 'Monasticism and Western Society: From Marginality to the Establishment and Back', *Memoirs of the American Academy in Rome*, 47 (2002), 87–90.

14 M.-D. Chenu, 'The Evangelical Awakening', in *Nature, Man, and Society in the Twelfth Century: Essays on New Theological Perspectives in the Latin West*, trans. J. Taylor and L. K. Little (Chicago, 1968), pp. 239–69.

15 M.-D. Chenu, 'Monks, Canons, and Laymen in Search of the Apostolic Life', in *Nature, Man, and Society*, pp. 202–38.

16 G. Constable, *The Reformation of the Twelfth Century* (Cambridge, 1996); and B. Bolton, *The Medieval Reformation* (New York, 1983).

17 J. Becquet (ed.), *Scriptores ordinis grandimontensis* (Turnhout, 1968), pp. 5–6, 66, 105–10.

18 C. H. Lawrence, *Medieval Monasticism: Forms of Religious Life in Western Europe in the Middle Ages* (New York, 1984), pp. 146–66.

19 Bernard of Clairvaux, *Epistolae*, 106 (*Patrologia latina*, 184, col. 217).

20 The seminar conducted by Michel Mollat at the Sorbonne on poverty and the poor in the Middle Ages ran from 1962 to 1977. Scores upon scores of papers presented by scholars from all over Europe and beyond, ranging from beginners to the seasoned, and on topics that

ranged widely across the Continent, produced an extraordinary consensus on the dating of this phenomenon. See Mollat's summing-up of this remarkable enterprise in his *Les Pauvres au moyen âge, étude sociale* (Paris, 1978); and the memorial minute in *Speculum*, 74 (1999), 903–4.

21 C. Morris, 'San Ranieri of Pisa: The Power and Limitations of Sanctity in Twelfth-Century Italy', *The Journal of Ecclesiastical History*, 45 (1994), 588–99.

22 R. I. Moore, *The War on Heresy* (London, 2012), pp. 184–203.

23 *Ibid.*, pp. 204–14, 220–4. P. Biller, *The Waldenses, 1170–1530: Between a Religious Order and a Church* (Burlington, VT, 2001); and 'Goodbye to Waldensianism?', *Past and Present*, 192 (2006), 3–33.

24 R. W. Southern, *Western Society and the Church in the Middle Ages* (Harmondsworth, 1970), pp. 103–31; C. Morris, *The Papal Monarchy: The Western Church from 1050 to 1250* (Oxford, 1989).

25 S. Kuttner, 'The Revival of Jurisprudence', in R. L. Benson and G. Constable (eds), *Renaissance and Renewal in the Twelfth Century* (Cambridge, MA, 1982), pp. 299–323; K. W. Nörr, 'Institutional Foundations of the New Jurisprudence', in Benson and Constable, *Renaissance and Renewal*, pp. 324–38; and J. A. Brundage, *The Medieval Origins of the Legal Profession: Canonists, Civilians, and Courts* (Chicago, 2008).

26 R. Brentano, *Two Churches: England and Italy in the Thirteenth Century* (Princeton, 1968), pp. 25–61.

27 Southern, *Western Society*, pp. 104–5.

28 *Ibid.*, pp. 131–3.

29 Kemp, *Canonization and Authority*, pp. 99–104.

8 Sainthood by community

1 C. Kleinhenz (ed.), 'Cremona', in *Medieval Italy: An Encyclopedia* (New York, 2004).

2 P. Tozzi and A. M. Ardovino, *Storia di Cremona: L'età antica* (Bergamo, 2003), pp. 118–27.

3 F. Menant, *L'Italia dei comuni (1100–1350)*, trans. E. Igor Mineo (Rome, 2011), pp. 60–1.

4 L. E. Boyle, 'Sicardus of Cremona', in *The New Catholic Encyclopedia*, Vol. VIII (New York, 1967), pp. 190–1; D. Piazzi, 'I tempi del vescovo Sicardo e di sant'Omobono', in A. Capriole, A. Rimoldi, and L. Vaccaro (eds), *Diocesi di Cremona* (Brescia, 1998), pp. 77–89.

5 A. Vauchez, *Omobono di Cremona (†1197): Laico e santo, profilo storico* (Cremona, 2001); and D. Webb, *Saints and Cities in Medieval Italy* (Manchester, 2007), pp. 46–53.

6 O. Hageneder and A. Haidacher (eds), *Die Register Innocenz' III*, 11 vols in 3 (Cologne, 1964–2010), Vol. I, pp. 761–4; Webb, *Saints and Cities*, pp. 54–6.

7 D. Piazzi, *Omobono di Cremona: Biographie dal XIII al XVI secolo* (Cremona, 1991).

8 E. W. Kemp, *Canonization and Authority in the Western Church* (Oxford, 1948), p. 102.

9 S. Boesch Gajano, *La santità* (Rome, 1999), pp. 80–1; A. Vauchez, *Sainthood in the Later Middle Ages*, trans. J. Birrell (New York, 1988), pp. 25–9, 85–6; Kemp, *Canonization and Authority*, pp. 99–104.

10 Vauchez, *Sainthood*, pp. 251–5; P. Delooz, *Sociologie et canonisations* (Liège, 1969), p. 338.

11 Vauchez, *Sainthood*, pp. 33–57; M. Gotor, *Chiesa e santità nell'Italia moderna* (Rome, 2004), pp. 17–18.

12 Excommunication and anathema were and continue often to be considered equal; however, see the discussion of the frequently employed phrase 'not only excommunicated but also anathematised' and of the canonical definition of anathema as eternal death in L. K. Little, *Benedictine Maledictions: Liturgical Cursing in Romanesque France* (Ithaca, NY, 1993), p. 33 and n. 47.

13 Delooz, *Sociologie*, pp. 350, 447–59; D. Weinstein and R. Bell, *Saints and Society: The Two Worlds of Western Christendom, 1000–1700* (Chicago, 1982), pp. 121–37.

14 Vauchez, *Sainthood*, pp. 232–5.

15 Boyle, 'Sicardus', p. 191; Piazzi, 'I tempi del vescovo Sicardo', pp. 80–4.

16 Menant, *L'Italia dei comuni*, pp. 47–100.

17 C. Bertinelli Spotti and M. Mantovani, 'Potere politico e vita religiosa nei secoli XIII–XIV', in Capriole *et al.*, *Diocesi di Cremona*, pp. 91–120.

18 P. Maioni, 'Le arti e l'economia urbana: Mestieri, mercanti e manifatture a Cremona dal XIII al XV secolo', in G. Chittolini (ed.), *Storia di Cremona: Il Quattrocento. Cremona nel Ducato di Milano (1395–1535)* (Cremona, 2008), pp. 116–47.

19 Vauchez, *Omobono di Cremona*, pp. 58–71; Webb, *Saints and Cities*, pp. 57–61.

20 Vauchez, *Omobono di Cremona*, pp. 73–107.

21 Webb, *Saints and Cities*, pp. 62–92. A. Vauchez, 'Raimondo Zanfogni', in I. Vizzini *et al.* (eds) *Bibliotheca sanctorum*, 12 vols (Rome, 1961–71), Vol. XI, pp. 26–9; and L. Canetti, *Gloriosa civitas: Culto dei santi e società cittadina a Piacenza nel medioevo* (Bologna, 1993).

22 *Acta sanctorum*, Iulii, VI, cols 649–50.

23 'Surger, age, diffidere noli; Romam, ubi tempus perdis et operam, desere, atque in patriam proficiscere.' *Ibid.*, cols 650–1.

24 R. Borgo, *Vita, morte e miracoli del beato Geroldo da un antichissimo libro latino in italiano nostra lingua transportati e con alcune spirituali meditationi ampliati* (Cremona, 1581).

25 A. Vauchez, 'Un modèle hagiographique et cultuel en Italie avant saint Roch: Le pèlerin mort en chemin', in A. Rigon and A. Vauchez (eds), *San Rocco: Genesi e prima espansione di un culto* (Brussels, 2006), pp. 57–69.

26 L. Gregorio, *Vita, morte e miracoli del beato Facio, estratto da alcune scritture antiche della Cattedrale e dell'Hospitale Maggiore di Cremona* (Cremona, 1606); A. Vauchez, 'Sainteté laïque au XIIIe siècle: La vie du bienheureux Facio de Crémone (v. 1196–1272)', *Mélanges de l'Ecole française de Rome, Moyen Age–temps moderne*, 84 (1972), 13–53. The few surviving documentary references to Facio written during his lifetime qualify him as a blacksmith, whereas the hagiographical works all make him out to be a gold- and silversmith.

27 C. M. Radding, 'Wergild', in *Dictionary of the Middle Ages*, Vol. XII (New York, 1989), pp. 617–18; and H. St L. B. Moss, *The Birth of the Middle Ages, 395–814* (Oxford, 1914), p. 66.

28 Vauchez, 'Sainteté laïque', pp. 21–3, 32, strains to make Facio consistently pro-Guelf throughout his life, but his early allegiance in Verona was to a pro-Ghibelline faction, and when adherents of the latter were expelled, one obvious place where they could expect to be well received was Cremona. See G. M. Varanini, 'Facio', in *Diz. Biog. Ital.*, Vol. XLIV, pp. 110–12; D. Waley, *The Italian City-Republics*, 3rd edn (London, 1988), pp. 91, 160–1; M. Miller, 'Verona', in Kleinhenz, *Medieval Italy*, p. 1135. The political sympathies of the clergy and the influential people who regularly worshipped at the cathedral of Cremona, where Facio seemed to fit in very well, lay with the imperial faction. Vauchez himself, in 'Sainteté laïque', p. 25 stresses the conversion Facio underwent in the 1250s and early 1260s, evident in his adoption of a proto-clerical form of life and his foundation of an intensely pro-Guelf religious and political consortium. This conversion eliminates the need for arguing in favour of life-long political sympathies.

29 Vauchez, 'Sainteté laïque', pp. 16–20, 33–4, 43–8.

30 This was of course a standard claim in saints' legends from other cities, for example that of Nevolone, a cobbler from Faenza who died in 1280, and who was said to have made eleven pilgrimages to Santiago. A. Vauchez, 'Nevolone', in Vizzini *et al.*, *Bibliotheca sanctorum*, Vol. IX, pp. 839–40.

31 D. Gallo (ed.), *Per André Vauchez: I miracoli di Antonio il Pellegrino (1267–1270)* (Padua, 2003), p. 7.

32 A. Puerari, in *Museo Civico Ala Ponzone, Cremona: Raccolte artistiche* (Cremona, 1976), p. 53, Figure 299; A. Ebani, 'Per l'interpretazione di

un altorilievo trecentesco del Museo Civico di Cremona', *Strenna dell' ADAFA* (1984), 59–68. The relief sculpture is also referred to below, in the Epilogue.

33 R. Rusconi, 'La predicazione: Parole in chiesa, parole in piazza', in G. Cavallo, C. Leonardi, and E. Menestò (eds), *Lo spazio letterario del medioevo*, Part I: *Il medioevo latino* (Rome, 1993), Vol. II, pp. 571–603; C. Delcorno, 'La predicazione', in P. Boitani, M. Mancini, and A. Varvaro (eds), *Lo spazio letterario del medioevo*, Part II: *Il medioevo volgare* (Rome, 2000), Vol. II, pp. 405–31. Vauchez, *Sainthood*, pp. 232–9.

34 J. C. Schmitt, *The Holy Greyhound: Guinefort, Healer of Children since the Thirteenth Century*, trans. M. Thom (New York, 1983).

35 S. Boesch Gajano, 'La certificazione del miracolo nel medioevo: Fonti e problemi', in R. Michetti (ed.), *Notai, miracoli e culto dei santi: Pubblicità e autenticazione del sacro tra 12. e 15. secolo* (Milan, 2004), pp. 31–53.

36 Vauchez, 'Sainteté laïque', p. 36.

37 Citing the testimony given by Salimbene and in the *Annals of Parma*, two historians at least have grasped the key role of the wine porters in creating the cult of Alberto: Vauchez, *Sainthood*, pp. 235–6; and M. Goodich, *Vita perfecta: The Ideal of Sainthood in the Thirteenth Century* (Stuttgart, 1982), pp. 194–5.

38 G. Casagrande, 'Un ordine per i laici: Penitenza e penitenti nel Duecento', in M. P. Alberzoni, A. B. Langeli, G. Casagrande, *et al.* (eds), *Francesco d'Assisi e il primo secolo di storia francescana* (Turin, 1997), pp. 237–55; and *Dizionario degli Istituti di Perfezione*, Vol. VI (Rome, 1980), pp. 780–815, Vol. IX, pp. 1042–50 and 1063–71.

39 L. Cavitelli, *Annales Cremonensis* (Cremona, 1588), pp. 98v–99r.

40 M. Lehmijoki-Gardner, *Worldly Saints: Social Interaction of Dominican Penitent Women in Italy, 1200–1500* (Helsinki, 1999), pp. 34–55.

41 M. Weber, *The Sociology of Religion*, trans. E. Fischoff (Boston, 1963), pp. 45–59.

9 Sainthood by the papacy

1 L. Cavitelli, *Annales Cremonensis* (Cremona, 1588), pp. 98v–99r. The painting by Giulio Campi now hangs in the Brera Gallery in Milan. The anonymous painting of Alberto dressed in the habit of a Dominican tertiary is in the Sanctuary of Blessed Alberto at Villa d'Ogna.

2 M. C. Gaposchkin, *The Making of Saint Louis: Kingship, Sanctity, and Crusade in the Later Middle Ages* (Ithaca, NY, 2008), p. 155; M. C. Gaposchkin (ed.), *Blessed Louis, the Most Glorious King: Texts Relating to the Cult of Saint Louis of France*, trans. Gaposchkin with P. B. Katz (Notre Dame, IN, 2012), pp. 29–30.

3 In addition to the works cited above in the first note in Chapter 7, see M. Gotor, *Chiesa e santità nell'Italia moderna* (Rome, 2004); the same author's *I beati del papa: Santità, inquisizione e obbedienza in età moderna* (Florence, 2002); S. Ditchfield, *Liturgy, Sanctity and History in Tridentine Italy: Pietro Maria Campi and the Preservation of the Particular* (Cambridge, 1995); and P. Burke, 'How to Be a Counter-Reformation Saint', in his *The Historical Anthropology of Early Modern Europe: Essays on Perception and Communication* (New York, 1987), pp. 48–62, 243, 261–76.

4 A. Vauchez, *Sainthood in the Later Middle Ages*, trans. J. Birrell (New York, 1988), pp. 138–9.

5 On the religious sensibilities of the later Middle Ages, see the classic 1924 work by J. Huizinger, *The Autumn of the Middle Ages*, trans. R. J. Payton and U. Mammitzsch (Chicago, 1996); as well as C. W. Bynum, *Christian Materiality: An Essay on Religion in the Later Middle Ages* (Cambridge, MA, 2011). For the catastrophes, see W. C. Jordan, *The Great Famine: Northern Europe in the Fourteenth Century* (Princeton, 1996); O. J. Benedictow, *The Black Death, 1346–1353: The Complete History* (Woodbridge, 2004); and on the changes in climate, the lecture series by Bruce Campbell referred to above in Chapter 4, n. 11: 'The Great Transition: Climate, Disease and Society in the 13th and 14th Centuries', www.econsoc.hist.cam.ac.uk/podcasts.html, consulted 18 July 2013.

6 D. Weinstein, *Savonarola: The Rise and Fall of a Renaissance Prophet* (London, 2011), p. 304.

7 D. Erasmus, 'A Pilgrimage for Religion's Sake', in *The Colloquies of Erasmus*, trans. C. R. Thompson (Chicago, 1965), Vol. I, pp. 285–312.

8 J. Huizinga, *Erasmus and the Age of Reformation*, trans. F. Hopman (New York, 1957); Gotor, *Chiesa e santità*, pp. 22–5.

9 Gotor, *Chiesa e santità*, pp. 30–3.

10 *Ibid.*, pp. 34–41.

11 *Ibid.*, pp. 75–93; Gotor, *I beati del papa*, pp. 320–30.

12 Gotor, *I beati del papa*, pp. 285–334.

13 *Ibid.*, pp. 335–41.

14 *Ibid.*, p. 325 for the fifty-year rule. Urban VIII, *Urbani VIII Pont. O. M. Decreta servanda in canonizatione et beatificatione sanctorum* (Rome, 1642).

15 Gotor, *I beati del papa*, pp. 289–91.

16 *Ibid.*, p. 335. In this context note that during the sixteenth and seventeenth centuries scholars in each of the major religious orders published repertories of legends and miracles of the saints of their respective orders.

17 J. Proctor (ed.), *Short Lives of the Dominican Saints* (London, 1901).

18 R. Po-chia Hsia, *The World of Catholic Renewal* (New York, 1998), p. 137; Gotor, *Chiesa e santità*, p. 95.

19 *Acta sanctorum quotquot toto orbe coluntur* (Antwerp and Brussels, 1643–); D. Knowles, *Great Historical Enterprises* (London, 1962), pp. 3–32; and H. Delehaye, *The Work of the Bollandists through Three Centuries, 1615–1915* (Princeton, 1922).

20 Knowles, *Great Historical Enterprises*, pp. 35–62.

21 S. Bertelli, *Erudizione e storia in Ludovico Antonio Muratori* (Naples, 1960).

22 R. Godding *et al.* (eds), *Bollandistes, saints, et légendes: Quatre siècles de recherche* (Brussels, 2007).

23 *Acta sanctorum*, Maii, II, col. 281.

24 G. Tromboni, *Vita, morte, e miracoli del glorioso santo Homobono* (Cremona, 1618).

25 R. Haynes, *Philosopher King: The Humanist Pope Benedict XIV* (London, 1970).

26 P. Lambertini, *De servorum Dei beatificatione et beatorum canonizatione*, 4 vols (Rome, 1747–48).

27 S. Boesch Gajano, 'Guarigioni di fede: Testimonianze, certificazioni e riconoscimento ecclesiastico del miracolo', in M. Borsari (ed.), *Salute e salvezza: L'elaborazione religiosa della malattia e della guarigione* (Modena, 2001), pp. 105–31.

28 A. Foglia, 'Istituzioni ecclesiastiche e vita religiosa nel XVIII secolo', in *Diocesi di Cremona* (Brescia, 1998), pp. 215–38; also 'Da San Carlo Borromeo a Napoleone: Vita religiosa dagli inizi del XVIII al 1814', in C. Capra (ed.), *Storia di Cremona: Il Settecento e l'età napoleonica* (Bergamo, 2009), pp. 152–71.

29 Foglia, 'Istituzioni ecclesiastiche', p. 220; M. Rubin, *Mother of God: A History of the Virgin Mary* (New Haven, 2009), p. 341; E. Muir, 'The Virgin on the Street Corner: The Place of the Sacred in Italian Cities', in S. Ozment (ed.), *Religion and Culture in the Renaissance and Reformation* (Kirksville, MO, 1989), pp. 25–42.

30 F. Arisi (ed.), *Cremona literata*, 3 vols (Cremona, 1741), Vol. III, pp. 52, 377–8.

31 I. Vizzini *et al.* (eds), *Bibliotheca sanctorum*, 12 vols (Rome, 1961–71), Vol. X, pp. 1318–21; *Enciclopedia Cattolica*, 12 vols (Città del Vaticano, 1948–54), Vol. X, pp. 429–30.

32 Cremona: Archivio Storico Diocesano, 'Processus Informativus et Examen Testius super Canonizzazione B. Stephane de Quinzanis', 1729. P. Guerrini, 'La prima "legenda vulgare" de la beata Stefana Quinzani d'Orzinuovi secondo il codice Vaticano-Urbinate latino 1755', *Memorie storiche della diocesi di Brescia*, ser. 1, 1 (1930), 65–186.

33 Anon., *De S. Alberto confessore bergomensi cremonae denato tertio ordini S. Domenicano adjudicando dissertatio historica* (Bologna, 1741).

34 Po-chia Hsia, *World of Catholic Renewal*, p. 132; Knowles, *Great Historical Enterprises*, pp. 15–17. Godding *et al.*, *Bollandistes, saints, et légendes*, pp. 105–8.

35 *Annales Parmenses*, Vol. IX of *Rerum italicarum scriptores, 500–1500*, 28 vols (Milan, 1726), pp. 759–880.

36 Anon., *De S. Alberto*, pp. 42–3. G. Berdu, *Tratado de la Tercera Orden del Glorioso patriarca Santo Domingo de Guzman, de sv origen, regal … y exemplos de santidad con que ha illustrado la Iglesia esta Tercera Orden* (Valencia, 1674), pp. 142–3; Cf. Balthasar de Arin, *Regla y practica de exercicios espirituales para los professores de la Tercera Orden de Predicatores* (Barcelona, 1683), p. 84. This research was kindly done for me by Nicolas Pluchot, doctorandus at the University of Lyons 2. The Dominicans, having brought the cult as far as Catalonia, may well have taken it further into Iberia. Indeed there is a clear indication of its presence, in the form of an image on a cloister wall, at the Dominican convent in Oaxaca, Mexico. Private communication from Don Giovanni Brembilla, whom I was able to contact thanks to the kind intervention of Dr Maria Teresa Brolis.

37 *Statuti dell'Università de' Brentadori della Città di Cremona* (Cremona, 1742).

38 Archivio Segreto Vaticano, Congregatio rituum, Processus 661, fos 14v–17r. The manuscript consists of 561 numbered folios.

39 Pro. 661, fos 8v–28v for the documents from the six groups authorising Todeschini to represent them.

40 Lambertini, *De servorum Dei*, Vol. I, p. 461.

41 Pro. 661, fos 38–195.

42 G. Bresciani, *Vita, morta, e miracoli di S. Alberto di Villa d'Ogna, territorio di Bergamo*, 2nd edn (Cremona, 1667). A handwritten note facing the title page says this is a revision of the 1637 original version. On p. 15 one finds the same image that was printed on the cover of the statutes of the wine porters' guild published in 1742, reproduced here as Figure 20.

43 Pro. 661, fo. 51v.

44 Saint Martin Porres (1579–1639), a Peruvian mulatto who became a Dominican lay brother. Proctor, *Short Lives of the Dominican Saints*, p. 351; Vizzini *et al.*, *Bibliotheca sanctorum*, Vol. VIII, pp. 1240–5.

45 Pro. 661, fos 464v–465.

46 *Ibid.*, fos 490–1.

47 P. M. Domaneschio, *De rebus coenobii Cremonensis ordinis praedicatorum* (Cremona, 1767); see below, n. 49.

48 James represented the papacy's hopes for the return of the British Isles to the Catholic fold. In addition to the annuity granted by Clement XI, Benedict XIV had a large marble monument made in honour of James's widow and placed in Saint-Peter's. In April 1746, just as the Rome phase of Alberto's beatification procedure was about to begin, the last serious military attempt by the Stuarts to regain the monarchy collapsed when James's son Charles – Bonnie Prince Charlie – suffered a crushing defeat in battle and fled to France.

49 T. A. Ricchini, *De S. Alberto confessore Bergomensi Cremonae denato tertio ordini S. Dominici adjudicando dissertatio historica* (Milan, 1746); Domaneschio, *De rebus coenobii Cremonensis*, pp. 363–98, 437.

50 *Positio super dubio* (Rome, 1748). Both the *positio* and the broadside were consulted at the Archivio Storica Diocesano of Cremona, where I was kindly received and ably assisted by Don Andrea Foglia.

51 Salimbene de Adam, *Cronica fratris Salimbene de Adam ordinis minorum*, Monumenta Germaniae Historica, Scriptores, 32 (Hanover, 1913), p. 503; and *The Chronicle of Salimbene de Adam*, trans J. L. Baird (Binghamton, NY, 1986), p. 514 (translation modified).

52 No information on the cost of the process or on how and by whom it was paid has emerged. There remains, though, a lingering doubt about the significance of an imperial decree that was drawn up in late 1741 and printed in the elaborate copy of the guild's statutes with the image of Saint Alberto on the cover, which came out in 1742. The premise of this decree by Maria Theresa (*Statuti dell'Università*, pp. 22–4) is that too many people who are poor have been admitted to the guild ('the number of those enrolled exceeds three hundred'), that they demand charity on the part of the guild (implying that that is why they join), and that thus the guild cannot perform adequately the acts of charity that one should be able to expect of it. Therefore she grants that the number of members can be doubled (to 600 or to *c.* 140?) so long as all those admitted own property in the city, have the means to pay all their debts, and pay double the usual amount required to join, 'which emoluments will result in greater glory for Saint Alberto, the protector of the brentatori'. The number of members stated in the decree does not match well with the number of those present at the meeting with the lawyer in May of 1742, nor does there seem to have been any need for more wine porters in Cremona at that time. Moreover, the phrase about 'the greater glory for Saint Alberto' matches a phase uttered by the lawyer in that meeting. Could this decree provide a way of allowing people of means, with no experience, desire, or intention of ever carrying a brenta of wine, to join so that they could help finance the coming campaign? It does not seem a likely explanation but the silence about finances raises the question.

Epilogue: Dignity and memory

1 R. Bergonzini, *Arte dei brentatori a Modena* (Modena, 1983), pp. 26, 36, n. 31. This Modena scene has some similarities with a painting executed by an unknown artist in mid-eighteenth-century Brescia that depicts the wine market of that city, where one can see a wine porter filling his brenta from a vat placed on a cart in the square, another wine porter who seems engaged in discussion or perhaps an argument about charges with a prospective client, and still others who appear to be headed off to make deliveries. The main difference is that the Modena scene evokes an imagined earlier time, whereas the Brescian work is a genre painting of its time, demonstrated clearly, for example, by the eighteenth-century dress of the gentlemen depicted (with their three-cornered hats). See V. Frati (ed.), *Brescia, Le città nella storia dell'Italia* (Rome–Bari, 1989), p. 123, Figure 115.

2 *Interno di cantina*, by Giovanni Battista Epis, 1855. For a reproduction, plus analysis by M. C. Rodeschini, see Banca Popolare di Bergamo, *I pittori bergamaschi dell'Ottocento*, 4 vols (Bergamo, 1992), Vol. II, pp. 179–80. Sandro Buzzetti kindly brought this work to my attention.

3 M. T. D'Azeglio, *I miei ricordi* (Florence, 1867), pp. 29–30.

4 E. De Amicis, 'I difensori delle Alpi', a section of his *Vita militare*, in *De Amicis*, ed. A. Baldini, 2 vols (Milan, 1945), Vol. I, p. 411.

5 Bergonzini, *Arte dei brentatori*, p. 40; B. Belotti, *Storia di bergamo e dei Bergamaschi*, 9 vols (Bergamo, 1989–90), Vol. III, p. 150, Vol. IV, p. 303.

6 G. Guidicini, *Cose notabili della città di Bologna*, 6 vols (Bologna, 1872), Vol. IV, pp. 188–91; A. Portioli, *Le Corporazioni artiere e l'Archivio della Camera di Commercio di Mantova* (Mantua, 1884); C. A. Levi, *Sopra alcune antiche scuole di arti e mestieri scomparse o ancora esistente a Venezia: Notizie storiche* (Venice, 1894); F. Pozza, 'Le corporazioni d'arti e mestieri a Vicenza', *Nuovo archivio veneto*, 10 (1895), 247–311; P. Sitta, 'Le università delle arti a Ferrara dal secolo XII al secolo XVIII', *Atti della Deputazione ferrarese di storia patria*, 8 (1896); G. Micheli, 'Le corporazioni parmensi d'arti e mestieri', *Archivio Storico per le provincie parmensi*, ser. 4, 5 (1896), 1–137; G. Alberti, 'L'antica corporazione dei portatori di vino a Trento', *Tridentum*, 2 (1899), 49–90, 149–65; M. Roberti, *Le corporazioni padovane d'arte e mestieri* (Venice, 1902), pp. 126–7, 136, 147–54, 213; R. Soriga, 'Sulle corporazioni artigiane di Pavia nella età comunale', *Bollettino della Società pavese di storia patria*, 15 (1915), 76–93.

7 Sitta, 'Le università delle arti', p. 7.

8 A. Scotti, 'I Brentatori', *Aurea Parma: Rivista di lettere arte e storia* 36 (1952), 100–2.

9 P. Petrocchi (ed.), *Nòvo dizionàrio universale della lingua italiana*, 2 vols (Milan, 1900).

10 For Andrea, see above, Chapter 4; for Carracci, see Chapter 6.

11 Como: Musei Civici di Como, 'Codice Carpani', p. 35 (formerly fo. 18r); for a printed facsimile of the same, C. Maspoli (ed.), *Stemmario quattrocentesco delle famiglie nobili della città e antica diocesi di Como, Codice Carpani* (Lugano, 1973), pp. xiv, 375. On the origins of the Brentano family: A. Engelmann, 'Die Brentano vom Comersee: Zu ihrer Soziallage und -entwicklung als Familie', in K. Feilchenfeldt and L. Zagari (eds), *Die Brentano: Eine europäische Familie* (Tübingen, 1992), pp. 17–28. Note the reference on p. 22 to Robertinus filius Roberti de Brenta in a notarial act of 1323.

12 *La Compagnia dell'Arte dei Brentatori* (Bazzano, 1976).

13 M. Mollat, *The Poor in the Middle Ages: An Essay in Social History*, trans. A. Goldhammer (New Haven, 1986).

14 C. Orelli, 'Emigrazione e mestiere: Alcuni percorsi di integrazione nelle città lombarde e toscane di "migranti" dalla Svizzera italiana (secoli XVI–XVIII)', in M. Meriggi and A. Pastore (eds), *Le regole dei mestieri e delle professioni: Secoli 15.–19.* (Milan, 2000), pp. 225–38, esp. p. 235.

15 The cases of Homobono and Alberto differ in so many ways that it comes as something of a surprise to see how their afterlives followed a similar pattern. The main impulse behind the spread of the cult of Saint Homobono outside Cremona was his fame as a tailor, for as tailors' guilds came to be formed in Italy and elsewhere in Europe, he was an obvious choice for those who went searching for a patron. He was able to satisfy the needs of guilds of merchants and of manual labourers as well. However, when the guilds were dissolved at the end of the eighteenth century, his utility as a guild patron also dissolved and he reverted to his original role as patron of his native city. *Mutatis mutandis*, this, too, was Alberto's fate. See A. Vauchez, *Omobono di Cremona (†1197), laico e santo: Profilo storico* (Cremona, 2001), pp. 111–12. For insightful reflections on various ways that saints' cults 'wear out' or decline and even die, see W. A. Christian, Jr, *Person and God in a Spanish Valley* (New York, 1972), pp. 64–5, 88–93.

16 G. Bertini, 'Un dipinto ritrovato di Antonio Bresciani', *Aurea Parma* 62 (1978), 30–2.

17 G. Guidicini, *Cose notabili della città di Bologna*, 6 vols (Bologna, 1872), Vol. IV, p. 189.

18 A. Masini, *La Bologna perlustrata*, Part I, Vol. II (Bologna, 1823), p. 15; Dr Aurelia Trafficante of the Archivio Storico Comunale of Modena kindly brought this work to my attention.

19 P. Scurani, *Storia della chiesa di San Giorgio (e della presenza dei Gesuiti) in Reggio Emilia* (Reggio Emilia, 1896), pp. 6–7.

20 D. Barilli, *I Pompieri e Parma: Storie parallele* (Parma, 1992). M. Dall'Aqua, 'Evoluzione artistico-culturale dell'antico convento del Carmine in Parma', in G. Piamonte and G. Nello Vetro (eds), *Parma Conservatorio di Musica, Studi e ricerche* (Parma, 1973), pp. 17–35; 'Sant'Alberto brentatore', in *Il vino e l'uomo: Lavoro e civiltà* (Parma, 1984), pp. 41–4; 'L'aria della città rende liberi nuove professioni e nuovi ceti sociali', in *Vivere il Medioevo: Parma al tempo della Cattedrale* (Milan, 2006), pp. 89–95.

21 A. Thompson, *Cities of God: The Religion of the Italian Communes, 1125–1325* (University Park, PA, 2005), p. 430. In a paragraph relating instances of friar-inquisitors successfully prosecuting lay saints for heresy in the years around 1290, the author comes to his final example, the case 'more notorious still' of Alberto, 'the wine porter of Cremona'. He gives a brief summary of what Salimbene tells us and then concludes: 'But Alberto was a drunkard, said Fra Salimbene, and his devotees were a pack of wine guzzlers and silly women. Thank goodness that a Franciscan inquisitor finally got around to suppressing his cult.' For another modern reading of the case of Alberto that makes essentially the same error by relying nearly exclusively upon Salimbene, see P. Golinelli, *Città e culto dei santi nel medioevo italiano* (Bologna, 1996), p. 113.

22 L. Arrigoni, E. Daffia, and P. C. Mariani (eds), *The Brera Gallery: The Official Guide* (Milan, 1998), p. 163.

23 For this information I am greatly indebted to Dr Marc Sureda, Conservator of the Episcopal Museum of Vich; Professor Lluis To Figueras, Professor of History at the University of Gerona; and not least to Professor Monique Bourin, Professor of History at the University of Paris I, who enlisted the assistance of these Catalonian colleagues on my behalf.

24 G. Carrara, *S. Michele al pozzo Bianco in Bergamo dopo i recenti restauri* (Bergamo, 1945), p. 12; see in particular n. 1: 'Which Saint Alberto? Saint Alberto of Villa d'Ogna, deceased in 1279? Saint Alberto the Carmelite, deceased in 1292? Or Saint Albertus Magnus, Doctor of the Church, deceased in 1282? The symbolic dove shown close to the head of the saint argues in favour of this third hypothesis.'

25 A. Puerari, in *Museo Civico Ala Ponzone, Cremona: Raccolte artistiche* (Cremona, 1976), p. 53, Figure 299; A. Ebani, 'Per l'interpretazione di un altorilievo trecentesco del Museo Civico di Cremona', *Strenna dell' ADAFA* (1984), 59–68.

26 D. Piazzi, 'Il Santorale della chiesa cremonese', in A. Caprioli, A. Rimoldi, and L. Vascaro (eds), *Diocesi di Cremona* (Brescia, 1998), pp. 414–18.

27 G. Locatelli, 'I più antichi documenti intorno alla chiesa ed all'ospedale di S. Alberto da Villa d'Ogna', *Bolletino della Civica Biblioteca di Bergamo*, 11:1 (1917), 24–8.

28 L. Ginami, *Il proprio dei santi della chiesa di Bergamo* (Rome, 1990), p. 131.

29 L. Ginami, *Il Beato Alberto di Villa d'Ogna: Esempio di santità laica nell'Italia dei Comuni* (Milan, 2000), pp. 105–6.

30 One is a seventeenth-century mural in Gandellino; the second is a seventeenth-century altarpiece in Piario; and the third is a nineteenth-century processional banner in Parre. Information on these works is found together with reproductions in the photographic collection of the Museo Adriano Bernareggi in Bergamo. On Discepoli, see S. Facchinetti, F. Frangi, and G. Vallagussa (eds), *Carlo Ceresa: Un pittore del seicento Lombardo tra realtà e devozione* (Bergamo, 2012), p. 160 and Plate 161; F. Frangi and A. Bernardini (eds), *Giovan Battista Discepoli* (Milan, 2001), p. 86.

31 In two rural villages in the plain, each about 10 km from Bergamo – Stezzano and Albegno (the latter being now part of Treviglio) – an attempt was made to launch the cult of Alberto in the early nineteenth century. Private communication from Don Giovanni Brembilla, whom I was able to contact through the kind intervention of Dr Maria Teresa Brolis.

32 R. Frost, 'The Death of the Hired Man', in his *North of Boston*, 2nd edn (New York, 1915), pp. 14–23.

Index

9 781526 116697